More Words of Wall Street:

2000 Investment Terms Defined

More Words of Wall Street:

2000 Investment Terms Defined

Allan H. Pessin
Joseph A. Ross

DOW JONES-IRWIN
Homewood, Illinois 60430

ISBN 0-87094-701-X

Library of Congress Catalog Card No. 86–70777

Printed in the United States of America

1 2 3 4 5 6 7 8 9 0 K 3 2 1 0 9 8 7 6

Preface

More Words of Wall Street, as was its predecessor, is aimed at two audiences:

- The individual investor who wants to learn more about the securities industry: its terms, its delivery systems, and the colorful slang that surrounds Wall Street usage.
- The industry professional who wants more specific information about a term or expression.

Again, this is not a how-to-do-it book; it will not make you rich, but it does teach the language of the financial services industry.

Although both this book and its predecessor are aimed at similar audiences, there are a number of differences.

First, to use a verbal analogy, *Words of Wall Street* is to *More Words of Wall Street* as beginning book is to advanced book. The present book expands on the previous book; it is more sophisticated—if you wish, more professional. This does not mean that it is more difficult to read or understand but that the words and concepts included are more advanced. For example, this book is full of the myriad of acronyms that have sprung up in recent years to describe the new packaged products of our industry. There are, for example, BITS, and CATS, and GAINS, and COUGARS, and OPPOSMS, plus a hundred others.

Second, we have added over 200 words from the original book to this book. We feel that these added words will help the reader to better understand some of the new words that have sprung up in our industry.

Third, we have placed the cross-references within the text, rather than at the beginning, as was the case with the previous book. We feel this makes reading and usage easier.

We hope that you enjoy this book and find it useful. Together with its companion volume, it forms the most extensive glossary of Wall Street terms available.

As you use this book, remember that, although we are the authors of these books, you are the authors of these words. After all, users determine what words mean; in fact, users determine whether a group of letters will become a word. After all, it will not become a word if it is not used. We ask you, therefore, to send us other words that you would like to see included in future editions of these books. In this way, you can help to maintain these two books as the premier dictionary of Wall Street usage.

Allan H. Pessin
Joseph A. Ross

Glossary

A

ABC
See AGENCY BACKED COMPOUNDER SECURITIES.

ABC AGREEMENT
New York Stock Exchange term to designate this situation: a member uses borrowed funds to purchase an exchange seat. So called because the exchange-approved agreement has three provisions: the member may (1) retain the seat and purchase another seat for a designee of the lender's choice, (2) sell the seat and remit the proceeds to the lender, (3) transfer the seat, at a nominal consideration, to another person in the employ of the lending member firm.

ABS AGREEMENT
ABS is an acronym for Associated Broker Service. The agreement is a contract between Trans Canada Options, Inc., and a U.S. broker/dealer with membership in the Options Clearing Corporation or an exchange on which equity options are traded. The agreement provides for daily and periodic reports by TCO to the U.S. firm and for clearance and settlement of Canadian options transactions.

ABOVE THE MARKET
Identification of an order to sell a security at a price that is greater than the present lowest offering price for that security in a particular marketplace. For example, if the present lowest

offering price for a security is $45 per share, an offer at $47 is above the market.

See also AWAY FROM THE MARKET (WWS*).

ACAT
See AUTOMATED CUSTOMER ACCOUNT TRANSFER SERVICE.

ACCELERATED DEPRECIATION
Accounting procedure whereby the cost of a fixed asset is amortized over the period of the useful life of the asset. Acceleration means that more revenues are set aside in the earlier years than in later years, thus reducing tax liabilities on income received by the corporation.

See also DOUBLE DECLINING BALANCE (WWS) and SUM-OF-THE-YEARS'-DIGITS (WWS).

ACCOUNT
General industry term for:
1. The bookkeeping record of a client's transactions and credit or debit balances of either cash or securities with the member firm. The term also is used of the conduct of such business relationships. For example, "Our firm emphasizes accounts productive to the firm and to client."
2. The books of an investment syndicate that indicate contractual relationships, the securities owned and sold, and the final financial balance between a participant in a syndicate and the syndicate.

ACCOUNT DAY
In England, the day on which securities transactions arranged during the preceding two-week period (the account) are due for settlement. Account day is usually seven business days after the end of the account period.

ACCOUNT EXECUTIVE
Commonly used term for an employee of a broker-dealer who has been registered with the NASD and/or one of the exchanges. Such employees are permitted to solicit buy and sell orders for securities and, in general, to handle client accounts.

---

*This reference—(WWS)—is to the authors' *Words of Wall Street: 2,000 Investment Terms Defined* (Homewood, Ill.: Dow Jones-Irwin, 1983), where the referred term is given its precise meaning.

Technically, the term applies to a registered representative, although some member firms use other designations for registered employees.

ACCREDITED INVESTOR
SEC term from Regulation D. In general, a person whose wealth or investment sophistication is such that they are not included in the enumeration of the 35 persons that forms the upper limit on an unregistered offering of securities.

Regulation D lists eight categories. Here are three examples of accredited investors:
1. A person with a net worth exceeding $1 million.
2. A person with income of at least $200,000 in the current year as well as in the last two years.
3. A person who purchases at least $150,000 of the offered securities and whose total cost does not exceed 20% of net worth.

ACCRUED INTEREST
Term designating the interest due on a bond or other fixed-income security that must be paid by the buyer of a security to its seller. Usual computation: coupon rate of interest times elapsed days from prior interest payment date (i.e., coupon date) up to but not including settlement date. Principal exceptions: money market securities that are sold at a discount do not have accrued interest.

Antonym: flat (i.e., without accrued interest).

Synonym: and interest (used as a qualifier). For example, The trade was made "and interest" (i.e., the accrued interest must be added to the contract price).

ACE
Acronym: American Commodities Exchange, Inc. ACE is a corporate affiliate of the American Stock Exchange and provides a market for the trading of futures contracts in selected financial instruments sensitive to interest rates.

ACH
See AUTOMATED CLEARINGHOUSE.

ACID–TEST RATIO
A measurement of corporate liquidity. Accepted measurement: subtract inventory from current assets; divide the remainder by

current liabilities. For example, a company has current assets of $10 million and inventory of $3 million. Net: $7 million. It has current liabilities of $3.5 million. Its acid-test ratio is:

$$\frac{\$7 \text{ million}}{\$3.5 \text{ million}} = \frac{2}{1}$$

Ratios below 1 to 1 are considered low. However, ratios that are extremely high may indicate that a company is not using assets effectively, may be cash rich, and is subject to a takeover by other companies.

ACQUISITION DATE

The calendar day, for legal and tax purposes, on which someone commits to the purchase of an asset.

Note: For assets received as a gift, the recipient normally uses the acquisition date on which the donor acquired the asset. Assets received as the result of a bequest are considered as acquired on the day of death of the previous owner.

ACTING IN CONCERT

Basic concept: two or more persons who, either collectively or through a common agent, endeavor to achieve an investment goal.

Basic restrictions against acting in concert: such persons may not (1) exceed the position and exercise limits set by the option exchanges, (2) work to change the management of a registered corporation without filing with the SEC, (3) accumulate a control position in the security of a corporation without reporting to the SEC, (4) manipulate the price of a security. Each of these restrictions also applies to individuals.

AN ACTUAL

Term used to identify the security underlying an option. For example, when discussing an option, the "actual" would be the security deliverable in satisfaction of the contract.

More common expression: "the underlying." Example: A call is an option to purchase the underlying at a stated price on or before a specified date.

ACTUAL VALUE OF REAL ESTATE

This is the dollar value placed on property by the economic forces of supply and demand. Accordingly, this value is volatile and generally is not used as a basis for property taxes.

See also ASSESSED VALUATION (WWS).

4

ADB
See ASIAN DEVELOPMENT BANK.

ADJUSTABLE RATE CONVERTIBLE NOTE
Debt security issued at a substantial premium over its redemption value at maturity. However, the note is exchangeable for a number of shares of common stock whose market value upon conversion is equal to the original issue price of the note; thus, it makes conversion economically more attractive than redemption.

Popular abbreviation: ARCN.

ADJUSTABLE RATE PREFERRED STOCK
An equity security that pays dividends at rates which change monthly or quarterly and are set at the highest of the then-prevailing rates for 90-day Treasury bills, 10-year Treasury notes, or 20-year Treasury bonds.

Also called "floating rate preferred stock."

ADJUSTABLE TENDER SECURITY
See ATS.

ADJUSTED EXERCISE PRICE
Term used of GNMA put and call options. Contract is for $100,000 unpaid principal balance on a GNMA pass-through security with an 8% nominal coupon. If GNMA pass-throughs with higher coupon rates are delivered, the exercise (strike) price will be so adjusted that the yield is the same. For example, the strike price on a GNMA call is 56. The yield will be 11%. If the call is exercised and the writer delivers a GNMA pass-through with an 11% coupon, the adjusted exercise price will be par, or 100.

ADVANCE REFUNDING
Term used to describe this situation: A municipality has outstanding bonds that are not yet callable (e.g., the earliest call date is 1988). If general interest rates drop, the municipality may find it advantageous to issue new bonds at a lower rate. The proceeds are invested in government securities that will mature in 1988, at which time the money will be used to call the earlier issue.

Also called "prerefunding."

ADVICE

1. A written acknowledgment by a broker/dealer or bank of receipt or delivery of money, or the transaction of securities business in a customer's account.

   In practice, a broker/dealer confirmation is an advice, and a statement is a summary of advices during an accounting period.
2. A recommendation by a salesperson, security analyst, or portfolio manager to buy, sell, or hold one or more specific securities issues.

AFFIDAVIT

A written statement of facts submitted voluntarily before a governing, judicial, or regulatory body. Affidavits must be signed in the presence of a court officer, notary public, or other designated person. For example, an executor of an estate files an affidavit of domicile of the decedent with an issuer's transfer agent to make a decedent's security certificate negotiable for sale.

AFFIDAVIT OF DOMICILE

Statement by executor or administrator of an estate attesting to the domicile of a decedent at the time of death. The affidavit is important for the transfer of securities from an estate because it, together with the tax waiver from the state of domicile, shows that no tax liens are outstanding against the securities about to be transferred.

AFFILIATED PERSON

General name for a person who can influence the management decisions of a corporation. Although legal advice may be needed in specific situations, the term includes: holders of 10% or more of the outstanding stock of a corporation, directors, elected officers (chairman, president, vice presidents, secretary, and treasurer), and members of their immediate family.

Also called "control person."

AFTERMARKET

General name for the trading activity in a security during the period of its initial offering to the public, and immediately thereafter, until the syndicate account is closed.

More popular name: secondary market.

AGENCY
1. A security, almost always debt, issued by a corporation sponsored by the U.S. government. Examples: bonds of the Federal Intermediate Credit Banks (FICB) or the Tennessee Valley Authority. Agency securities are exempt from registration under the Securities Act of 1933.
2. The act of buying or selling for the account and risk for another person.

AGENCY BACKED COMPOUNDER SECURITIES
Trademark of Kidder Peabody & Co., for zero-coupon bonds backed by Ginnie Mae and Fannie Mae securities. Sold at a discount from face value, ABCs pay no current interest. The difference between purchase price and redemption value at maturity represents compound interest at a rate prevailing at the time of purchase.

Popular abbreviation: ABC.

AGENCY FOR INTERNATIONAL DEVELOPMENT
AID is a U.S. governmental entity organized to assist developing countries in financing low-cost housing. Bonds issued under the sponsorship of AID are backed by the full faith and credit of the U.S. government. These bonds are exempt from registration, have maturities as long as 30 years, and are taxable as foreign-source income to U.S. investors.

AGENCY NOTES
One- to two-year obligation offered at a discount from par by U.S. government agencies, such as the Federal National Mortgage Association, the Federal Home Administration, and the Farm Credit System. Such notes generally represent interim financing prior to the issuance of long-term bonds.

AGENT
1. A person who buys or sells for the account and risk of another. Generally, an agent takes no financial risk and charges a commission for his services.
2. In state securities law, any person who represents an issuer or a broker-dealer in the purchase or sale of securities to, or for, a person domiciled in that state.

AS AGENT
Term describing the role of a broker/dealer organization when it acts as an intermediary, or broker, between its customer and a

market maker or contra broker. For this service, the firm generally negotiates with its customer for a reasonable commission or fee.

Synonym: as broker.

AGENT BANK

A commercial bank that acts as an intermediary between a customer and the customer's broker/dealer. For example, an agent bank may serve the customer by settling securities transactions with the broker/dealer, by acting as a custodian of securities purchased, by entering orders to buy or sell, and by acting as an investment adviser to the customer.

AGGREGATE EXERCISE PRICE

Term in security options: the exercise (strike) price times the number of securities involved in the contract. For example, a call is purchased at 50 for 100 shares. The aggregate exercise price is $5,000. Exception: GNMA options and T-bill, T-note, and T-bond options, in which the aggregate exercise price is the strike price times the face value of the underlying contract. For example, a GNMA call at 68 is 68% times $100,000, the face value of the underlying contract.

See ADJUSTED EXERCISE PRICE.

AGGREGATE INDEBTEDNESS

Term used by the SEC in the computation of broker/dealer compliance with the SEC's net capital requirements. Best definition: the total of the broker/dealer's indebtedness to customers. For example, a broker/dealer owes $200,000: $50,000 is owed to a partner in the business and $150,000 is owed to customers for their credit balances in their accounts. The broker/dealer's aggregate indebtedness is the $150,000 owed to customers.

AIBD

See ASSOCIATION OF INTERNATIONAL BOND DEALERS.

AID

See AGENCY FOR INTERNATIONAL DEVELOPMENT.

AID AND ABET

Legal term: to help, encourage, and incite. The term often is used in the statement of charges brought against someone who is alleged to have facilitated a violation of federal securities law.

AGREEMENT AMONG UNDERWRITERS

The formal contract between the members of an underwriting, or syndicate, account.

In general, the agreement among underwriters appoints one or more syndicate managers, defines the powers of the manager(s), and sets the rules for the conduct of the account.

A/K/A

Abbreviation: also known as. Often used in securities brokerage offices to identify short titles of customer accounts maintained by that firm.

Synonym: an alias.

Note: A/K/A is a different name for a person or entity. D/B/A is used if a person does business under a different name. For example, William Smith A/K/A Bill Smiley, as opposed to William Smith D/B/A Scimitar Company. Both sets of letters often are used lowercase.

ALL OR ANY PART

Order instruction sometimes given by a customer for the execution of a block transaction, either a purchase or sale. With this instruction, the trader is advised to execute when, and as, offers or bids become available, regardless of quantity provided the original parameters of the order as established by the customer are observed.

Abbreviation: AOAP.

ALL OR NONE

1. Used of an underwritten offering: it is conditional to a total subscription of the shares offered. If every share is not subscribed, issuer has the right to cancel the offering. Example: The Women's Bank offered shares on an all-or-none basis.
2. Used of an order ticket by a buying or selling customer: buy or sell the entire amount on a single transaction. Do not execute a partial transaction. Order entry symbol: AON. All-or-none instructions that require immediate execution must be marked fill or kill (FOK). Thus, AON restricts the size but not necessarily the time of the transaction.

ALLOTMENT LETTER

In England, a term for a temporary stock certificate issued to persons entitled to a stock dividend or stock split. The notification of the allotment of the stock dividend or split is in the form of a letter; hence, the name.

ALL–SAVER CERTIFICATE

Name used of special one-year CD that was exempt from federal taxation if the deposit was made between September 1981 and the end of December 1982. Up to $1,000 of interest income was exempt.

All-saver certificates have been discontinued.

AMERICAN DEPOSITORY RECEIPT

Negotiable receipt, registered in the name of the owner, for shares of a foreign corporation held in the vault of a foreign branch of an American bank. The receipt may or may not be on a share-for-share basis with the underlying security. ADRs, if sold in the United States, are subject to the securities laws of the United States, and many foreign corporations sell their securities in the United States in the form of ADRs. Because of ease of transfer and resale, ADRs are a popular form of domestic equity ownership of foreign corporations.

AMERICAN OPTION

Term used of a put or call if it is necessary to distinguish from a European option, many of which do not have the same exercise privileges during the life of the option.

AMERICAN STOCK EXCHANGE MARKET VALUE INDEX

This is a market index for all common stocks listed on the American Stock Exchange. It is prepared daily, and often within the day. Subgroupings are by geography and industrial categories.

AMERICUS TRUST

A five-year unit investment trust into which holders of American Telephone & Telegraph common stock could deposit their shares. Upon divestiture of AT&T in 1984, the trust held the original shares and the shares of the old AT&T subsidiaries. Unit holders also had the option to split their interest in the trust into two components: The PRIME component was to receive all dividends; the SCORE component was to receive all capital gains over $75 per share based on the original telephone stock.

AMORTIZED LOSSES
Accounting technique used by banks if they sell debt instruments at a loss. The technique permits the bank to prorate the loss over what would have been the remaining life of the instrument, thereby reducing taxable income over that period.

AND INTEREST
Term used in conjunction with the trading of most outstanding bonds. It signifies that the buyer must pay (and the seller receive) the interest that has accrued from the last interest payment by the issuer up to, but not including, the settlement date for the contract.

Antonym: flat—that is, no accrued interest is payable by the buyer to the seller.

See also ACCRUED INTEREST, FLAT (WWS).

APARS
See AUTOMATIC PRICING AND REPORTING SYSTEM.

APPROVED PERSON
NYSE term: a person who is a director of a member corporation, or an owner of 5% or more of the voting stock thereof, but who is neither a member of the NYSE nor an allied member. An approved person must be qualified by the NYSE to serve in such a position.

See MEMBER CORPORATION.

See also ALLIED MEMBER (WWS).

ARBITRAGE
1. Verb: The act of buying and selling the same security in different marketplaces to profit from a disparity in market prices.
2. Verb: The act of buying one security coupled to a short sale of the same security to profit from a disparity of prices.
3. Noun: An offsetting security position that has a built-in profit.
4. Adjective or as past participle: To describe a security position that establishes a profit. Example: His long position was arbitraged by a short sale.

ARCN
See ADJUSTABLE RATE CONVERTIBLE NOTE.

ARCO
Acronym: Atlantic Richfield Company. ARCO also is used as the company's commercial logo.

ARM'S-LENGTH TRANSACTION
Any business arrangement negotiated by an unrelated or un-affiliated party to the transaction. Such a transaction avoids conflicts of interest and thus is not detrimental to the interest of a third party with whom either or both of the transactors is associated.

ARP
See ADJUSTABLE RATE PREFERRED STOCK.

ASIAN DEVELOPMENT BANK
An international financial institution established to foster economic growth and social development in countries in Asia and in the perimeter of the Pacific Ocean. Headquartered in the Philippine Islands, the bank lends money to smaller or less developed countries in that region of the world for projects designed to assist their economic growth.
Acronym: ADB.

ASPIRIN COUNT THEORY
A lighthearted leading indicator of general market price movement. Concept: About a year after aspirin production rises in the United States, the market will fall, and vice versa if aspirin production decreases.

ASSOCIATED PERSON
General term: any person associated with a broker/dealer as a proprietor, partner, officer, director, branch office manager, investment banker, or salesperson. Persons who perform minis-terial or clerical functions are not associated persons.

ASSOCIATION OF INTERNATIONAL BOND DEALERS
AIBD, domiciled in Switzerland, is composed of banks and broker/dealers engaged in primary and secondary markets for international debt securities. The members of AIBD act as under-writers and marketmakers and settle transactions in accord with the procedures set forth by the association. AIBD is similar in function and responsibility to the NASD in the United States, but it lacks governmental backing.

ATS

Acronym: adjustable tender security. ATS is a variable rate municipal security developed and sold by Smith Barney Harris Upham & Company, a prominent broker/dealer and investment banker. The municipality resets its interest rate daily. There is a put option attached to the instrument that enables the holder to redeem the debt at face value. However, the put can only be exercised weekly or monthly; this gives the issuer some flexibility in its debt structuring and some protection against volatile yield curve aberrations.

See also AUTOMATIC TRANSFER SERVICE ACCOUNT.

ATTEST

To swear or affirm as true. The term is used in legal documents when it is necessary to swear that the information contained therein is true.

AT THE MONEY

Term used of a security option if the strike (execution) price and the market price are the same. Example: a put at 35 on ABC if the market price of ABC is 35.

The term abstracts from premiums paid or received and from the cost of executing the option contract. Thus, at the money should not be confused with the client's break-even point—either as holder or seller—on the option contract.

ATTORNEY-AT-LAW

Any legally qualified person authorized to represent clients in court or in other proceedings requiring the services of a lawyer.

ATTORNEY-IN-FACT

Any person, acting as agent, who has the written authority to represent someone in out-of-court proceedings. The person who acts as attorney-in-fact need not be a lawyer. For example, by signing a stock power, the registered holder authorizes the broker to act as attorney-in-fact to facilitate the transfer of the security to the new owner.

ATTORNEY GENERAL

Official title for the chief law enforcement officer of the U.S. government or of one of the United States. Frequently used abbreviation: AG.

AUTEX SYSTEM

A communications network using electronic screens to enable broker/dealers and other subscribers to show their trading interest in specific blocks of stock. If a mutual interest is found, the transaction is completed on a securities exchange or in the over-the-counter market.

AUTO–EX

Acronym: Automatic Order Execution System. This American Stock Exchange system is used in conjunction with the exchange's AMOS system. AUTO–EX provides instant execution of the most active series in the exchange's Major Market Index options (XMI). AUTO–EX can immediately execute market and limit orders at the market in quantities of up to 10 contracts at a single price.

AUTOMATED CLEARINGHOUSE

A process provided by the Federal Reserve Banking System whereby funds are transferred electronically without the need to handle paper checks.

Popular abbreviation: ACH.

AUTOMATED CUSTOMER ACCOUNT TRANSFER SERVICE

Acronym: ACAT. A service of the National Securities Clearing Corporation (NSCC) that enables members to transfer customer accounts automatically via NSCC computerized facilities. Within five business days following the written instruction from the customer, and the validation thereof, the losing broker's account will be debited and the receiving broker's accounts will be credited with the customer's security and money positions.

As a general rule, option and investment company positions are outside this procedure.

AUTOMATIC PRICING AND REPORTING SYSTEM

System used in conjunction with the Designated Order Turnaround (DOT) system on the NYSE for the pricing of odd-lot orders.

Concept: APARS accepts and stores orders from 1 to 99 shares until a round-lot transaction takes place in that stock. When the round-lot transaction occurs, the system prices those orders that are capable of execution and directs them back to the originating firms.

AUTOMATIC TRANSFER SERVICE ACCOUNT

Banking term for those savings accounts from which funds can be transferred quickly and electronically to customers' checking accounts to cover checks. By using this system, the customers' savings accounts continue to earn interest until a check is written against savings balances.

Acronym: ATS.

AXE

Shortened form of "an axe to grind." Slang expression used by securities traders when they solicit business without disclosing to securities salespersons whether they are interested in buying or selling. In this way, the traders can get an indication of market interest before they commit themselves to one side of the market or the other.

B

BABY BOND

A debt instrument with a face value of less than $1,000. Example: ATT has many $100 face value bonds outstanding. Baby bonds were designed to appeal to the small, public investor in the early 1800s as the railroad industry used massive financing for their expansion efforts. "Baby" was created on the floor of the New York Stock Exchange to differentiate it from the regular ($1,000) obligations of those railroads traded there.

See CITIZEN BONDS and CONSOL.

BACK–END LOAD

Slang for a hidden sales charge by a no-load mutual fund in the form of higher operating expenses. In this way, the purchaser of the no-load fund pays an indirect charge.

Note: In practice, the expenses of most no-load funds are comparable to the expenses of funds with a sales charge. Do not confuse the term *back-end load* with the redemption fee that some no-load funds charge, or that are charged if funds are withdrawn before a certain period following purchase.

BACK–END RIGHTS

A term from corporate finance to designate management's gift to stockholders in a company that has become a takeover target. The privilege enables holders to exchange one right and one share for cash, preferred stock, and/or debt securities in that concern in the event an acquirer obtains a predetermined percentage of the outstanding stock and does not promptly consummate the takeover at a value at least equal to management's distributed package of cash and securities. Back-end rights serve to protect the financial interests of shareholders in an about-to-be-acquired company.

BACKING AWAY
Market maker fails to honor a firm bid for the minimum quantity. Action violates the Rules of Fair Practice of the National Association of Securities Dealers (NASD).

BACKSPREAD
A reversal of the popular ratio-spread technique. Most ratio spreaders buy one call and sell two calls with a higher strike price. A backspread also can involve the purchase of one call and the sale of two calls with a lower strike price.

BACK UP
1. Verb: Describes the market action of debt securities when dollar prices rise and yields fall. Example: The bond market is backing up.
2. Verb: Describes the action whereby a bond portfolio manager sells one bond and purchases another of equal quality with a shorter maturity date.

Note: Do not confuse with the noun backup—that is, a person or system that will substitute for another.

BACKWARDIZATION
English trade term that describes the situation in commodities markets when spot prices are higher than futures prices.
Synonym: inverted market.

BAIT AND SWITCH
The unsavory, and at times unethical, practice of advertising an item at an advantageous price. When potential customers inquire about the item, they are pressured into buying higher-priced substitutes that are more advantageous to the salesperson.

BALANCE SHEET EQUATION
Total assets = Total liabilities + Stockholders' equity (net worth). It is this equation, graphically represented in the balance sheet, that makes double-entry bookkeeping possible.

BALLOON INTEREST

Feature of serial bond issue in which earlier years' coupons are lower than coupon interest rates for later serial maturities.

BANK CHECK

A draft drawn by a bank upon itself. In the securities industry, a bank check is considered one of several forms of good trade settlement because payment is assured by the bank's obligation to honor the check. If requested by a third party, the bank normally will charge a fee for the issuance of a bank check.

Note: Do not confuse with a check drawn by a bank on its account with the Federal Reserve System. Such checks are a form of federal funds.

See also FEDERAL FUNDS (WWS).

BANK GUARANTEE LETTER

A letter from a commercial bank to a broker/dealer stating that a customer has funds on deposit and that these funds will be paid to the broker/dealer if certain activities occur in the customer's brokerage account.

A bank guarantee letter can serve as acceptable collateral for the writing of a short put in the customer's account.

BANK HOLDING COMPANY

A corporation engaged in many businesses through control of other corporations. However, the holding company's principal asset is ownership of a commercial bank. This form of business enterprise often is used to establish subsidiaries that are outside the restrictions of state banking laws.

BARE ASS

In the securities industry, this colorful term is used of the Boeing Company, the largest manufacturer of jet aircraft in the world. The term is derived from the company's stock symbol: BA.

BARGAIN

1. Verb: Used as a synonym for negotiate. Example: They bargained back and forth.
2. Noun: In the United States, a security that is underpriced in terms of other securities of the same class or industry. Example: XYZ is a bargain at today's prices.

3. Noun: In England, a completed securities transaction.
   Example: They struck a bargain on the sale.
4. Adjective: Used to describe an "as is" sale. Example: That was a bargain sale and may not be rescinded.

BARREL OF OIL
A standard measure of crude oil volume, equal to 42 U.S. gallons of oil at 60 degrees Fahrenheit.

The term has extensive usage in economic reports; its price, for example, is a major component in the consumer price index (CPI). The term also is used in conjunction with certain tax-sheltered investments involved in oil exploration and development.

BASIC
1. Noun, in capitals: A simple computer language used by the general public and other noncomputer specialists. Example: "My computer is programmed in BASIC."
2. Adjective: Used as a synonym for elementary or essential. Example: Timely purchase is a basic investment strategy.

BASIS BOOK
Published by Financial Publishing Company of Boston, book contains coupon interest rates and time remaining to maturity. From these, one can compute yield to maturity given dollar price, or dollar price given yield to maturity.

BASIS TRADING
Also called "yield trading." It is a term associated with wealthy or institutional-type investors who establish large underlying stock and index option futures positions. If index futures look cheap, relative to the underlying stocks, they buy the futures and sell the stocks short. When futures become overvalued, they do the opposite. The purpose of this very aggressive trading is to generate an overall rate of return on invested capital that is greater, and safer, than can be achieved in only one marketplace.

BASKET TRADING
A practice used by some portfolio managers and investment partnerships with substantial investment capital. Rather than attempt to outperform the market, they try to match the performance of a particular market index or average. To do this, they assemble a portfolio—a basket of securities—that in composition and share volume will tend to track the index or average they want to follow.

Many variable annuities use such trading and often assemble a portfolio of mutual funds to achieve the desired effect.

Also called "market basket trading."

BB

An employee of the Chicago Board Option Exchange. He or she makes a memorandum of option orders that are away from the market and, thus, are not capable of execution at the present time.

See also BOARD BROKER (WWS).

BBI

An index that measures yield levels of municipal bonds.

See also BOND BUYERS INDEX (WWS).

BCC

Acts as court of first instance for trade practice complaints made under the NASD's Code of Procedure.

See also BUSINESS CONDUCT COMMITTEE (WWS).

BD

Written Bd and used as an abbreviation for bond.

In newspaper transaction tables for U.S. government securities, the lowercase symbol b is used instead of Bd.

BEARDING

The practice of splitting a large order into smaller pieces for execution by a number of brokers. In this way, corporate raiders and large institutional investors can mask their strategies and discourage others who may want to piggyback their activities.

Bearding, of course, does not absolve the acquiror from complying with the provisions of SEC Rule 13D as it applies to the acquisition of 5% or more of the equity securities of a registered company.

BEAR HUG

Slang term used in describing a takeover offer. Concept: The raiders' offer is sufficiently attractive to draw protests from shareholders if the board turns it down, but it really is not that attractive. Thus the board of directors is caught in a "squeeze play"—they're damned if they do and damned if they don't accept the offer.

BEAR MARKET
Colorful, and metaphorical, term used to describe the fact that securities prices generally are declining. Term also may be used of an individual security. Example: Although the stock market is generally rising, there is a bear market for high-technology stocks.

See also BEARISH (WWS).

BEAR SPREAD
An option strategy that involves the purchase and sale of options of the same class. Example: The purchase and sale of calls, or puts, on the same underlying.

Such a strategy is called "bearish" if the holder/writer will profit from a drop in the market. The term is used correctly only of vertical spreads.

In a *call* bear spread, the long leg has the higher strike price. In a put bear spread, the short leg has the higher strike price.

The strategy works because, as the market drops, the premium on the leg with the higher strike price will drop faster than the premium on the lower leg.

See OPTION SPREAD STRATEGY.

BED AND BREAKFAST TRANSACTION
English expression for the profitable sale of a security late in the day with a next-day repurchase, possibly at a lower price.

BEDBUG LETTER
Facetious expression for the deficiency letter sent by the SEC in response to the filing of a preliminary registration statement by a corporation about to distribute securities.

Concept: The SEC wants the "bugs" taken out of the registration statement before the securities are issued.

BELLS AND WHISTLES
1. Used of special features attached to a security to attract investor attention. Example: The company put a lot of bells and whistles on that issue of preferred stock by adding subscription warrants.
2. Used pejoratively of sales presentations in which the salesperson emphasizes minor features of an investment and thus distracts the customer from features that may be disadvantageous for the purchaser.

BELLY UP

Slang term to describe a company, or its securities, that threatens to go bankrupt, and thus be worthless. Example: When faced with the low cost of foreign labor, many smokestack industries may go belly up.

Concept: a fish that has died in the water often floats in this position.

BELOW THE MARKET

A bid to purchase a security that is lower than the then highest bid price. For example, if the highest bid for a security is $23 per share, a bid at $21 is below the market.

Synonym: away from the market, although this expression also is used of offers above the market.

BENCHMARK

A standard for quantitative measurement. For example, the benchmark for the quarterly dividend rate on the variable rate preferred stock was set at 75% of the two-year Treasury note auction rate during that period. Or, the London Interbank Offer Rate (LIBOR) is the benchmark for Eurodebt securities.

Note: Benchmark is a quantitative norm. To express a qualitative norm, use hallmark. For example, concern for the customer's needs and investment objectives is the hallmark of business ethics in the securities industry.

BESSIE

Nickname for Bethlehem Steel Corporation, derived from its stock symbol: BS.

BEST EFFORTS

Term used of an underwriting conducted on an agency basis. The distributor promises to do his best to sell the security but does not guarantee the sale by purchasing the security from the issuer. If the security is not sold, the underwriter receives no fee, but he has no further financial obligation to the issuer.

BETA

An analysis of price volatility of a security in terms of Standard & Poor's Index. The S&P Index is given a value of 1. Securities with a beta greater than 1 have in the past been more volatile than the S&P; those with a beta less than 1 have been less volatile. It is anticipated that this trend will continue, although the beta is subject to factual revision in terms of current comparisons of the security and the S&P Index.

BG
Meaning: bank guaranteed. This symbol often is used of debt securities if a commercial bank has guaranteed either the payment of principal or interest, or both, on a security.

Because the bank guarantee does not represent a deposit there is no insurance. Thus, the value of the bank guarantee for this security should be based on the credit rating of the bank.

BID AND ASKED
The highest price (bid) at which someone is willing to purchase a security and the lowest price (offer) at which the same or another person is willing to sell a security here and now.

Synonyms: bid and offer; quote; quotation; market.

BID–IN–COMPETITION
An institutional investor solicits bids from several dealers for a block of bonds that it wants to sell. The bonds will be sold to the dealer with the highest bid.

BID WILL IMPROVE
Expression used by OTC traders in response to a request for a market from a seller. It signifies that the trader can pay more than the represented bid price, but first he or she wants a counter proposal from the prospective seller.

Acronym: BWI.

BIGI
See BOND INVESTORS GUARANTY INSURANCE COMPANY.

BIG MAC
See MUNICIPAL ASSISTANCE CORPORATION FOR THE CITY OF NEW YORK.

BIG STEEL
Colloquial name for United States Steel Corporation, or for its shares.

BILL STRIP
A Treasury bill auction in which the Treasury Department simultaneously offers bills of different maturities at one average price.

BINDER
A written memorandum of the terms and conditions of a contract that is meant to serve as a temporary agreement until a formal contract can be drawn and signed.

BITCH BOX
An unfortunate colloquialism for open, two-way, telephonic communication within a member firm.

See SQUAWK BOX.

BITS
Acronym: Bond Interest Term Security. This is a municipal security product developed and sold by Smith Barney Harris Upham, a prominent broker/dealer and investment banker. The product features a variable rate interest coupon and a put feature so the holder can redeem the bond at par if the daily rate is not satisfactory to the holder.

BITSY
A word based on the phonemes of BTSI (Brokers Transaction Services, Incorporated). BTSI sells trade processing, surveillance, and reporting services to broker/dealers.

BLACK KNIGHT
In corporate finance, a party who makes a tender offer or merger proposal that is hostile to present management of a company.

Antonym: white knight—that is, a tenderer who overcomes the unfriendly actions of a black knight.

BLANK CHECK PREFERRED STOCK
Slang for the authorization given to company management to issue, at various rates and times, preferred shares without further specific approval of the common shareholders.

BLANKET FIDELITY BOND
Insurance coverage required of brokers to protect firm against fraudulent trading, check and securities forgery, and security

misplacement or loss. Minimum coverage is required by industry rules and varies with firm's SEC net capital requirement.

Synonymous with blanket bond.

BLIND AD

Promotional material that reaches a mass audience through public media without identifying the name of its sponsor. Help wanted ads that describe a job to be filled but do not identify the hiring company would be included in this definition.

Blind ads are not unethical, but they could become illegal if they are used to disguise discriminatory hiring practices.

BLIND BROKERING

The use of an intermediary for an unnamed principal to bring borrower and lender together in a collateralized financing transaction. Often used in repurchase agreements (REPO) when an institution's money is loaned to an unidentified dealer against securities in that dealer's inventory.

BLIND POOL

Monies collected from many persons are managed for their profit. Periodic reports of profits are made to these contributors, but the contributors have no authority to manage the money nor to know how the money is employed.

In most states, blind pools are illegal except under the most stringent regulatory control.

BLOCKED

Exchange floor terminology to advise block traders that their block cannot be crossed under existing market conditions at the trader's specified price. Generally, the condition exists because the spread is too narrow to permit a cross, or because another broker with time priority is willing to pay as much or offer as little as the trader in question. Example: Our cross at 57½ is blocked by a broker with 1,000 to sell at that price.

BLOCK ORDER

As a general rule, an order to buy or sell 10,000 or more shares of the same security, or of any quantity if the dollar value is $200,000 or more.

BLOTTER

A record of daily activity transacted at a broker/dealer. The SEC requires that the broker/dealer keep separate records to reflect purchases and sales, money received and disbursed, securities accepted and delivered, and the location of all securities under that firm's control.

The term *blotter* had its origins in the days before automation when these records were handmade pen-and-ink entries.

BLUE–SKYING

General term used for the qualification of securities for sale in any of the United States under their securities laws. Also used for the registration of broker/dealers or their agent.

The expression blue sky means lacking in substance (e.g., right out of the blue—having no worth). These state laws provide that new securities issuers qualify by providing information about the issue and the issuer so buyers may judge the issue's value.

Generally, issues senior to securities already blue-skied (or a further issuance of securities already listed on a national exchange) are exempt from blue sky procedures. Legal advice is needed.

BO DEREK

Slang for the U.S. Treasury bonds 10s of May 2010. Term derives from the title of a popular movie (*10*) and the name of its star whose beauty and figure ranked at the top of a 1 to 10 scale.

BOND

1. Any debt security, such as an IOU or a corporation promissory note.
2. A debt security with a maturity of more than 7 to 10 years. Used in distinction to note, a debt security with a shorter time to maturity. Often an issuer will describe a debt security as a bond that other issuers would call a note.
3. Money or property deposited as a pledge of good faith.
4. Usually, bonds are secured by a mortgage.
5. One's word given as a pledge of future performance. Example: "My word is my bond."

BOND INTEREST TERM SECURITY

See BITS.

BOND INVESTORS GUARANTY INSURANCE COMPANY

An insuror of the timely payment of interest and the repayment of principal to holders of selected municipal securities. BIGI is equally owned by American International Group, Bankers Trust, Xerox Credit, and Phibro-Salomon.

This group not only competes with MBIA and AMBAC, it also insures municipal unit investment trusts, municipal bond funds, and substantial municipal portfolios. Premiums are set as a percentage of the par value of the securities insured.

BOND WASHING

Term used of an unethical, if not illegal, procedure associated with bond trading in England.

Background: Some English bonds trade ex-interest, rather than on an accrued interest basis. To avoid taxes, these bonds are sold before ex-date to nontaxable holders. After ex-date, the bonds are repurchased at a price that represents the original price plus the interest amount. In this way, the "interest" becomes a capital consideration, rather than a currently taxable event.

BOOK VALUE

Take total assets minus intangibles, subtract all liabilities and the par value of preferred stock. Divide by the number of outstanding common shares. Quotient is the book value.

Although book value can be a deceptive measurement, it is used by many to make a gross selection of common shares that may be underpriced. Book value should not be an ultimate criterion for security selection.

Also called the "net tangible value" or the "liquidating value per common share."

BOOT

Acronym: branch operations and orientation training. A program of training and development for new employees who will work in the operations side of a branch brokerage office.

Generally, the BOOT program is more detailed and suited to customer relations and problems than to training headquarters operations personnel.

BOOTSTRAP ACQUISITION

Term used in conjunction with a friendly corporate takeover. First, when threatened with a takeover, the target company exchanges some of its assets for outstanding shares held by the dissident shareholders. Then, the target company sells the rest of the firm to a friendly acquirer. In this way, the friendly acquirer obtains 100% of the target company for less than it would have paid. In effect, the target company has helped to finance part of its own takeover.

BOTTOM

Term used by traders and chartists to refer to a price level through which an issue, or the market in general, is not expected to fall without encountering substantial buying pressure by investors.

If used historically, the term often is used in conjunction with qualifying terms, such as double bottom, triple bottom, and so on.

BOTTOM LINE

1. The net profit, after interest and taxes, of a corporation or other business enterprise.
2. The result of any endeavor. Example: "If we do it right, the bottom line will be a quality product."

BRACKET

The ranking of individual investment bankers in an underwriting. The term refers to the financial responsibility of the firm, in terms of takedown, in the distribution; thus, the higher the bracket, the greater the financial responsibility.

Typical bracket terminology, from highest to lowest, is: manager (co-manager), special, major, mezzanine, submajor, first regional, second regional.

Occasionally, the term is used to show a special business relationship with the manager of the underwriting or the issuer.

BREAKUP VALUE

1. English term: net asset value per share. American synonym: book value.
2. The value of the component parts of a corporation if they were to exist as independent entities. Example: The breakup value of American Telephone & Telegraph is $78 billion.

BRIDGE LOAN

Short-term financing provided while borrower seeks longer-term loan.

BROAD TAPE

Colloquial: wire news services whose news is printed on wider paper than the traditional stock ticker tapes. Examples: the news services provided by Munifacts, Dow Jones, and Reuters.

BROKEN CONVERTIBLE

A convertible bond or preferred that is selling at a yield competitive with yields on nonconvertible securities of the same class. This occurs if the market has no prospects for a rise in the value of the common stock; thus, the market is unwilling to pay extra for the conversion feature. When this occurs, the price of the convertible will tend to fall to a level to provide a yield that is competitive with nonconvertible fixed-income securities and the convertible is said to be "broken."

BROKERS TRANSACTION SERVICES INCORPORATED
See BITSY.

BTSI
See BITSY.

BUCK
1. Jargon: a U.S. dollar or multiple thereof.
2. U.S. government securities trading term for an even dollar quote, either for the bid or the asked. For example, a U.S. Treasury bond has been trading in the 97–98 range. The quote could be: 28 to a buck. Meaning: bid $97^{28}/_{32}$, asked 98.

BUDGET
1. The anticipated cost of a project or enterprise. For example, we have a budget of $4 million for the rollout of the new computers.
2. The difference between revenue and expenses for a specific time period, usually one year, for a corporation or government. For example, XYZ Corporation expects a budget deficit in the first quarter.
3. The act of allocating assets for the initiation or completion of a project. For example, we have budgeted $10 million for the project.

BUG
1. Noun: slang—an unanticipated problem in the programming of a computer that does not show up until processing begins.
2. Verb: slang—to pester or annoy others to do an action that they have previously refused to do. Example: "He is a successful salesperson because he bugs his clients until they buy."

BULLDOG SECURITIES

Debt securities of foreign issuers that trade in England and whose face value and interest payments are denominated in pounds sterling. Typically, these securities are investment grade with longer-term maturities.

U.S. analog: Yankee bonds.

BULL MARKET

A market for stocks, bonds, or commodities that is generally marked by rising prices.

The origin of the metaphor is unknown, but the concept is clear: a period marked by general enthusiasm, often thoughtless and overly speculative, for the value of financial assets.

BULL SPREAD

An option strategy that involves the purchase and sale of options of the same class. Example: The purchase and sale of calls, or puts, on the same underlying.

Such a strategy is called "bullish" if the holder/writer will profit from a rise in the market. The term is used correctly only of vertical spreads.

In a *call* bull spread, the long leg has a lower strike price. In a *put* bull spread, the higher strike price.

The strategy works because, as the market rises, the premium on the leg with the lower strike price will rise faster than the premium with the higher strike price.

See OPTION SPREAD STRATEGY.

BUNNY

Colloquial name for Playboy Enterprises, Inc., a well-known magazine publisher, hotelier, and operator of entertainment clubs. The name comes from the company's popular commercial logo.

BUSINESS CYCLE

1. Term used of time from top of one rise in gross national product through one fall in GNP back to original base line. In past, business cycles have tended to average about 2½ years.
2. Time it takes a manufacturing company to turn raw materials into sold finished products.

BUST–UP PROXY PROPOSAL

Term for the request made to shareholders to approve the sale or liquidation of a company. Usually, this request is made by dissident shareholders who seek to oust present management or who wish to gain control of the company or its parts.

BUY AT BEST

This is the trade instruction underlying a market order to buy.

In practice, this substitute instruction is used in over-the-counter trading if the purchaser wants a large block of securities and wants the broker/dealer to act as an agent. There is no requirement that all of the purchases be made at the same price.

BUY–DOWN LOAN

Term for a mortgage loan in which the builder subsidizes a portion of the buyer's interest payments for the first three years or more. To make monthly mortgage payments more appealing to the buyer, the builder, for example, agrees to pay the difference between a lower rate of interest, let's say 9%, and the then prevailing mortgage interest rate, let's say 13%. This is a mortgage interest savings of 4% for the first three years.

BUYERS' MARKET

Condition in which the anticipated supply so exceeds demand that buyers can dictate prices and terms of sale. For example, the world surplus of oil has produced a buyers' market.

Antonym: sellers' market.

BUYER'S OPTION

Securities contract between two broker/dealers in which the seller attempts to settle before the date agreed upon at the time of the contract. In this case, the buyer has the option of agreeing to settle before the agreed upon date or of refusing to do so without prejudicing its rights in this transaction.

BUYING SIGNAL

A point in a sales presentation to a potential buyer where the buyer shows interest in the product. For example, a salesperson is presenting the benefits of a particular convertible security and the client asks: How many shares of stock will I receive if I convert?

Generally, an efficient salesperson will, if the product is otherwise suitable to the client, ask for the order if the client gives a buying signal.

BUY SIGNAL

A term used by chartists. It means that their technical measurements of previous price movements indicate the appropriateness of a purchase at the present time.

Generally, buy signals occur when the price of a security does not break through a support level, or when the price of a security penetrates a preestablished moving average. Market volume is also an important consideration.

BUZZ WORD

Jargon: a word or expression that is considered state of the art and is used by experts to identify a problem or its solution. As this word or expression flows into current usage by nonexperts, it is called a buzz word.

Buzz words are often misunderstood by their users. Many buzz words are neologisms. Example: Telephone sales can often be time-consuming.

A rapid method of screening potential clients by telephone is called "telemarketing." This buzz word now becomes the expression to solve all sales problems.

C

CABINET BID/OFFER

On option exchanges, a procedure used to make accommodation transactions in relatively worthless option contract positions. It is a nonauction procedure enabling investors to close out option positions, either long or short, for 1¢ per share.

CABINET BONDS

NYSE term for listed corporate bonds that are infrequently traded. So called, because current bids and offers, if any, are filed in cabinets by price and time of entry. The infrequent trades are completed when a buyer or seller uses the cabinet entries to find the other side of the trade.

CABS

Acronym: Capital Appreciation Bonds. This is a service mark of Salomon Brothers Inc for zero-coupon municipals.

CAES

Acronym: Computer Assisted Execution System.

CAES is an NASD-sponsored communication system that links stock exchange broker/dealers to OTC marketmakers. CAES permits these broker/dealers to automatically direct order flow for exchange-listed securities to the OTC market for execution, if this is a better market.

CALENDAR SPREAD

Option spread endeavoring to profit from the purchase of an option in a farther month and from the sale of an option of the same class in a nearer month. Example: buy October 50 call, sell closer July 50 call; or buy October 45 put, sell closer July 45 put.

Called "horizontal spread" if strike (exercise) prices are the same. Called "diagonal spread" if strike prices are different.

Calendar spreads are bullish if investor will profit from upward movement of underlying stock; bearish if investor will profit from downward movement of stock.

CALLABLE PREFERRED

Term identifying a preferred issue that may, at the option of the issuer, be retired at a preestablished redemption value. The prospectus of the issue will outline the call price and the conditions under which the issue, or a portion thereof, may be retired by the issuer. Most preferred issues are callable.

CALL LOAN

Loan made by broker, upon deposit of appropriate collateral, to finance margin activities of customers. Loan is callable at any time by either party.

Also called "broker loan," or "broker's collateral loan."

CALL LOAN RATE

The rate of interest charged by banks when brokers deposit margined securities as collateral for loans used to finance client margin accounts. The margin interest, in turn, will be based on the call loan rate.

The process of depositing margined securities is called "rehypothecation."

Synonym: broker's (collateral) loan rate.

CANADIAN DOLLAR

The primary unit of currency in Canada.

Frequent abbreviations: Can$ or $C.

CANADIAN INSTITUTE OF CHARTERED ACCOUNTANTS

A nationwide body in which public accountants in good standing in Canada are granted membership. Although CICA makes accounting practice announcements affecting corporate audit practices, professional ethics are regulated under provincial control. To be a member of CICA, a public accountant must have a college degree and practical working experience, and must pass a series of local examinations.

CAP

Term used in the preliminary discussions of a new security offering. The "cap" is the highest interest rate the issuer is willing to pay on a bond issue, or the highest price at which the underwriters are willing to attempt to make an offering of stock.

CAPITAL APPRECIATION BONDS

See CABS.

CAPITAL APPRECIATION AND PROTECTION INSURANCE

See CAPTN.

CAPITAL ASSET

For IRS purposes, all equity and debt issues of value. Profits and losses realized from trading in capital assets are accorded special tax treatment if they were held more than six months.

Money market securities are not considered capital assets. Exception: A sale of Treasury bills before maturity can generate a capital gain or loss if sold above or below the ratable value in terms of purchase price and maturity value. Tax advice is needed.

CAPITALISM

An economic system in which private ownership dominates and determines the production and distribution of goods and services for financial profit.

Capitalism can coexist with socialism—that is, a partial ownership of certain industries or public services.

Antonym: Communism—that is, an economic system in which all, or practically all, means of production are owned by the state.

CAPITALIZATION

General term for sources of a company's funds that are evidenced by either longer-term bonds or stock. Current liabilities (in which bonds that will mature in one year or less are numbered) are excluded from capitalization. In addition to the par value of outstanding preferred and common stock, paid-in surplus and retained earnings are included in capitalization.

See CAPITALIZATION RATIO.

CAPITALIZATION ISSUE

In England, a free distribution of stock to common shareholders in proportion to their existing holdings in the company. Also called "scrip" or "bonus issue."

In the United States, such distributions are known as stock dividends, split-ups, or spin-offs.

CAPITALIZATION RATIO

Measurement of longer-term sources of funds used by a corporation in terms of funded debt (bonds), preferred stock, and common stock.

Normally stated as a percentage. For example, company has longer-term debt of $10, preferred stock of $5, and common stock of $35 (including surplus). Total capital is $50. Bond ratio is 20%, preferred stock ratio is 10%, common stock ratio is 70%.

CAPITAL STRUCTURE

1. The component parts of a corporation's permanent or relatively permanent sources of funds. In practice, the practical breakdown is made between funded debt (bonds with maturities of more than one year), preferred stock, and common stock. In the computation of the relative value of common stock, par value, paid-in surplus, and retained earnings are used.
    Synonym 1: capitalization.
2. The total capital of a company from all sources, including current liabilities.

CAP ORDERS

Term applied to large buy or sell orders left with an exchange specialist that authorize the specialist to use market judgment in their execution.

Technically, the use of such discretion by a specialist violates exchange rules. Nevertheless, such orders persist because they save time for floor brokers, allow specialists to earn floor commissions, and permit the buyer or seller to avoid missing the market or unduly influencing prices.

Also called "hook" or "on the hook" orders.

CAPPING

Term used to describe the manipulative practice whereby a person who has previously sold call options sells the underlying stock to depress its value and thus prevent, or discourage, the exercise of the calls against the account.

The practice is illegal.

CAPS

See CONVERTIBLE ADJUSTABLE PREFERRED STOCK.

CAPTIVE INSURANCE COMPANY

Term identifying an affiliate of a company that insures plant and equipment of the parent company. In effect, the establishment of a captive insurance subsidiary is a form of self-insurance that may result in significant savings.

Many captive insurance subsidiaries are set up outside the United States (offshore) for tax and regulatory purposes. Often, such subsidiaries also insure other companies.

CAPTN

Acronym: capital appreciation and protection insurance. A form of variable life policy that enables the owner to switch investment premiums between several investment choices. These choices may include a number of mutual funds or zero-coupon bonds. Yields and realized profits remain tax sheltered as long as they remain undistributed.

Variously known as universal life, directed life, multipurpose life policies.

CARP

See CONTROLLED ADJUSTABLE RATE PREFERRED STOCK.

CARRYOVER

Provision of tax law of United States that permits individual taxpayer, who sustains net capital loss in excess of annual deduction of $3,000 against income, to carry over the remainder into the subsequent tax years until it is offset against either capital gains or income.

CARS

See CERTIFICATE FOR AUTOMOBILE RECEIVABLES.

CARTEL

Italian: *cartello,* a letter of defiance.

A group of countries or businesses, usually international, that band together to control prices or distribution of a commodity, thus assuring a great profit in most cases.

Practical synonym: a monopoly.

CASH AND NEW

English stock exchange term. Concept: A person buys and sells a stock during the same account period, thereby avoiding a commission, and then repurchases the same security during the next account period.

See ACCOUNT DAY.

CASH FLOW

Accepted measurement is earnings after interest and taxes, and preferred dividend if applicable, to which the annual depreciation charge for fixed assets is added.

The cash flow measurement is indicative of the earning power of a company, but can be deceptive. Many recent articles in scholarly journals dispute accepted measurement standards.

Cash flow is calculated as follows: company has annual after-tax earnings of $50 million. Company also had depreciation charge of $5 million and preferred stock dividend of $2 million. Cash flow is:

$50,000,000	
− 2,000,000	For preferred dividend
$48,000,000	For common stockholders
+ 5,000,000	Depreciation
$53,000,000	Cash flow

CASH IMMEDIATE MARKET

Term is analogous to regular way settlement in the corporate bond market, but the term is restricted to trades in pass-through securities. In the case of conventional pass-throughs, settlement must be no later than seven business days following the trade date.

A cash immediate market for GNMA pass-throughs permits the trade to be settled any time in the current month, but no substitution of comparable GNMA issues is permitted; only the issue that is the subject of the contract is deliverable.

CASH MANAGEMENT ACCOUNT
Proprietary service mark of Merrill Lynch & Company for its central brokerage accounts that permit securities trading, provide a checking account, and a debit/credit VISA card.

Generally, CMA accounts are margin accounts, but cash accounts also are permitted for custodians, trusts, estates, and corporations.

CASH MANAGEMENT BILL
A short-term U.S. Treasury bill occasionally offered by the Treasury Department to restore depleted cash balances or to meet current debt obligations.

CASH ON DELIVERY
Used typically on buy orders entered by institutional investors, many of whom are prohibited from delivering cash unless an asset is received in its place. Example: "If I give you $1 million, you must give me something worth $1 million."

Also called "delivery against cash" (DAC).

CATNIPS
See SERIAL CATS and CATS.

CATS
Acronym: Certificate of Accrual on Treasury Securities. These securities, which are proprietary to Salomon Brothers Inc , represent ownership interest in future interest and principal payments on selected U.S. government securities. The underlying securities are placed in trust with a commercial bank.

CATS are listed on the NYSE and have an active secondary market. In effect, CATS are zero-coupon bonds and are taxed accordingly.

CAVEAT EMPTOR
Latin: let the buyer beware.

Term frequently used in the securities industry to warn anyone who eagerly purchases any security without an appropriate consideration of risk or without adequate diligence about the issuer.

CAVEAT VENDITOR
Latin: let the seller beware.

In effect, a warning by regulators of the securities industry. It is directed toward broker/dealers and their agents: Obey federal, state, and industry rules and regulations, or face criminal, civil, or economic sanctions.

CBI
See CERTIFICATE OF BENEFICIAL INTEREST.

C&D ORDER
Abbreviation for a "cease and desist" order.

C&D orders often are sought by the SEC and CFTC to halt an ongoing practice by someone acting against the federal securities or commodities trading laws. This is required because the SEC and the CFTC do not have civil or criminal jurisdiction.

C&D REIT
See CONSTRUCTION & DEVELOPMENT REIT.

CEDE
This is the nominee partnership entity of the Depository Trust Company (DTC), the quasi-cashiering department of the securities industry. The partnership name is used as the registration form for stocks and bonds left in DTC's custody. This greatly simplifies the transfer of securities following a trade.

CEDEL
An institution headquartered in Luxembourg that serves banks and broker/dealers as a clearing corporation for Eurobond transactions.

CENTRAL REGISTRATION DEPOSITORY
Acronym: CRD. The CRD, sponsored by the NASD, is a computerized system for the maintenance of registration records for all registered personnel. The system also encompasses many state blue sky registrations. Centralization permits easy record-keeping and especially the annual renewals required by many of the states.

CEO
Acronym: chief executive officer.

The corporate officer, reporting only to the board of directors, whose responsibility it is to carry out policies established by the board. How much of the day-to-day responsibilities the CEO exercises depends on how much has been delegated to other management officials.

CERTIFICATE

1. Any document representing equity or debt of the issuer.
2. A debt instrument with an original maturity of one year or less. Exception: Some certificates of deposit have longer maturities.

CERTIFICATE FOR AUTOMOBILE RECEIVABLES

"CARS," as they are popularly called, are two- to three-year debt securities collateralized by pools of bank and finance company car loans. Because CARS give higher than comparable Treasury security interest rates, they are attractive to institutional investors.

CERTIFICATE OF ACCRUAL ON TREASURY SECURITIES

See CATS.

CERTIFICATE OF BENEFICIAL INTEREST

A CBI is evidence of an undivided ownership interest in a business created under a legal trust. As such, a CBI differs little from common stock and is often called "a share of beneficial interest." However, unlike common stockholders, owners of CBIs do not elect successors to the trustees. The trustees elect their own successors.

CERTIFICATE OF INDEBTEDNESS

A short-term, fixed-coupon debt security formerly issued by the U.S. Treasury with maturities of 90 days to one year. CIs have been replaced by 180-day and one-year Treasury bills.

CERTIFICATE OF (TIME) DEPOSIT

A debt security issued by a commercial bank in exchange for funds that are to be left on deposit for a period of 30 days to one year, although longer-period CDs are available. Generally, the interest rate is fixed and is paid at maturity, or at more frequent intervals.

Holders of nonnegotiable CDs generally have to pay a penalty for premature redemption. Negotiable CDs are issued in bearer form and are readily marketable at prevailing money market rates.

CERTIFICATE ON GOVERNMENT RECEIPTS

See COUGARs.

CERTIFIED CHECK

A personal check drawn on a commercial bank that the bank guarantees to honor upon presentation. The bank, upon certification, sets aside sufficient funds from the writer's account to redeem the certified check.

Note: Do not confuse with bank check, a check drawn by the bank on itself, or with Federal Funds check, a check drawn by the bank on its account with the Federal Reserve. Certified checks are clearinghouse funds.

CFO

See CHIEF FINANCIAL OFFICER.

CHA–CHA

Colloquial name used to identify both the company and the common stock of Champion International, Inc., a prominent manufacturer of building materials. Name is derived from the symbol for the stock: CHA.

CHARTIST

A market technician who makes buy/sell decisions based on the plotted price movements of a security.

See also POINT AND FIGURE CHART (WWS).

CHATTEL MORTGAGE

A loan agreement that places a lien on such personal property as furniture, automobiles, jewelry, or other personal possessions that are pledged as collateral for the repayment of the loan.

CHEAP

Term often used to indicate that the price of a particular security is relatively low when compared to previous prices for the same security, or when compared to the securities of other companies in the same industry.

Cheap tends to be a judgment of present price in terms of present value. Underpriced tends to be used of present price in terms of future value.

Common antonym: fully priced.

CHEAP STOCK

Corporate shares distributed while the concern is still in a developmental or promotional stage, or issued to promoters for a consideration well below the proposed public offering.

CHERRY PICKING

Slang expression for choosing the best of something while ignoring what is less attractive.

The SEC uses the term regarding Rule 14b-1 and the intent of issuers to be fair and reasonable in soliciting names of beneficial owners. If issuers solicit names, they should do so from all broker/dealers and banks; in this way, the issuers would not show discrimination by forcing only large brokerage firms to search their records for the names of beneficial owners.

CHIEF FINANCIAL OFFICER

In a corporation, the individual who has the responsibility to oversee the management of the company's money, investments, and tax liabilities. Included also is the responsibility of overseeing, planning, and supervising the corporate budget.

CHIEF OPERATING OFFICER

In a corporation, the individual responsible for the day-to-day management of the company. If the chairman is the chief executive officer, the president normally will be the chief operating officer.

CHINESE ARBITRAGE

See REVERSE HEDGE (WWS).

CHINESE MARKET

Term used by traders to signify that they are willing to buy above the lowest offer, or sell below the highest bid, but only in significant quantities.

CHINESE WALL

Slang expression to describe the communications barrier between the trading/sales side of a broker/dealer and the finance (investment banking)/research side of the firm.

The barrier is ethical, rather than real. The purpose is to prevent the sales/trading side of the firm from taking advantage of the nonpublic (inside) information that is often possessed by the investment banking or research side of the firm.

CHIPS

Acronym: Clearing House Interbank Payment System. CHIPS is an electronic, international check-transfer system that can move dollar balances between participating U.S. and foreign financial institutions anywhere in the world.

CHURNING
Excessive trading in an account, with connotation that buy/sell activities are against financial interests of customer. Unethical activity and often actionable at law by offended party. Courts judge degree of control over the account, broker profits versus customer profits, and turnover of original capital to decide if churning has occurred.

CI
See CERTIFICATE OF INDEBTEDNESS.

CIB
See COMPOUND INTEREST BONDS.

CICA
See CANADIAN INSTITUTE OF CHARTERED ACCOUNTANTS.

CIS
Acronym: Computer Information Services. CIS sells trade processing, surveillance, and reporting services to broker/dealers and commodity futures merchants.

CITIZEN BONDS
Originated by Prudential-Bache Securities, these are municipal bonds that can be purchased in denominations of $1,000 or less to provide greater public participation. A single jumbo-sized certificate is issued, held by the Depository Trust Company, and ownership, transfer, and secondary market transactions are made in the Prudential-Bache computerized operations system.

CITY, THE
That region in the eastern portion of London wherein is concentrated England's principal financial services organizations. It is the counterpart of New York's Wall Street.

CLASS
1. Used of securities with similar features. For example, bonds are a class of security.
2. Used of options with similar features. For example, all calls of an underlying security are one class, all puts are another class. Definition is important because option position and exercise limits generally are determined by class.

CLASS OF OPTION

This term identifies all put options on the same underlying security as a class. All call options on the same underlying security constitute a second class.

CLASS 1 RAILROAD

Industry category used to distinguish those railroads in the United States that have annual revenues of more than $10 million. Practically, these are the only railroads that can borrow money through debt securities without either a commercial bank assurance or a parent company guaranty.

CLAYTON ANTITRUST ACT

Passed in 1919, this federal law is designed to prevent business monopolies, unfair competition, or restraint of trade in any domestic industry.

CLEAN

Term used by block positioners if they are able to match buy-and-sell orders from customers without the need to take the security into inventory. Example: "We did a clean trade for 50,000 ABC." In other words, they had a seller of 50,000 and found a buyer without taking inventory risk.

"Clean on the tape" is often used if the transaction appears on an exchange tape.

The term *natural* is often used as a synonym for clean. Example: "We did a natural for 50,000 ABC."

CLEAN ON THE PRINT

Expression used by block positioners of exchange-listed stocks. The expression is an announcement to the firm's sales force that it brought buyers and sellers together in sufficient quantity so the block trade may be executed on the floor without a need for the firm to act as principal to facilitate the trade.

CLEARING AGREEMENT

1. A contract between broker/dealers in which one agrees to execute, compare, confirm, and settle the other's securities transactions on a fee basis.
2. A contract between banks whereby one agrees to honor, accept, and process the other's checks through the Federal Reserve Banking System.

CLIENT SERVICE REPRESENTATIVE
CSR is an alternate title for registered representative or account executive. The inference is that the CSR is a salaried employee, while the RR works on a salary plus adjustment or directly on a commission basis.

The term *CSR* originated with discount brokerage firms, although some full-service brokerage firms use CSRs to screen walk-ins, to handle one-time transactions, or to execute orders for house accounts.

CLOSING SALE
Term used of exchange-traded options if a transaction reduces or eliminates a long position in an option series. Example: A client purchases 5 XYZ JAN 65 puts. A subsequent sale of 5 XYZ JAN 65 puts would constitute a closing sale and would eliminate the position.

"CLUB" FINANCING
Term used in Eurobond underwritings. The term is used to designate an underwriting by a group of similarly sized banks each of whom subscribes to an equal amount of the issue.

CMTA
Acronym: Clearing Member Trade Agreement. The agreement is a standard Options Clearing Corporation form that permits exchange members to execute, clear, and settle contracts through a clearing member. This procedure facilitates record-keeping of the opening and closing of options contracts and the collection of execution brokerage expenses.

CNS
A prevalent method of clearing and settling securities transactions.

See also CONTINUOUS NET SETTLEMENT (WWS).

COBOL
An approximate acronym for: Common Business Oriented Language. This is a popular business-oriented computer language developed especially for typical commercial activities.

CODM
Acronym: call option deutsche marks. This is a conventional currency contract arranged as a European option to enable the

holder to buy a predetermined amount of West German currency at a fixed price stated in U.S. dollars.

As a European option, the option may be exercised only on a specific date in the future; thus, it differs from an American option that can be exercised any time between purchase and expiration date.

COD TRANSACTION

Frequently used designation on institutional client buy orders. Broker buys for client's account and will deliver to client's agent. Upon delivery, agent will pay for cost of purchase.

Also called "DVP" (deliver versus payment) and "DAC" (deliver against cost).

COLLAR

In connection with a new issue of securities, this term signifies the lowest interest rate that bond purchasers may accept, or the lowest price an issuer may accept as a guarantee from the underwriters of stock.

Antonym: see CAP.

COLLATERALIZED MORTGAGE OBLIGATION

A CMO is a debt security collateralized by a portfolio of other securities—for example, a portfolio of GNMA modified passthroughs. In effect, they have the same credit rating as the collateral.

CMOs are normally issued in denominations of $1,000, pay semiannual interest, and semiannual partial repayments of principal.

COLOR

Jargon: background information. Used in the financial services industry to describe market conditions, investor preferences, price levels for yield spreads between benchmark issues, or between alternative investments.

COMBINATION

Long call and long put, or short call and short put, on same underlying security having different expiration months or different strike prices. For example, buy XYZ April 50 call, buy XYZ July 45 put. Order ticket will give the net debit, on long combination, or the net credit, on short combination, that is acceptable to customer. Order will be executed only if conditions can be met.

COME BACK

1. Verb: Used as two words—the act of returning to an original state. Example: The market is temporarily depressed and will come back to its old high.

   Note: In England, the expression implies a return to a lower state. Example: The market will come back.

2. Noun: Used as one word—the result of the act of returning. Example: "That was quite a comeback." Implication is that the return is a repetition of a former success.

COMFORT LETTER

Letter of indemnification often given by an issuer or seller of a security to its investment banker as underwriter or sales agent. In a comfort letter, the offeror agrees to reimburse the investment banker for realized litigation losses and expenses resulting from material omissions or misrepresentations in a registration statement, merger proposal, or tender offer.

COMING TO ME

Qualifying language used by over-the-counter traders when they represent a quote that is not their own. For example, the price is 19½–20, coming to me.

The price expresses another dealer's firm market, but it does not represent the market at which the trader is willing to buy or sell.

COMMERCIAL BANK

A national or state chartered institution that accepts savings, time, or demand deposits. These deposits, in turn, are used to finance short- and intermediate-term loans to individuals, businesses, and governments.

COMMITMENT FEE

1. Money paid as an incentive to investors by an issuer of securities to be distributed some time in the future. The issuer has no current need for the money but is willing to pay a fee for the certainty that the funds will be available when needed.

2. Points paid by a prospective borrower to a bank to guarantee the availability of funds in the future. Often used with mortgages on residential property. As such, points represent a form of interest and are tax deductible.

COMMITTEE FOR AN INCOMPETENT

Term used for a court-appointed person or institution directed to handle the legal, personal, or financial affairs of someone judged to be physically or mentally unable to handle their own affairs.

The term generally is shortened to committee. Example: The court appointed a committee to handle her affairs while she is recovering from a stroke.

Security transactions effected by a committee constitute a "legal" transfer and require supporting documentation.

COMMITTEE ON UNIFORM SECURITIES IDENTIFICATION PROCEDURES

Its numbering system—nine characters, seven numbers, and two letters—permits a standardized computer identification of any security issued in the United States after 1970.

Acronym: CUSIP (WWS).

COMMODITY EXCHANGE INCORPORATED

Acronym: COMEX, a commodity exchange in New York City. Formed by merger of four prior exchanges, Comex trades futures in metals, petroleum, coffee, sugar, and financial instruments.

COMMODITY POOL OPERATOR

Acronym: CPO. Any person or enterprise that solicits funds to pool them for trades in commodities futures contracts on behalf of the owners of the funds. Such pool operators must register with the National Futures Association (NFA) and comply with the provisions of the Commodities Exchange Act.

COMMODITY TRADING ADVISER

Acronym: CTA. A person who provides others, for a fee, with advice on futures contract tactics or strategies. CTAs must register with the National Futures Association (NFA) and comply with the provisions of the Commodities Exchange Act.

COMMON LAW

1. Legal precedents derived from court decisions over a period of years, rather than from specific legislative decrees.
2. Used to distinguish such precedents from statute law.
3. Used to distinguish general legal statutes from specific laws. Example: The law of agency derives from common law, rather than from securities law.

COMMON MESSAGE SWITCH

Acronym: CMS. CMS is an electronic switching device that links member firms with the floors of the New York and American Stock Exchanges. Order instructions are routed electronically, that is, switched to the appropriate floors for execution. Executed orders are returned to the initiating member firm by the same system.

COMMUNISM

1. As a political system, the centralized control of social and economic forces by a strong and totalitarian political faction that is self-perpetuating.
2. As an economic theory, a transition phase between capitalism and socialism. It is characterized by governmental control of production facilities and the distribution of goods and services. Ultimately, production facilities should be transferred to the workers who produce the goods and services.

COMMUNITY PROPERTY

Legal concept: Assets acquired during a marriage are deemed to be acquired half and half by each party to the marriage. As a result, in those states that have community property laws, the consent of both parties is required to effect transfer or other disposition of such assets.

COMPARISON

Notice exchanged between brokers who are parties to a trade to verify and confirm details of the trade prior to settlement.

Also called "comparison sheet."

COMPETITIVE OPTIONS TRADER

Acronym: COT. A COT is a NYSE-registered options trader. The COT provides liquidity to the marketplace by augmenting the dealer activities of the specialist. Comparable to the market maker function on most other option exchanges, the COT will bid and offer, or buy and sell, for personal accounts to accommodate public orders in all option series dealt in on the NYSE.

COMPO

Contraction for: in competition.

An invitation to a dealer by a customer that the dealer, in competition with other dealers, submit a competitive bid/offer for a block of securities. The dealer with the best bid/offer then completes the trade in an over-the-counter transaction.

COMPOUND INTEREST

Also called "interest on interest," it is a borrowing charge calculated on the principal amount of a loan *plus* the unpaid interest from preceding interest periods. For example, the interest on margin debit balances is compounded monthly.

Future value tables will show the amount owed, or owned, at varying compound rates of interest. To program a pocket calculator, key: CE; 1; +; rate of interest as a decimal; x. Each time the = is keyed, it will compound the interest for the designated number of interest periods. Multiply by the principal amount in dollars to get the future value.

COMPOUND INTEREST BONDS

Used of municipal bonds issued at a significant discount from face value that pay no periodic interest. At maturity, the bond is redeemed at par. The difference between the original purchase price and par value represents interest income.

See also ZERO–COUPON BOND (WWS).

COMPUTER–ASSISTED EXECUTION SYSTEM

See CAES.

COMPUTER INFORMATION SERVICES

See CIS.

CONCESSION

1. Corporate underwritings: dollar remuneration per share or per bond given to members of selling group who successfully market the securities.
2. Municipal underwritings: dollar discount from public offering price. Given to members of the Municipal Securities Rulemaking Board (MSRB) who are not members of the account if they purchase bonds for their own or the accounts of customers.

CONDITIONAL SALES AGREEMENT

Often used in the private placement of equipment trust certificates. The issuer pledges a minimal amount of equity; however, title to the equipment does not pass to the issuer until the entire debt is repaid.

CONDOR SPREAD

Slang used by professional traders in index options to designate certain vertical spreads. It is a condor if it is a vertical bull and bear (four positions, therefore). Condor spreads may be put or call positions.

Condor spreads do not have any strike prices in common. The two long legs are in the middle, with the short legs bounding them to imitate the wide wingspan of the condor. The spread, therefore, covers a wide range of index volatility. Example: With the OEX at 197.57, a condor spread would be long the OEX 195 and 200, and short the OEX 190 and 205. All expirations would be the same month. The four positions could be puts or calls.

CONDUIT–TYPE CUSTOMER

Term used to describe an institutional client doing business with a broker/dealer who does not disclose the principals for whom it is transacting business. Typical conduit-type customers include banks and trust companies.

Frequently used synonym: omnibus account on an undisclosed basis.

Conduit-type customers are required to represent to the broker/dealer that they know their customers and that federal securities laws and industry regulations are not being violated.

CONFIRMATION

Commonly called a "confirm."

The confirmation is a notice to a customer that payment is due on a purchase, or that net proceeds are available on a sale of securities.

Federal securities law requires that a confirmation be sent promptly following each purchase and sale. Notices for dividend reinvestment programs, however, may be sent on a periodic basis.

CONFLICT OF INTEREST

Term used to describe a financial situation where a person prejudicially places personal affairs before those of constituents that the person is supposed to serve or represent. The term is not limited to financial profit; it also may include social or political conflicts.

One example of a conflict of interest would be for a registered representative to purchase a security for a personal account just before recommending it to customers.

CONGLOMERATE

Description of a corporation that controls a number of other concerns in unrelated business fields. The term is descriptive only. In practice, many companies diversify business activities to moderate the effects of economic cycles without being called conglomerates.

CONSERVATOR

A court-appointed fiduciary whose responsibility it is to manage the assets of someone legally deemed to be incompetent.

In practice, the distinction between a conservator and a committee is semantic. Usually a committee is appointed if a person is physically or mentally incompetent. A conservator may be appointed for a person who is a compulsive gambler or a spendthrift.

See COMMITTEE FOR AN INCOMPETENT.

CONSIDERATION

1. Money or other item of value transferred at the time a contract, either written or oral, is made.
2. Funds or securities used to acquire title to equity or debt securities of an issuer.

CONSOL

An infrequently used term for a bond with a face value of less than $1,000.

See BABY BOND.

CONSOLIDATED BALANCE SHEET

A financial document showing the combined assets, liabilities, and net worth of a parent organization. The combined balance sheet does not break out the components that come from subsidiary corporations.

Most American parent corporations use consolidated balance sheets, although the annual report may represent the input, or profitability, of the subsidiaries.

CONSOLIDATED QUOTATION SYSTEM

Acronym: CQS. A system that collects from all market centers the current bid and asked prices, with sizes, of listed stocks. These bids and sizes are then disseminated to subscribers. For example, the Quotron Financial Data Base is a CQS. Line 20 of Quotron represents current bids and offers not only from the NYSE but also from the other exchanges or the Third Market if these are better than the NYSE quotes.

CONSOLIDATED TAPE (SYSTEM)

Acronym: CTS. An electronic system that receives and disseminates volume and last sale prices for listed stocks from all markets in which they are traded.

There are two networks: A, for trades of NYSE-listed stocks; B, for ASE-listed and regional-exchange-listed stocks. The tape display does not give the location of the trade, although it formerly did so.

CONSTANT RATIO PLAN

A program of formula investing. The investor establishes a ratio of fixed income to equity securities to be maintained in a portfolio, and fixed time schedule for portfolio adjustment. Example: An investor sets a 60–40 bond to equity ratio with a semiannual period of adjustment. Every six months, the investor will sell either bonds or stocks and reinvest the proceeds to return to the original preestablished ratio. The procedure presumes that bond and stock prices move in opposite directions.

CONSTRUCTION & DEVELOPMENT REIT

A mortgage real estate investment trust that lends short-term funds to builders and developers of commercial and residential properties.

Abbreviation: C&D REIT.

CONTANGO

1. In the English securities markets, an arrangement whereby a trader can carry over a long or short securities position from one account trading period to another without payment or delivery.

   See ACCOUNT DAY.
2. In American commodities markets, term is used if futures contracts trade at higher prices than spot prices. The difference is usually the carrying charges involved in a future delivery of the commodity.

CONTANGO DAY

In the English securities markets, the day on which a contango is arranged. Usually, it is the last day of the trading period, which is also called "account day."

CONTEMPT OF COURT

An action, or the omission of an action, that interferes with the orderly administration of justice. Persons declared in contempt of court may be fined or imprisoned.

Generally, contempt of court is a misdemeanor. Do not confuse with obstruction of justice—such as perjury, falsification of evidence, suborning a juror, and the like—which is usually a felony.

CONTRA BROKER
The broker who represents the opposite party to a trade. Example: To a buying broker, the selling broker is the contra broker.

Also spelled as one word.

CONTRACT NOTE
In England, the equivalent of the confirmation notice sent by American broker/dealers following a purchase or sale.

See CONFIRMATION.

CONTRACT SHEET
Prepared daily by Securities Industry Automation Corporation (SIAC) from information given by brokers and contra brokers. Brokers compare their transaction records to prepare for settlement. Items not in agreement with records are DKd, slang for don't know, or marked QT, questioned trade. Discrepancies are usually resolved quickly so settlement may be made on proper day.

CONTRA PARTY
The party to the other side of a trade. Example: To a seller, the contra party is the buyer.

In practice, contra broker is the more commonly used expression.

CONTROLLED ADJUSTABLE RATE PREFERRED STOCK
Acronym: CARP. A preferred stock whose dividend is periodically adjusted to reflect current Treasury security rates plus a premium.

"Controlled" adds this concept: The issuer promises to maintain a base of assets to ensure that the company will be able to pay the adjusted rate dividend.

CONTROLLER
Term that designates the work area of a broker/dealer responsible for preparing, maintaining, and auditing the firm and

customer financial reports, and the records and statements of accounts, as prescribed by federal law and SEC rules.

Often spelled: comptroller.

CONTROL PERSON

Generic term for someone who can influence corporate decisions. Control can arise from voting power, because person owns 10% or more of corporation's voting shares, or because person is director or elected officer of corporation.

Also called "affiliated person" in certain contexts.

CONVENIENCE SHELF

An abbreviated registration statement for a public offering of securities. A convenience shelf can become effective under SEC Rule 415 without pricing information and the names of nonmanaging underwriter; however, the size of the offering cannot be increased.

Often called "phantom shelf."

Note: Do not confuse with the traditional shelf registration, which requires more information and also permits greater versatility to the registrant.

See SHELF REGISTRATION STATEMENT.

CONVENTIONAL PASS–THROUGH

A security, issued by a savings bank, a savings and loan, or a commercial bank, that represents an interest in a pool of mortgages. There is no government guarantee of interest and principal payments, although such conventional pass-throughs often are insured commercially.

Antonym: modified pass-through, which is U.S. government guaranteed.

CONVERSION

1. Feature permitting owners of certain bonds and preferred stock to exchange these securities for a fixed number of common shares.
2. Feature of many mutual funds whereby owners of one fund may exchange shares for shares of other funds under same management without additional sales charges.
3. Illegal use of assets held in trust for another for one's personal advantage.

See CONVERSION RATIO and FAMILY OF FUNDS.

CONVERSION PARITY

Mathematical statement of equality between value of underlying common stock and theoretical value of convertible security. Example: If a bond is convertible into 40 shares of common stock and stock has market value of $22 per share, conversion parity is $880, that is, 40 times $22.

See CONVERSION PREMIUM and CONVERSION RATIO.

CONVERSION PREMIUM

Dollars in excess of market price of a convertible security over conversion parity. May also be stated as a percent. Example: Convertible bond is selling at $990. Conversion parity is $880. Premium is $110, $990 minus $880. Or, premium is 12.5%, $110 divided by $880.

Percent of conversion premium provides critical insight into risk of ownership of convertibles. Low premium centers risk on changes in market value of underlying common stock; high premium centers risk on convertible as a fixed income security.

CONVERSION PRICE

Fixed dollar value often used by corporation to state conversion ratio of convertible securities. For example, a bond is convertible into common shares at $40 per share. Thus, conversion ratio is par value, $1,000, divided by $40, or 25 shares.

Conversion price is theoretical and presumes convertible selling at par. Conversion feature goes with security, and convertible may be exchanged for common stock at option of holder.

As a general rule, if company splits stock or pays a stock dividend, the conversion price will change because convertible will be exchangeable for a larger number of shares.

CONVERSION RATIO

Statement of the relationship between a convertible bond and the number of common shares into which it is convertible. Example: A bond with a face value of $1,000 is convertible into 40 shares of common stock. As a ratio:

$$\frac{\$1,000 \text{ (1 bond)}}{40 \text{ (shares)}} = X$$

This shows that the theoretical conversion price of the common stock is $25.

See CONVERSION PARITY to find the practical application of conversion ratio to the actual market prices of the convertible bond and the underlying common stock.

CONVERTIBLE ADJUSTABLE PREFERRED STOCK

Acronym: CAPS. A class of preferred stock that (1) has an adjustable dividend rate that is periodically pegged to Treasury security rates and (2) permits the holder to exchange the CAPS for common stock equal in market value to the par value of the preferred.

CAPS usually permit the issuer, if CAPS are tendered, to redeem for cash, rather than cause an undue dilution of the common stock of the company.

COOKED BOOKS

Slang: The financial records of a company have been falsified to persuade investors to purchase or to achieve unrealistic profits. Generally, the expression implies an intent to deceive.

Note: Do not confuse with legitimate accounting practices that temporarily provide a more profitable picture of the company. Such accounting practices always are included in the footnotes to the financial statements.

CORPORATE EQUIVALENT YIELD

Yield on a corporate bond selling at par that must be achieved to equal the yield on a government security selling at a discount. Cash flow on discounted government security reflects tax on interest income and maximum corporate tax on capital gains.

Used by government bond dealers in their offering sheets to show possible advantage, or disadvantage, of an investment in government bonds at the offered price.

CORPUS

Latin: body.

1. The assets underlying a trust agreement.
2. Of a debt security, the principal amount, as opposed to the coupons representing future interest payments.

CORRESPONDENT

A broker/dealer, bank, or other financial services organization that provides services to other organizations in markets to which the other organization does not have access.

Securities firms may have correspondents in foreign countries or on exchanges of which they are not a member. Usually correspondents are linked by private wire.

COST OF GOODS SOLD

Accounting entry that represents the costs of material, labor, and other production costs of goods sold during an accounting period.

General practice is to make a separate entry on corporation income statements of depreciation of plant and equipment, and sales and administrative expenses. In this way, the cost of goods sold can be compared more exactly from one accounting period to another.

COST PURCHASE ACCOUNTING

An accounting system that permits a corporation that owns less than 20% of another corporation's stock to include in its own income only the cash dividends received from this investment.

Antonym: equity purchase accounting.

COT

See COMPETITIVE OPTIONS TRADER.

COUGARS

Acronym: Certificates on Government Receipts. Trade name for A.G. Becker Paribas's instruments evidencing interests in principal or coupon payments to be made in the future on specific issues of U.S. Treasury bonds. Modeled on the Merrill Lynch TIGRs and Salomon Brothers CATS.

COUNTRY OF ORIGIN

Term used in the foreign currency option market to designate the sovereign government that issues the particular currency underlying an option.

COUPON ROLLOVER DATE

The quarterly or semiannual date on which a new interest rate will be established for payments on a floating-rate security. Depending on the issuer, the new rate will be pegged at a specific percentage above LIBOR for Eurofloaters, or above the U.S. Treasury bill rate for domestic floaters.

COVENANT

Those portions of indenture or bond resolution in which issuer promises to do, or not to do, certain activities. Covenants are for benefit of bondholders and may, with permission of bondholders, be voided or changed.

Also called "restrictive covenant."

COVER BID

This is the second highest bid in a competitive distribution. The spread between the winning bid and the cover bid gives an insight into the validity of judgments of value made for the underlying security.

CQS

See CONSOLIDATED QUOTATION SYSTEM.

CRAZY MARY

Nickname for the common shares of Community Psychiatric Centers, a large corporate owner of mental hospitals. The nickname is derived from its NYSE ticker symbol: CMY.

CRD

See CENTRAL REGISTRATION DEPOSITORY.

CREDIT AGREEMENT

Document prepared by a broker/dealer and presented to every customer who uses credit to purchase, carry, or trade securities with that firm. A copy of this agreement—which details the terms, conditions, and arrangements by which credit will be provided, the margin to be deposited or maintained, and when and how interest is charged—must be given to each credit customer of the firm. SEC Rule 10b-16 obligates the broker/dealer to give this document to the customer.

CREDIT DEPARTMENT

1. General term for the margin department of a broker/dealer. See also MARGIN DEPARTMENT (WWS).
2. Specific term for the work area of a broker/dealer or a commodity broker who investigates the creditworthiness and the line of credit to be extended to customers.

CREDITOR

A person, whether real or legal, to whom a debt is owed. Example: In a margin account, the broker/dealer becomes a creditor.

CREDIT SPREAD

A long and short position in options of the same class (puts, or calls). It is called a "credit spread" if the net premiums (plus the premium received minus the premium paid) results in a credit in the client's account.

Also called a "money spread."

Credit spreads become profitable if the premium differential so narrows that the client can close the position at a lower cost than the proceeds of the spread.

CREDIT UNION

A state or federally chartered savings institution that is owned, managed, and operated as a cooperative association by its members for their own financial benefit. Eligible member depositors and borrowers are linked by a common interest, be it occupational, fraternal, educational, or residential. The primary purpose of a credit union is to lend money to its member depositors at relatively low rates of interest.

CREEPING TENDER OFFER

Term used by the SEC to describe the private or open market purchase of a significant percentage of an issuer's stock by one or more persons acting in concert. The purpose is to gain control without the benefit of a prior public notification by means of a proxy statement.

CROP

A person registered as options principal who is responsible for a firm's compliance with options rules and regulations.

See also COMPLIANCE REGISTERED OPTIONS PRINCIPAL (WWS).

CROSS

Broker acts as agent for both a buyer and a seller in a completed transaction. Example: A floor broker with both a buy and sell order for the same amount of shares, after following proper floor procedures, completes both transactions by having her customers buy and sell to each other.

CROSSED MARKET

If any broker's bid is higher than the lowest offer of another broker, or vice versa, the market is said to be crossed. This occasionally happens. The rules of the National Association of Securities Dealers (NASD) for NASD Automated Quotations (NASDAQ) forbid dealers to cross the market intentionally.

CROSS HEDGE

An attempt to limit or prevent monetary loss in an established security or commodity futures position by buying or selling another security or futures contract in a different instrument which has similar market reactions. Example: A client has a long position in GNMA pass-throughs. A cross hedge could be effected by the sale of U.S. Treasury note futures. A client who has written a call on 90-day CDs could cross hedge by purchasing 13-week U.S. Treasury bill put options.

CROSS-TRADING

An illegal practice in the futures marketplace. It is a prearranged transaction between two customers of the same futures merchant, executed outside the specific trading pit for that commodity. In effect, it is not a public trade.

CROWN JEWEL DEFENSE

A management strategy to thwart a hostile takeover. The strategy centers on an agreement to sell to a third party the company's most valuable asset, or assets—hence the term—to make the company less attractive to the raider.

Such a defense will bring stockholder suits if the asset is sold for less than its fair market value.

CRT

Initials for cathode ray tube. Although in recent years other video display devices have been used to project prices and news, the initials CRT are still in use. A form of CRT is in use to administer the principal examination to officers of broker/dealer organizations.

CRUMMEY TRUST

A legal instrument, named for its originator, which enables its beneficiary to accept valuable assets on a continuing basis from any person and to provide that donor with an annual exclusion from federal gift taxes. Characteristically, this trust is drawn for the benefit of a minor and it has the power to receive additional donations by parents and relatives over the ensuing years. Each contributor is entitled to the yearly maximum $10,000 gift exclusion.

CRWNS

Acronym (pronounced "crowns"): currency related warrants to acquire certain U.S. Treasury note securities. These warrants, with one- and two-year expiration dates, permit purchase of U.S. Treasury $11^5/8$s of '94 at designated fixed prices. The exercise price, while stated in U.S. dollars, is denominated in deutsche marks at the exchange rate of 3.152 per dollar.

CS
A frequently used abbreviation for common stock.

CSA
See CONDITIONAL SALES AGREEMENT.

CSR
See CLIENT SERVICE REPRESENTATIVE.

CT
Abbreviation for certificate—that is, a debt instrument with an original maturity of up to one year.

CT also is used interchangeably with CTF, the more common abbreviation for certificate. Here certificate means the engraved paper used to evidence equity or debt participation in the issuer.

CTA
Acronym: Consolidated Tape Association.
See CONSOLIDATED TAPE (SYSTEM).

CTF
Abbreviation: certificate.
See CT.

CTM
See COMING TO ME.

CTS
See CONSOLIDATED TAPE (SYSTEM).

CUFF QUOTE
Slang: an educated guess about the bid and asked prices for an issue. A cuff quote is given without actually checking the current market with market makers.

CULPEPPER SWITCH
The computerized message switching center located in Culpepper, Virginia, to transfer federal funds and U.S. Treasury securities between member banks of the Federal Reserve System.

CUM

1. Abbreviation for cumulative preferred stock. The abbreviation is used in Moody's and in Standard & Poor's stock guides. Generally, however, the abbreviation is omitted in newspaper listings because almost all issues of preferred stock are cumulative.
2. Latin: with. Used to designate that a transaction will be accompanied by a distribution. For example, cum rights, or cum dividend.

CUR YLD

Abbreviation: Current yield. Used in newspaper tables of bond transactions on the NYSE and ASE to show the simple interest an investor will receive if the bond is purchased at current prices. Formula:

$$\frac{\text{Annual interest payment}}{\text{Current market price}}$$

Note: Newspaper bond tables often give to maturity yields for government, agency, and municipal bonds. Thus, CUR YLD is only used if current yield is being computed.

CURRENT MATURITY

Used to designate the remaining lifetime of an already outstanding bond. For example, a bond with an initial 20-year maturity has a current maturity of 15 years at the end of its first 5 years.

CURRENT SINKER

Slang: a bond with a sinking fund obligation that is presently operative. A corporation is currently obligated to retire a portion of an outstanding bond issue either by a call or by an open market purchase.

If a bond is selling at a discount, the fact that it is a current sinker will tend to enhance its market value because the issuer will tend to buy through an open market purchase, rather than call a portion of the issue at the call price.

CURRENT YIELD BASIS

One of two acceptable methods used to determine the return on capital of a mutual fund. The method adjusts the current price by the previous distribution of capital gains and compares this number with the net distribution of dividend and interest income during the previous year.

Formula:

$$\frac{\text{Net dividend/Interest income}}{\text{Current offer price} + \begin{array}{l}\text{Capital gain paid}\\ \text{in last 12 months}\end{array}}$$

Antonym: historical yield basis.

CURTSY

Slang: the legal interest a man has in the real property held in the estate of a deceased wife.

Alternate spelling: curtsey.

CUSHION BOND

A bond, currently callable, whose market price—in terms of competition with other bonds of similar coupon and rating—is artificially suppressed because of its call price. Example: A bond, callable at 105, that should sell at 120; it is selling at 107, however, because the marketplace fears it will be called. Its price is said to be cushioned.

Although cushioning works against the bondholder as interest rates decline, it works for the bondholder if interest rates rise. In other words, the bond will, in many cases, tend to remain stable during a period of interest-rate changes because the call price and the market price are close.

CUSTOMER

1. Any person for whom, or with whom, a broker/dealer executes a transaction, or for whom it holds funds or securities in an account created for that purpose. As a general rule, principals of the broker/dealer, even if they have brokerage accounts with the broker/dealer, are not considered customers.
2. Any person who may become a customer of a broker/dealer. Many of the rules and regulations of the industry are written to cover the ethical conduct that must govern relationships not only with present customers but also future customers.

CUSTOMER'S MAN

A term used in prior times to describe a man or woman who served as a registered representative.

See also REGISTERED REPRESENTATIVE (WWS).

CUSTOMER STATEMENT
See STATEMENT (OF ACCOUNT).

CUTTING A MELON
Slang: any distribution of profits by means of cash or stock dividends. The term is not restricted to distributions to equity owners; it also includes bonuses paid to employees.

CV
Abbreviation for convertible. Used in newspaper stock and bond tables, and in stock and bond guides, to designate any security that may, at the option of the owner, be exchanged for a fixed number of common shares, usually of the same issuer.

D

DAILY ADJUSTABLE TAX EXEMPT SECURITIES
Acronym: DATES. A type of municipal industrial development revenue bond designed by Salomon Brothers Inc. Key feature: The interest, which is calculated daily and distributed monthly, is based on an index of 30-day tax exempt commercial paper published by the Munifacts Wire System. Added feature: DATES can be tendered to the issuer at any time at face value plus accrued interest to the day of redemption.

DAMAGES
The monetary compensation awarded to someone who was injured by the negligent action of another. As a general rule, court-awarded damages, unless they are punitive, are not taxable income to the recipient.

DARTS
Acronym: Dutch Auction Rate Transferable Securities. An adjustable rate preferred stock originally issued by Goldome Florida Funding Corporation. This preferred stock is nonconvertible. Its dividend rate is reset every 49 days by competitive bids (Dutch auction). Each party submits a rate at or above which the holder is willing to "buy"—that is, continue to hold the stock. The maximum rate is 125% of the 60-day, AA commercial paper yield.

DATED DATE

The date from which accrued interest is calculated on bonds and other debt instruments that are newly offered. Example: If the dated date is May 1 and when issued settlement is May 25, the buyer will pay 24 days of accrued interest to the issuer. This money will be regained when the first interest payment is paid.

DATE OF DECLARATION

The day on which a dividend distribution is announced by the board of directors of a corporation.

DATE OF PAYMENT

The date set by the board of directors of a corporation for the distribution of a cash, stock, or other distribution.

More frequently: payment date.

DATE OF RECORD

The date set by the board of directors of a corporation for its securities transfer agent(s) and registrar to close their books to further changes in ownership registration. Those identified as owners at the close of business on the date of record will be the recipients of the distribution declared by the board of directors.

DATES

See DAILY ADJUSTABLE TAX EXEMPT SECURITIES.

DAWN RAID

See PREMIUM RAID.

DAY LOAN

A one-day loan made by a broker/dealer to finance the purchase of securities. The securities thus purchased are used as collateral for the loan while more permanent financing is being arranged.

DAY-TO-DAY REPO

This is an open-ended repurchase agreement that has a one-day effective life. The agreement is cancelable on 24-hour notice; but if not canceled, the REPO is automatically renewed at an interest rate adjusted to current market conditions.

D&B

See DUN & BRADSTREET.

DBCC

This committee is empowered by the NASD to hear trade practice complaints against a member of the NASD or a person associated with a member.

See also DISTRICT BUSINESS CONDUCT COMMITTEE (WWS).

DBL

Initials for Drexel Burnham Lambert, Inc. Often used on corporate and municipal calendars to represent this major underwriter.

DEA

See DESIGNATED EXAMINING AUTHORITY.

DEADHEAD

Slang term unfortunately used by securities traders to identify, from its stock ticker symbol DH, the securities of Dayton Hudson Corporation.

DEALER BANK

1. A commercial bank that makes a continuous market in government and agency securities.
2. A separately identifiable department of a bank that is registered as a municipal securities dealer with the Municipal Securities Rulemaking Board (MSRB).

DEALER FINANCING

An economic arrangement between a marketmaker and a financial institution whereby a collateralized loan is made by the financial institution to the marketmaker to carry its inventory of stocks and bonds. Through such loans, a securities dealer can provide sizable liquid market positions with a minimum amount of its own capital.

DEALER LOAN

A collateralized loan by a bank to a marketmaker in corporate, municipal, or government securities to finance its trading position. Dealer loans are arranged on a day-to-day basis, and the interest rate is negotiated according to competitive conditions.

DEALER MARKET

A securities market in which virtually all transactions are effected between principals acting for their trading or investment accounts. Thus, few agency transactions are effected. Both the municipal securities and the U.S. government securities markets are predominately dealer markets.

DEALER PAPER

Commercial paper sold by its issuer to a broker/dealer who, in turn, sells it to institutional investors for a small markup. The presumption on dealer paper is that the dealer will maintain a secondary market for the commercial paper.

DEALER'S TURN

Jargon for the profit a broker/dealer, acting as a marketmaker, realizes if he or she buys at the bid and sells at the offer price for a security. Generally, a dealer's turn is available only if there is a relatively stable market prevailing for a security.

DEALING FOR NEW TIME

Term from the English securities market designating a purchase or sale of securities for the next account trading period. This activity is permitted during the last two days of the present account period.

See ACCOUNT DAY.

DEALING WITHIN THE ACCOUNT

In English securities markets, a purchase and a sale, or a short sale and an agreement to repurchase, executed within the same two-week account period. Because these trades offset one another, only one commission is charged, and settlement can be made by a single check for the differences.

DEB

Abbreviation for: debenture.

DEBIT SPREAD

A long and short position in options of the same class (puts, or calls). It is called a "debit spread" if the net premiums (plus the premium received minus the premium paid) results in a debit in the client's account.

Debit spreads become profitable if the premium differential so widens that the client can close out the position with greater proceeds than the original cost of the position.

DEBT CEILING

The maximum dollar debt limit a government, agency, or municipality may incur legally without specific further authorization of a higher debt limit by Congress or other legislative body.

Also called "debt limit."

DEBT–EQUITY SWAP

Concept: An issuer, using the distribution facilities of a broker/dealer, exchanges a newly registered issue of stock for outstanding bonds of the same issuer. As a general rule, a debt-equity swap will improve the corporation's balance sheet by lowering the amount of long-term debt and will often increase earnings after interest and taxes.

DEBTOR

A person, either real or legal, who owes money, or other assets, to another. For example, persons who purchase securities or who sell short in a margin account are debtors.

DEBT SERVICE

1. The annual interest payment on a debt that is not self-amortizing.
2. The annual interest and principal payment on a debt that is self-amortizing.

The second meaning is more common.

DECEDENT

Legal name for a person who is deceased. Because death causes the property of the decedent to pass to his or her estate, industry rules require that, upon notification of the death of a customer, the member firm must cancel all open security orders and take no further action in the account without the advice of counsel or the legal representative of the decedent's estate.

DECK

Nickname derived from the stock symbol DEC for Digital Equipment Corporation, a leader in the electronic computer industry.

DECLARATION DATE

See DATE OF DECLARATION.

DECLARATORY JUDGMENT
Judicial pronouncement that expresses the opinion of the court about a matter of law without ordering anything to be done about it.

DEEP BID (OFFER)
Trader's jargon for a bid or offer of significant size that is somewhat away from the prevailing market. It is used as an advisory to salespersons that a large order may be executed if and when market prices reach that level.

DEEP POCKET
Colloquial term for a person of wealth. In context, the term is used of securities liability litigation where the defendants are usually those most likely to be able to afford payment of a sizable judgment. For example, in our litigious society, lawyers for the plaintiff will sue the deepest pocket.

DEFALCATION
Legal term: the misappropriation of funds or other assets by a fiduciary or other person in a position of trust. Depending on the amount involved, defalcation may be a misdemeanor or a felony, and may subject the perpetrator to civil and criminal penalties.

Reasonable synonym: embezzlement.

Also used of the funds misappropriated.

DEFEASANCE
Used in finance, either municipal or corporate, of the action whereby a present debt is effectively removed from the balance sheet by pre-refunding.

Concept: An issuer has an outstanding debt. Additional money is borrowed and escrowed to maturity in U.S. government securities with a maturity that is the same as the previous issue (or its call date). Because funds are in hand for the previous debt's retirement, the debt, and any restrictive covenants attached thereto, are effectively removed from the issuer. Only the requirement of the new debt remains.

DEFEASED BOND/EQUITY SWAP
Procedure used by many corporate guarantors of industrial development bonds (IDB) to pre-refund the bonds. Under this procedure the guarantor arranges to swap its common stock for a similar dollar amount of U.S. Treasury securities. The bonds are escrowed to maturity, or to earliest call to pre-refund the issue of

IDB. The dealer who arranged the swap then sells the common stock and thereby recovers its costs for the U.S. Treasury securities.

DEFERRED CHARGES
Expenses incurred by a corporation to improve or promote the long-term prospects of the business. These expenses are summarized on the corporation's financial statements and are charged off against earnings over a time period. If prepaid, such charges become an asset until they are charged off. For example, prepaid insurance that overlaps a fiscal year. If unpaid, they become a liability. For example, the discount at which an issue of bonds was sold by the issuer.

DEFERRED PAYMENT NOTES
A Eurodollar security combining some features of a debt security with some features of a securities option. The debt security is fixed rate, but requires only a 25% initial payment, with final payment due several months later. If, during the period, interest rates rise dramatically, thus dollar value falls, the purchaser can refuse further payment, thus limiting loss to the initial 25% payment. If interest rates fall, the purchaser will complete payments and will have a leveraged play on interest rates during the period between initial and final payment.

DEFERRED PROFIT–SHARING PLAN
Acronym: DPSP. Permits corporations registered with Revenue Canada to sponsor employee retirement plans. Under such plans, the employer can contribute the greater of 20% of wages or $3,500, thereby reducing taxable income for the year.

DEFICIT REDUCTION ACT OF 1984
Popularly called: DEFRA, or DRA. This 1984 tax act:
1. Reduced long-term holding period from more than 12 months to more than 6 months.
2. Changed from 16 days to 46 days the minimum holding period for corporate investors to be eligible for the 85% dividend exclusion.
3. Requires holders of newly issued market discount bonds to treat some of the discount annually as ordinary interest income.
Tax advice is needed.

DEFINED BENEFIT PLAN

Under ERISA rules, a participant receives a guaranteed pension at retirement. Thus contributions to each participant's plan will vary according to age and actuarial assumptions. The amount of the pension is specified and varies with salary. Typically, the pension is 60% of average wages over a predetermined time period.

See DEFINED CONTRIBUTION PLAN.

DEFINED CONTRIBUTION PLAN

Under ERISA rules, specified annual payments, usually based on a percentage of salary, are made to the retirement account of participants. The retirement benefits, therefore, will vary according to the investment experience of contributions made to the plan.

Also called "dollar purchase plan."

See DEFINED BENEFIT PLAN.

DEFINITIVE SECURITY

A permanent stock or bond certificate issued to replace a temporary certificate. Occasionally issuers will give temporary certificates at the time of a new issue or stock split/dividend.

See GLOBAL CERTIFICATE.

DEFLATION

An economic period generally marked by a period of lowered consumer prices and, thus, marking an increase in the purchasing power of money.

More commonly used: disinflation.

Antonym: inflation.

DEFRA

See DEFICIT REDUCTION ACT OF 1984.

DELY

Abbreviation: delivery.

DEMAND LINE OF CREDIT

Arrangement made with a commercial bank whereby a customer may borrow, up to a preset maximum dollar amount, on a daily basis (i.e., upon demand).

DEMAND LOAN

A loan with no fixed maturity date which is payable upon demand—that is, immediately—by the party granting the loan.

In practice, the terms *demand loan* and *call loan* are synonyms.

DEPOSITORY INSTITUTIONS DEREGULATION ACT OF 1980

DIDA is a federal law that provides for the orderly phaseout of the restrictions on interest and dividend rates paid on accounts maintained for customers by banks and other thrift institutions. A special committee (DIDC) has been authorized to develop new government-insured interest-bearing deposits to compete with money market mutual funds.

DEPOSITORY INSTITUTIONS DEREGULATION COMMITTEE

DIDC is an ad hoc group authorized by federal law to develop government-insured interest-bearing deposit accounts at banks and other thrift institutions that can compete with money market mutual funds.

DEPOSITORY PREFERRED STOCK

Term used for an issue of high par value preferred stock that is deposited with a bank. The bank, in turn, issues many more shares of a lower par value preferred stock that is entitled to a proportionate interest in the deposited security. This technique could be used to circumvent share limitations imposed on the corporation by corporate bylaws.

DEPRESSION

Term used to describe the long-lasting period of curtailed business and economic activities in the United States from 1929 through the 1930s. For example, during the Depression many banks and businesses failed. Usually called the "Great Depression."

The term also is used of any continued period marked by deteriorating securities and commodities prices coupled to a period of depressed personal savings and decreased industrial production.

DESIGNATED EXAMINING AUTHORITY

Acronym: DEA. A self-regulatory body with responsibility for oversight of a particular broker/dealer. Because most broker/dealers have memberships on several exchanges and in the NASD and MSRB, it often is confusing if several authorities exercise surveillance. Under DEA, one of the regulators assumes the job for the others, thus, duplication of effort, confusion, and contradictions are avoided.

DESIGNATED NET
Order given to a municipal security syndicate by a nonmember of the MSRB, for example, by an insurance company to a municipal underwriting syndicate. The order, executed at the public offering price, directs that the concession be credited to the accounts of at least three members of the syndicate designated by the insurance company.

Frequently used by institutional municipal investors to reward account members who have presented sales ideas or other valuable research information.

DESIGNATED ORDER TURNAROUND
Electronic switching service for NYSE members whereby market orders for 1 to 5,099 shares are routed directly to the specialist, who represents such orders in the crowd, before the opening and 2,099 afterward.

See also DOT (WWS).

DEVALUATION
A decrease in the value of one nation's currency in relation to some preestablished norm. The norm may be a specified amount of gold, silver, or a basket of currencies.

If the issuing government unilaterally lowers such currency values, it usually is an endeavor to spur its own exports and to stem exports of another country's goods and services.

DEWAP
Acronym: Department of Water and Power of the city of Los Angeles, California. Used also of the municipal revenue securities issued by that municipal entity.

DIDA
See DEPOSITORY INSTITUTIONS DEREGULATION ACT OF 1980.

DIDC
See DEPOSITORY INSTITUTIONS DEREGULATION COMMITTEE.

DIME

When used in connection with the yield on a debt security, this slang expression designates 10 basis points, or .10%. Example: "I will buy if you will raise it a dime."

DINGO

Acronym: discounted investment in negotiated government obligations. This is the Australian version of government-issued securities stripped of interest coupons. The securities, which are sold at deep discounts, are similar in concept to TIGRs, CATS, and the newly issued Treasury STRIPS.

DIRECT PAPER

Term used of commercial paper that is sold by a corporation to investors without the use of a broker/dealer or a bank as an intermediary.

DIRECT PARTICIPATION PROGRAM

General term used by National Association of Securities Dealers (NASD) for partnership agreements that provide a flow-through of tax consequences to the participants. Subchapter S corporations, which provide tax consequences similar to partnerships, are usually included in this concept.

REITS, pension, and profit-sharing plans, individual retirement accounts, annuities, and investment companies are usually excluded from the definition of direct-participation programs.

DISC

Acronym: Domestic International Sales Corporation. The term is used of an offshore entity created by a U.S. corporation to provide tax advantages for foreign exporters of U.S. merchandise to foreign countries. DISCs enable U.S. companies to compete effectively with subsidized foreign competitors. The IRS permits certain tax exemptions under complex, closely controlled rules.

DISCO BROKER

Contraction for: discount broker—that is, an SEC-registered broker/dealer that charges substantially lower commissions than full-service brokers. As a general rule, discount brokers do not provide securities research options and often curtail the other ancillary services that are associated with securities brokerage services.

DISCOUNT
1. Noun: the dollar (or point) difference between the price of a security and its redemption value. Example: A bond with a face value of $1,000 is selling at a $50 discount if its current market value is $950.
2. Adjective: used to describe a security selling at a discount or offered for sale at a discount. Example: Treasury bills are discount securities.
3. Verb: the act of factoring the long-term effects of news into one's estimate of the present value of a security. Example: The stock has gone down in value because the market is discounting the news of a threatened labor strike.

Also used as a past participle. Example: The news is discounted.

DISCOUNT SECURITIES
Debt instruments issued without a fixed interest rate that are offered and traded until maturity at a value below the face amount of the security. Common examples: U.S. Treasury bills and commercial paper. At maturity, the difference between the purchase cost and maturity value represents interest income.

If longer-term, such securities are called "original issue discounts."

Note: Do not confuse with securities issued at or near face value that are currently selling at a market discount.

DISCOUNT YIELD
Measurement of return that computes interest on face value of security rather than on dollar amount invested. Used in figuring yield on U.S. Treasury bills. The formula is:

$$\text{Yield} = \frac{\text{Discount}}{\text{Face amount}} \times \frac{360 \text{ days}}{\text{Days until maturity}}$$

Example: If a client buys a $10,000 Treasury bill for $9,500 when 180 days remain to maturity, the discount yield is calculated as follows:

$$\text{Yield} = \frac{500}{10000} \times \frac{360}{180}$$

$$\text{Yield} = 0.05 \times 2$$

$$\text{Yield} = 10\%$$

Also called "discount basis."

DISCRETIONARY ACCOUNT
Brokerage account that permits a designated employee of the member firm to make investment decisions on behalf of a client. The investment decisions include buying and selling, the selection of the securities, and the time and price of the trade.

Authorization for such accounts must be given in writing by the customer and must be accepted by an officer of the member firm.

Member firm customers may verbally give discretion about time and price for specified trades. This limited discretion does not require written authorization.

DISINTERMEDIATION
Term describing the action of an investor who has left funds on deposit with a portfolio intermediary (e.g., a bank, savings and loan, or insurance company), removes those funds, and makes a direct investment in other securities. Example: A bank depositor who receives $5\frac{1}{4}\%$ on a passbook deposit withdraws funds to purchase Treasury securities paying 11%.

Disintermediation occurs when rates on direct security investments are substantially higher than the rates paid by portfolio intermediaries.

DISPROPORTIONATE IN QUANTITY
Term used by the NASD in its interpretation of the allocation of a "hot issue" by a broker/dealer. The term applies to sales of more than 100 shares, or $5,000 face value of bonds, to persons in these occupational categories:
1. The managing underwriter's finder for this offering, its accountants, attorneys, financial consultants, and members of their immediate families.
2. Senior officers, securities department employees of commercial banks, savings banks, insurance companies, and investment companies, or other persons who influence the investment decisions of these institutions.

DIVERSIFIED COMMON STOCK COMPANY
A management investment company that has substantially all of its assets invested in a portfolio of common stocks of companies engaged in a wide variety of industries.

Often called "a diversified common stock fund."

DIVERSIFIED MANAGEMENT COMPANY

An investment company that has at least 75% of its assets represented by: (1) cash and cash items; (2) government securities; (3) securities of other investment companies; and (4) other securities, limited to securities of one issuer having a value not greater than 5% of the management company's total assets and no more than 10% of the voting securities of the issuing corporation.

DIVIDED ACCOUNT

A corporate underwriting agreement in which syndicate members sign a contract with the issuer as a group but limit their individual liability to the specific quantity of shares or bonds that they individually underwrite.

See also WESTERN ACCOUNT (WWS).

DIVIDEND DEPARTMENT

Work area in a broker/dealer organization that accepts, allocates, pays, and claims dividend and interest distributions associated with securities that are in the firm's custody or within the firm's responsibility.

DIVIDEND/INTEREST DISBURSING AGENT

An institution, usually a commercial bank, that distributes dividend or interest checks to the holders of specific securities upon instruction from that issuer's directors or trustees.

The disbursing agent uses the official record of the registrar to identify the appropriate recipients.

DIVIDEND RECORD

A widely used publication of the Standard & Poor's Corporation that contains statistical information about dividends and dividend payment policies of publicly held security issuers.

DJ

See DOW JONES & COMPANY, INC.

DM

Initials for: deutsche mark. DM is the primary unit of currency in the Federal Republic of Germany (West Germany).

The initials also are used to designate the currency options in deutsche marks that are traded on the Philadelphia Stock Exchange.

DNE

Order ticket initials standing for: discretion not exercised. This situation arises when the customer has given discretion to an employee of the member firm but, in this particular case, the customer initiated the trade, not the registered representative.

DOCUMENTARY STAMP TAX

A state or local tax imposed on the transfer of real property.

In Florida, the tax also is effective on the transfer of debt and equity securities within that state. It is paid by the seller.

In England, the tax is payable by the buyer of ordinary (common) shares to reregister certificates.

DOCUMENTED DISCOUNT NOTES

Acronym: DDN. Commercial paper pledged by member banks as qualified collateral at a Federal Reserve District Bank. To qualify as acceptable collateral, the DDN must be accompanied by a letter of credit written by a commercial bank, or guaranteed by a private insurance company not related to the commercial paper issuer.

DOEA

Acronym: Designated Options Examining Authority. A self-regulatory organization responsible for inspecting member firm compliance with the rules of the various option exchanges. Under the SEC's present plan, only the ASE, CBOE, NASD, and NYSE can be DOEAs.

DOG AND PONY SHOW

Colloquial term for an informational seminar used to introduce a new product or service. Such seminars are often given by broker/dealers to stimulate the interest of its own registered representatives. Frequently, the seminars center on particular companies, and participants, who may include potential customers, have an opportunity to discuss company policies and products with corporate officials. Generally such seminars are given in many different locations.

Dog and pony show is an allusion to old time vaudeville acts that traveled from place to place.

DOING BUSINESS AS

Acronym: D/B/A.

DOL

Acronym: Department of Labor. The DOL is the cabinet-level agency that has jurisdiction over pension and profit-sharing plans subject to ERISA laws. The DOL establishes the rules and reporting requirements for such plans. It also regulates the relationship of such plans with bankers, brokers, and investment advisers.

DOLLAR AVERAGING

Incorrect contraction of the expression "dollar cost averaging." As such, securities regulators consider its use objectionable.

See DOLLAR COST AVERAGING for the correct usage.

DOLLAR BONDS

1. Long-term municipal revenue bonds usually quoted in dollars (i.e., in points), rather than in yield to maturity.
2. Bonds of foreign issuers sold in the United States and denominated in U.S. dollars.
3. Bonds, denominated in U.S. dollars, they are issued, bought, and sold in foreign countries.

    Also called Eurobonds, although such bonds are traded in Mexico and Japan.

DOLLAR COST AVERAGING

Method of formula investing based on the periodic investment of equal dollar amounts in the same security. The result in every case will be an average cost per unit that is less than the average of the prices paid. Method, however, does not guarantee a profit. There will be a profit only if sale price exceeds average cost per unit.

Dollar cost averaging can be used for the purchase of management investment company shares (mutual funds) and in the sharebuilder plans offered by many broker/dealers.

DOLLAR PRICE

Term used of the quote for a bond that is expressed as a percentage of that instrument's face value. Example: A bond quoted at 98½ means that the dollar price will be 98.5% of the bond's face value; that is, $985 if the bond has a face value of $1,000.

Term is used to distinguish from basis price; that is, a bond quote given in terms of yield to maturity. For example, the bond is priced at 10.72%.

DOMICILE

In law, one's principal home and permanent residence. The law is complex, and legal advice is needed.

The term is important for income and estate tax considerations. In general, to probate an estate and to transfer securities for a decedent, it is necessary to have an affidavit of domicile and a tax waiver from the state in which the decedent was domiciled.

DORMANT ACCOUNT

A customer securities account in which there has been no securities or money activity for an extended time.

It is not uncommon for the brokerage firm to determine that such an account is dormant and to cease doing business with the customer.

If the customer cannot be found, there may be a presumption of death of the customer, or abandonment of the assets. In such cases state "escheat" (pronounced "ess-cheat") laws take over the ownership of the assets.

DOUBLE-BARRELED

Use of municipal revenue bonds if the payment of interest and the repayment of principal is further guaranteed by another municipality that will make the payments from general taxes. For example, a housing authority issues revenue bonds. The bonds are double-barreled if a city or state pledges to pay interest and principal if rents from the housing project are insufficient. Do not confuse with overlapping debt (i.e., a bond with two issuers).

DOUBLE DIPPING

1. Any conflict of interest.
2. Slang: the practice whereby a corporation finances construction through an issue of industrial revenue bonds by the municipality in which the property will be located. The corporation double dips in that it raises capital at lowered rates and uses accelerated depreciation to recover costs. Pending legislation would eliminate one of the "dips" by requiring straight-line depreciation.

DOUBLE EXEMPTION BOND

Colloquial expression for a bond whose interest payments are not subject to federal and state taxation. This privilege is generally limited to municipal bonds if the holder is domiciled in the same state as the issuer of the bond.

DOUBLE TAXATION
Feature of the tax law in the United States whereby the income of dividend payers is taxed before the distribution of dividends. The dividends, in turn, are again taxed at the recipient's level. Example: The earnings of a corporation are taxed. The corporation then pays dividends that are taxable to the individuals receiving them.

Exception: dividend recipients to whom the "conduit" theory applies. Example: certain trusts and regulated investment companies, who pass through the dividend untaxed. The final recipient pays the taxes.

DOWER
Term used for the legal interest a woman has in the estate of her deceased husband.

DOW JONES & COMPANY, INC.
Publisher of research and advisory services to the securities industry. DJ is the publisher of *Barron's* and *The Wall Street Journal* and is the proprietor of the Dow Jones Averages, which is the most popular of the measurements used to track the general movements of stock market prices.

DOWN–AND–OUT OPTION
Term used of a block of at least 10 call options with the same exercise price and expiration date carrying this provision: If the underlying stock declines by a predetermined, agreed-upon amount in the marketplace prior to the expiration date, the exercise privilege is immediately canceled and the option becomes worthless.

Listed options are not subject to the down-and-out provision.

DOWN UNDER BONDS
Eurobonds denominated in Australian or New Zealand dollars. Such bonds are offered originally in European markets. Because they are not registered in the United States, they may not be acquired by U.S. investors until they are "seasoned"—that is, are actively traded for a time and are thus no longer subject to U.S. legal restrictions.

DOWPAC
Acronym: Dow Jones Put and Call Option. An over-the-counter option contract developed by Oakley, Sutton Investment Corporation, an investment adviser. The contract permits the holder to

buy, or sell in the case of a put, a package of eight stocks, in different predetermined quantities, most of which are issues used to calculate the Dow Jones Industrial Average.

DR
Abbreviation from the Latin *debetur:* it is owed.

The abbreviation designates a debit balance owed to a broker/dealer and is used in customer statements to show the net dollar amount owed. For example, $2,165.78 DR.

DRA
See DEFICIT REDUCTION ACT OF 1984.

DRAW BACK
The expression signifies that an underwriter's retention in a specific syndicate offering has been reduced by the manager. In other words, the underwriter has fewer shares or bonds to offer to its own customers from its underwriting commitment, because the manager has drawn back shares or bonds into the "pot" for sale to institutional accounts.

DREW'S ODD–LOT THEORY
A hypothesis, on a theory of Garfield Drew, that one may predict a general market trend opposed to the trend of odd-lot transactions. Thus, if odd-lotters are buying, sell; if selling, buy. The theory has no present value.

See also ODD–LOT THEORY (WWS).

DRIP
Acronym: dividend reinvestment plan. Program whereby some corporations offer current shareholders the option of using dividends to purchase more shares in the corporation. Often such shares purchased through dividend reinvestment are purchased at a discount, typically 5%, from current market value.

More than 800 companies whose shares are listed on the NYSE offer such plans. Because the shareholder has the option of taking the dividend in cash or reinvesting, the dollar value of the reinvestment is taxable in the year of purchase.

DROP–LOCK
Colloquial term for a feature that often accompanies the issuance of floating-rate note. Using this feature, the holder may convert the floating-rate note into a fixed-rate note if prevailing

interest rates drop to a specified level during the life of the instrument.

See also FLOATING–RATE NOTE (WWS).

DROP–LOCK SECURITY

A floating-rate security with interest payments pegged to changes in a popular interbank loan rate as they occur. LIBOR is commonly used. However, if the rate used as the peg falls to a predetermined level, the drop-lock security automatically changes to a fixed-rate security until its maturity date.

DRT

Abbreviation: disregard tape. This designation is used on orders sent to exchanges if the buyer/seller wants to authorize the floor broker to use personal judgment to determine the time or price, or both, of the execution.

More popular usage: NH—that is, order not held.

DUAL CURRENCY YEN BONDS

Japanese-issued securities, offered in the European market-place, in which the periodic interest is payable in yen. The principal amount, however, is repayable in some other currency at a specified rate of exchange.

DUAL LISTING

A misnomer for a security that is listed on one exchange and is also traded on a second or third exchange. Generally, an issuer does not file a listing application with more than one exchange. If a second exchange trades the security, it usually means that the SEC has permitted the second exchange to conduct unlisted trading on its premises.

The term is not used of a security listed for exchange trading that also is traded over the counter. In this case, the over-the-counter trading is referred to as "the third market."

DUAL–PURPOSE COMPANY

A form of closed-end management investment company that initially distributes two classes of securities in equal amounts in a single offering. Generally, one class will be designated capital shares, and the other will be designated income shares. Each class will have its own privileges. By issuing equal amounts of each class of shares, an investor of $1 in one type may reap the results of $2 worth of investment because all income goes to one class of security and all capital growth to the other class.

DUAL SERIES ZERO–COUPON DEBENTURE

Two distinct securities offered by the same issuer at the same time in an endeavor to appeal to different segments of the market. Typically, one security is a short-term (1 to 5 years) zero-coupon note; the second is a long-term (20 to 30 years) fixed-coupon bond. The issuer, by offering both bonds at the same time, hopes to achieve a net interest cost that will be less than the cost of issuing each security separately.

DUAL TRADING

1. In securities markets, the simultaneous trading of the same security on two or more exchanges.
   See DUAL LISTING.
2. In commodities markets, it refers to a contract in which a futures commission merchant (FCM) and its customer are on opposite sides of the transaction.

DUE BILL CHECK

A due bill for a cash dividend on stock or an interest payment on registered bonds. The due bill check is postdated and can be deposited on the payment date designated by the issuer of the underlying securities. For example, a stock was purchased with the dividend. However, the certificate cannot be delivered to the buyer in time to make the buyer the holder of record. The buyer will not accept the certificate unless a due bill check for the amount of the dividend to which the buyer is entitled has been attached to the certificate.

DUE DILIGENCE MEETING

A meeting held to discuss and review the detailed information included in the registration statement and to begin negotiation for the formal underwriting agreement. SEC rules require that such a meeting between officers of the issuing corporation and prospective members of the underwriting syndicate be held between the filing of the preliminary registration statement and the effective date of the offering.

DUE–ON–SALE CLAUSE

Clause often contained in a mortgage instrument whereby the full balance due the lender must be paid at the time there is a sale of the underlying real estate. This clause precludes the assumption of the existing mortgage, which often has very favorable terms, by the new purchaser of the property.

DUFF AND PHELPS
A Chicago-based research organization that rates debt securities of many utility, bank, finance company, and industrial issuers. Duff and Phelps uses a numerical rating, 1 through 14, rather than the alphabetical ratings used by Standard & Poor's, Moody's, and Fitch.

DUMP
1. To sell a security at a sacrifice price. Example: "Let's dump it."
2. In computer terminology, to erase a database, or to transfer a portion of data from one base to another to detect program errors.
3. The nickname used for Dome Petroleum, a large Canadian producer of crude oil, derived from its American Stock Exchange ticker symbol: DMP.

DUMPING
1. The removal of stored information from the database of an automated computer system. Dumping is normally done when the system's capacity is reached.
2. Slang for a practice prohibited by the CBOE. Dumping is the sudden entry of a large number of market and immediately executable limit orders for options on the order book official (OBC). This practice can excessively burden or impede trading in a particular option series. In practice, it may even lead to a trading halt.

DUN & BRADSTREET
A corporation, headquartered in New York City, that specializes in credit reporting and collection. Its subscription services are widely used by broker/dealers and other commercial enterprises to obtain credit information about current and prospective customers.

DU–OP SECURITY
Contraction of: dual option. A warrant that contains two options: the holder may subscribe either to an issue of common stock or an issue of preferred stock. In this way, the holder may profit if the common stock rises in value, or may elect to choose preferred stock for income.

DURABLE POWER OF ATTORNEY

An authorization to act on behalf of another, including the purchase and sale of securities, in which the designee's power will survive the disability or incompetence of the grantor. As usual, this power of attorney terminates upon the death of the grantor.

DUTCH AUCTION

An auction in which the seller offers the property at a price above its fair market value. Then the price is gradually lowered until a buyer is found.

If the property being offered is in multiple units, the price is lowered until buyers for all of the property are found. The weekly auction of Treasury bills is a classic Dutch auction.

DUTCH AUCTION RATE TRANSFERABLE SECURITIES

See DARTS.

DVP TRANSACTION

Initials: deliver versus payment.

A purchase of securities on behalf of a customer who promises full payment at the time the certificates are delivered to an agent bank or broker/dealer.

Synonym: COD (cash on delivery) transaction.

In practice, such transactions are permitted only in institutional-type accounts.

DWR

When used on corporate or municipal calendars, these initials stand for Dean Witter Reynolds, a subsidiary of Sears Roebuck and Company, and a major underwriter of securities.

E

EAGLE

NYSE title for its computer command system for on-line retrieval of information stored in its FOCUS, LEGAL, and REGIS subsystems. Access to this information is highly restricted and is tightly controlled by the exchange.

EARLY BIRD RECEIPTS
Similar in concept to CATS and TIGRs, this name is given to stripped U.S. government securities issued by Lazard Freres & Co.

See CATS and TIGRs.

EARLY EXERCISE
Term used if an option holder chooses to buy (call) or sell (put) before the expiration date of the contract.

From the viewpoint of the writer of the option, early exercise results in an early assignment.

EARNINGS REPORT
Popular name for the income statement of a corporation—that is, a statement showing the corporation's revenues and expenses over a given period. Generally, earnings reports are issued quarterly and annually.

EARN–OUT
Merger and acquisition terminology for future supplementary payments that must be made for the acquisition of a business. These payments are not part of the original purchase price; instead, they are extra payments to be made if future earnings of the acquired business excess a specified minimum dollar threshold.

EARN–OUT RIGHT
Term used to describe the entitlement given to the seller of a business to additional compensation based on the level of future earnings of the company. Thus, the seller receives an immediate payment for control of the business, but more remuneration may be forthcoming if the company meets specified revenue or net income goals.

EASIER
Term used by industry professionals to designate that bid prices (or transaction prices) are falling in value. For example, the market is easier.

Also used as a participle. Example: Bond prices are easing.

EASTERN ACCOUNT
Commonly used underwriting account for municipal securities. Basic concept: syndicate as a group assumes financial responsibility for success of the venture. Thus, gains or losses for partici-

pants in the account are not dependent on what they sell, but on their participation in the account. Example: In a divided account, member A has a 10% participation. Member A sells 15% of the bonds, but the entire syndicate only sells 80% of the bonds it bought. Member A would be responsible for 10% of the remaining bonds despite overselling his percent participation.

Also called "divided account."

EASYGROWTH TREASURY RECEIPTS

Acronym: ETR. Stripped U.S. Treasury bonds made into zero-coupon debt securities by Dean Witter Reynolds, Inc. There is a single payment of cash at the maturity of the certificate. ETRs are similar in concept and function to TIGRs, CATS, and COUGARs.

EASY MONEY

Slang term for an economic situation in which interest rates are low and the money supply is plentiful. The most popular criterion for easy money is the Federal Funds Rate: the interest rate banks pay one another for the loan of overnight funds. The Federal Reserve Board, through the powers granted to it, is probably the greatest influence on whether money is easy or not.

ECONOMIC LIFE

The time period within which the cost of a fixed asset can be depreciated against current earnings. Theoretically, the economic life represents the time frame within which that asset will yield useful service to the business. Land has an infinite economic life; hence, it may not be depreciated. The economic life of most other assets is fixed by the tax code and ACRS (Accelerated Cost Recovery System).

ECONOMIC RECOVERY TAX ACT OF 1981

See ERTA.

ECU

See EUROPEAN CURRENCY UNIT.

EDGAR

Acronym: Electronic Data Gathering, Analysis, and Retrieval. EDGAR is a computer program sponsored by the SEC. The program permits registered issuers to file electronically, rather than by hard copy, the required reports to the SEC. As a result, public subscribers to these reports can have instant access to this updated information by means of a computer interface.

EDGE
1. Slang: an advantage. Example: Federal securities law forbids the use of inside information because it would give the edge to one person over another.
2. Used as a short form for the Edge Act, or securities issued thereunder.

EDGE ACT
Federal law, passed in 1919, permitting commercial banks to conduct international business across state lines. As a general rule, domestic banks may only conduct business in the state where they are chartered.

Often, you will hear securities related to such interstate banking activities called "Edge Act securities."

EDR
See EUROPEAN DEPOSITORY RECEIPT.

EFFECTIVE DATE
Date when a registered offering may begin to be made. Usually it is the 20th day following the filing of a registration statement with the SEC, unless the SEC has issued a deficiency letter requiring the issuer to make certain adjustments in the registration statement.

SEC, either on its own initiative or upon request by the issuer, may set an earlier effective date.

EFFECTIVE LIFE
1. The time remaining on an unexecuted open order entered by a customer. For example, at many member firms good-till-canceled orders have an effective life of 31 days.
2. The expected life of a self-amortizing security based on the experience of other securities of the same class. For example, although GNMA pass-through securities are based on 30-year self-amortizing mortgages, the expected life may be much shorter.

EFH
Initials often used on municipal and corporate calendars to represent E. F. Hutton & Company, a major broker/dealer and underwriter of securities.

EFP PROGRAM
See EXCHANGE–FOR–PHYSICAL PROGRAM.

EIGHTY–FIVE PERCENT EXCLUSION
Commonly written: 85% exclusion.

Feature of the federal tax law that permits 85% of the cash dividends received by one domestic corporation from another domestic corporation to be excluded from taxable income. Taxes are paid at corporate rates on the remaining 15%.

Tax advice is needed because dividends from some domestic corporations are not eligible for the exclusion.

EITHER/OR ORDER
An exchange order that combines a limit with a stop order for the same security. Execution of one instruction requires cancellation of the other, that is, either the limit or stop order because each is on an opposite side of the market.

See also ALTERNATIVE ORDER (WWS).

EITHER WAY MARKET
A market situation in which there is an identical bid and offer (asked) price for a security. Term also is used if there are identical interest rates on bank deposits.

Common synonym: locked market.

ELBOW
Designation of a sharp change in the slope of a yield curve. Example: If there were a steady rise in yields for maturities from 1 to 7 years, then a pronounced flattening of the slope from 7 out to 30 years, the change at 7 years would be called "an elbow."

ELECTRONIC ACCESS MEMBER
A person who has purchased from the NYSE the right to use the trading floor facilities to buy and sell securities through the electronic communications and execution capabilities of a regular member organization. The current fee is $18,500 per year.

ELECTRONIC DATA GATHERING ANALYSIS & RETRIEVAL
See EDGAR.

ELEEMOSYNARY INSTITUTION
Greek: *eleemosyne,* meaning mercy or alms. A legal or recognized charity that may be religious, social, or political. Such organizations are philanthropic and nonprofit and, as such, are tax-

exempt. Great care must be exercised if brokerage accounts are opened for such institutions to make sure that all recommendations are suitable and that the institution is properly empowered to have securities accounts.

ELIGIBLE SECURITY
Widely used term, which may refer to:
1. Securities traded by Federal Open Market Committee.
2. Securities that Federal Reserve will accept for loans at discount window.
3. Securities that have loan value under Regulation T, whether in the general or special subscription accounts.
4. Securities that a carrying broker may deposit at the Options Clearing Corporation as collateral for short option positions.
5. Securities that exchange members may trade in the OTC market although they are listed on the exchange.

ELLIOTT WAVE THEORY
A popular technical analysis of trends in the Dow Jones Industrial Averages, formulated in 1938 by the late Ralph Elliott. Using a system that counts and measures price changes in the DJIA, an Elliott analyst predicts future trends in the average. From this, one then can deduce the next likely broad market movement for most stocks.

EMBEZZLEMENT
Misappropriation of a customer's or firm's assets, often in the form of checks or securities certificates. Persons associated with the securities industry who embezzle, even if full restitution is made, generally are barred from future employment in the industry. By industry rule, brokerage firms must carry a blanket fidelity bond to protect it from such unlawful actions by employees.

EMINENT DOMAIN
The sovereign right of government to appropriate the assets of a private party for the general welfare of the public. Just and equitable compensation must be paid for the property taken. Eminent domain usually is associated with real estate transactions, and it could affect paydowns on GNMA, FHLC, and conventional mortgage loans in some circumstances.

EMPLOYEE RETIREMENT INCOME SECURITY ACT OF 1974
See ERISA FIDUCIARY.

EMPLOYEE STOCK OWNERSHIP PLAN
See ESOP.
Also referred to as: employee stock ownership trust.

ENDORSEMENT FEE
Money paid by put and call brokers and dealers to an **NYSE** member organization for its guarantee of client performance in connection with the writing of a conventional OTC option. Generally, the fee is about $6.25 per contract, although higher fees may be negotiated.

ENGLISH AUCTION
Marketing method occasionally used by issuers for public offerings of their securities. Each of the bidding broker/dealers independently submits a bid for a specific quantity of the issue at a price it deems reasonable for investment or profitable resale. The issuer sells the securities to as many of the best bidders, at their prices and quantities, as are needed to distribute the entire offering. Example: In a 300,000-share offering, if an issuer received five 100,000 share bids at 39, $39\frac{1}{8}$, $39\frac{1}{4}$, $39\frac{3}{8}$, and $39\frac{1}{2}$, it would sell 100,000 to each of the top three bidders. The bidders, in turn, would establish their own reoffer prices.

ENTREPRENEUR
French: a person who undertakes. In practice, a person who undertakes a business enterprise.

The connotation of the word is that the enterprise entails a considerable amount of ingenuity and risk. Hence, the adjective, entrepreneurial, meaning inventive and risky.

E&OE
Initials for: errors and omissions excepted. This legend often appears on customer statements and is intended to absolve the broker/dealer of liability if an accidental mistake is made in preparing the statement.

EOM LOANS
Acronym: early ownership mortgages. EOM loans are marked by these provisions: During the first 6 years the payments are sufficient to pay off the mortgage in 30 years. After the 6-year period, the payments increase, although the rate stays the same; as a result the loan is paid off in less than 30 years. Thus, there is early ownership.

EQUALIZING SALE

Term formerly used of a short sale executed on a national securities exchange at a minus tick or zero-minus tick. This was allowable under SEC rules if that price constituted a plus or zero-plus tick had the sale been made on the principal exchange where the issue was traded. The current SEC reference price for short-sale transactions is the last published sale on the consolidated tape.

EQUITY KICKER

Slang for an offering of debt securities that is convertible or that is accompanied by a warrant to subscribe to common stock in the company. The company usually can sell the bonds at a lower interest rate and the purchaser has the opportunity to share in the future financial success of the company.

See also EQUITY (WWS).

EQUITY NOTES

Also called "a security purchase contract." Equity notes are debt instruments that will automatically become shares of common stock of the same issuer after a set time period. This financing technique originated in 1982 and was popular for a time with some large commercial banks.

EQUITY PURCHASE ACCOUNTING

Accounting practice that permits a company holding 20% or more of another company's stock to include in its own net income a percentage of the other company's income equal to its percentage share in the other company. For example, if Company A held 25% of Company B, and Company B reported annual earnings of $2 million, Company A could include $500,000 in its net reported income.

EQUITY–TYPE SECURITY

Securities that are neither common nor preferred stock but that are capable of conversion, subscription, or exercise for either of these securities. Equity-type securities would include convertible bonds, rights, warrants, and long calls.

Also called "common-stock equivalents," and the term is important because the purchase of such equity-type securities during the "tainted" period of a sale of the underlying security as a loss will constitute a wash sale.

EQUIVALENT BOND YIELD

Used to compare the discount yield on money market securities to the coupon yield on government bonds. Example: A Treasury bill with a 90-day maturity is sold at a discount yield of 12%. The purchase price is $97,000, the discount is $3,000. The equivalent bond yield is:

$$\frac{\$3,000}{\$97,000} \times \frac{365}{90} = 12.54\%$$

The number 365 is used because interest on government bonds is computed on a 365-day year rather than the 360-day year used for T-bills.

EQUIVALENT TAXABLE YIELD

Comparison of the nontaxable yield on a municipal bond to the taxable yield on a corporate bond at a client's tax bracket. For example, a client in the 40% tax bracket is offered a municipal bond with a yield of 12%. What is the corporate bond yield after tax that equals the nontaxable yield on the municipal is calculated thus:

$$\frac{\text{Municipal yield}}{1 - \text{Tax bracket}} = \frac{12}{1 - .40} = \frac{12}{.60} = 20\%$$

ERD

Acronym: Escrow Receipt Depository program. This is a book-entry system administered by the Options Clearing Corporation to facilitate the handling of escrow receipts issued by custodian banks. Through the use of a multientry rollover form, custodian banks can readily deposit, withdraw, and reallocate escrow receipts collateralizing options on different series of the same class. The program sharply reduces the movement of securities and the issuance and reissuance of escrow receipts.

ERISA FIDUCIARY

A person who provides a pension or other employee benefit plan covered by the Employee Retirement Income Security Act with investment advice, or who has discretionary authority over the management of the assets of the plan. Such fiduciaries have an obligation to act solely in the interest of the plan, and to work for the exclusive purpose of providing it with benefits and prudent administration.

ERR
Symbol used in the futures marketplaces to designate quotations deemed to be erratic. Such a designation may be used if bid and asked prices fluctuate wildly, or result in "locked" or "crossed markets."

ERRORS AND OMISSIONS EXCEPTED
See E&OE.

ERTA
Acronym: Economic Recovery Tax Act of 1981. ERTA was a broad-based law designed to encourage savings and investments. It did this by introducing "All Saver" certificates, lowering capital gains taxes, raising the threshold for gift and estate taxes, and by granting retirement savings incentives—particularly the IRA account. The law contains many other features.

ESAE
See EXCHANGE SUPERVISORY ANALYST EXAM.

ESCROW RECEIPT
A paper often used by writers of call option contracts who have underlying securities on deposit with an exchange-approved bank. The bank issues an escrow receipt to broker, thereby guaranteeing delivery of shares to broker if call is exercised against writer.

ESCROW RECEIPT DEPOSITORY PROGRAM
See ERD.

ESOP
Acronym: employee stock ownership plan. Also called "employee stock ownership trust" (ESOT).
Plan whereby employees of a corporation can buy out all or part of the corporation for which they work. Tax advice is needed.

ETC
Commonly used abbreviation for: equipment trust certificates—that is, serial debt obligations secured by a lien on movable equipment, such as diesel locomotives, railroad cars, buses, and the like.

ETR
See EASY GROWTH TREASURY RECEIPTS.

EURO CLEAR
A Brussels-based organization that serves member banks and dealers with clearing facilities for transactions in Eurobonds and Yankee bonds.

EURO CURRENCY
Bank deposits in a country other than the one in which those monies are denominated. Example: U.S. dollar deposits in a London bank are Eurodollars; French franc deposits in an Italian bank are Eurofrancs, and so on.

EURODOLLAR SECURITY
A stock or bond of a United States or foreign issuer that is denominated in dollars, and the dollars are deposited in one or more European banks. Such securities may not be initially offered to U.S. persons because they are not SEC-registered in accord with U.S. securities laws.

EUROLINE
A line of monetary credit made available to a customer by a bank located outside the United States. Euroline credit terms are stated in the specific currency of a European country.

EUROPEAN CURRENCY UNIT
Also used: ECU. ECUs are a weighted package of currencies of the member nations of the European Economic Community—that is, the Common Market. The weighting is periodically adjusted to reflect the trade balances of the countries. By using ECUs to settle trades between nations, the member nations partially diversify the risk of volatile currencies.

EUROPEAN DEPOSITORY RECEIPT
Commonly abbreviated: EDR. A negotiable instrument issued by a European bank to represent ownership of a specific number of shares in a non-European corporation. The bank holds the underlying shares. The receipts are traded, and the bank's records are changed to reflect these transactions.

EUROPEAN OPTION
A put or call privilege that has this restriction: it can be exercised by its holder only on the expiration date or during the five-day period prior to that date.
Such options may be for stocks or bonds.

EUROPEAN TERMS

Expression used in currency transactions. It states the number of units of a foreign currency required to purchase one U.S. dollar. Example: If Swiss francs were offered at 2.0181, European terms, it would mean that a Swiss franc is worth $.4955—that is, $1 divided by 2.0181.

EVALUATION

Term commonly used of the endeavor to estimate the worth of an investment portfolio. Listed stocks are valued at closing prices; OTC stocks, at the bid price. The value of infrequently traded bonds is based on third-party estimations. The same is true of fixed assets that have no established marketplace.

EVEN–BASIS SWAP

A sale of one fixed-income security and the purchase of another effected without any change in the yield on the investor's portfolio. Such a swap may change average maturities, or face value, but it does not change yield.

EVEN KEEL

Nautical term used to describe the fact that the Federal Reserve's monetary policy will remain unchanged. Example: Despite the recent refunding of $20 billion in notes by the U.S. Treasury, it seems that the FED will maintain an even keel.

EVERGREEN PROSPECTUS

Term used when an offering of securities registered with the SEC will be made on a continuous basis. Classic evergreen prospectus: those used to offer open-end investment company shares.

An evergreen prospectus, while remaining substantially the same, will be periodically updated to reflect changing company conditions.

EXCESS MARGIN ACCOUNT SECURITIES

As defined in SEC rules, excess margin account securities are those above and beyond the value of what is necessary to finance the debit balance in a client's margin account.

In practice, securities worth more than 140% of the client's debit balance must be segregated; thus, they are identifiable and will not be jeopardized if the broker/dealer becomes insolvent.

EXCHANGE FOR PHYSICAL PROGRAM

Common acronym: EFP. A trading technique that involves futures on an index and the component stocks. The stock index is used as a benchmark. Sophisticated computer programs show aberrations in the spread between the futures and the stocks. The trader will try to profit by arbitraging—that is, by buying the index future and selling the stocks short, or vice versa. As the spreads return to their historical norms, the positions are closed out at a profit.

EXCHANGE RATE

This is a price, or value factor, at which the currency of one country can be exchanged for that of another. For example, the exchange rate of U.S. dollars for French francs is 5.0674; this value factor means that a person with one U.S. dollar can purchase 5.0674 French francs.

In the past, the exchange rate often has been artificially pegged by the countries involved. At the present, most exchange rates are determined by market forces.

EXCHANGE SUPERVISORY ANALYST EXAMINATION

A qualification test that must be passed by member-firm employees responsible for the approval of research reports that will be distributed to the public. It is a two-part exam that tests the knowledge of financial statement analysis; the second part of the exam tests the candidate's knowledge of NYSE and ASE research standards of suitability.

EXCHANGE–TRADED OPTION

Technical term for what is popularly called "a listed option."

EXCHANGE–TYPE COMPANY

In the past, persons could exchange their personal holdings of securities for shares of diversified mutual funds without a capital gain tax liability. The management companies that permitted such exchanges were commonly called "swap funds."

Such exchanges are no longer permitted by the IRS.

EX CLEARING HOUSE

Expression used to identify a transaction that is completed between the contrabrokers without the use of a clearing facility.

Such transactions are infrequent. Ex clearing house transactions usually arise when the buyer requires guaranteed physical delivery of the security.

EXECUTRIX

A female named to act in a valid will. The term *executor,* without any designation of the sex of the person, is now commonly used.

EXEMPT SECURITIES

1. Securities exempted from the registration requirements of the Securities Act of 1933. Example: government and municipal securities.
2. Securities exempted from certain provisions of the Securities Exchange Act of 1934 in terms of margin, registration of dealers who make a market in them, and certain reporting requirements. Example: A class of equity securities of a corporation that now has less than 300 holders is exempted from quarterly and annual reporting.
Also called "exempted securities."

EXPORT–IMPORT BANK OF THE UNITED STATES

Common acronym: EXIMBANK. The bank, which is an independent agency of the United States, aids in the financing of exports and imports between the United States and foreign countries.

The debt obligations of EXIMBANK are guaranteed by the full faith and credit of the United States.

EXPOSURE

235342.

1. The dollar amount of financial risk involved in an investment.
2. The maximum dollar amount of credit that a broker/dealer will extend to a customer between trade and settlement date. By extension, if ultimate settlement is not to be completed until a future date; such as, short option contracts and commodity futures, the total dollar amount of risk that a broker/dealer will undertake on behalf of a customer.

EXTENDABLE DEBT SECURITY

A debt obligation that gives the holder the option at maturity of redeeming at face value or continuing to hold the security for a predetermined time. If the holder chooses to retain ownership, the interest rate will be adjusted according to a preset formula. Generally, the formula is based on a spread over Treasury issues of comparable maturity.

EXTENSION SWAP

A purchase of one debt security and the sale of another, with the result that the client's time to maturity is lengthened.

Common synonym: maturity swap.

EXTRAORDINARY INCOME/CHARGES

A one-time expense entry on the income statement of a company. Called "extraordinary," with the implication that there will be no similar entry in the future.

See also NONRECURRING CHARGES (WWS).

EYE BEEM

Jargon used by traders and exchange members for the common stock of International Business Machines (IBM).

Also used: Big Blue. This is based on the characteristic color of the company's logo.

F

F

1. Fast. Used in commodities markets to describe a condition of exceptionally rapid price fluctuations with large volume. Condition may excuse a broker who misses the market.
2. Flat—that is, dealt in without accrued interest paid by buyer to seller of a bond. Generally, such trading marks bonds that are in default.

FACE AMOUNT CERTIFICATE COMPANY

A type of investment company that issues debt instruments obligating the payment of a stated sum of money (face amount) on a date in the future in return for deposits made by an investor. May be lump sum or period payments. Minimum maturity: 24 months. Generally, the investor will receive a fixed rate of interest, but the company will often pay additional interest if its investment income warrants it.

FACE VALUE

Of bonds, the dollar amount that appears on the face of the bond certificate. It is the dollar amount the issuer promises to pay to the holder at maturity.

Face value and par value are synonyms when these terms are used of bonds.

FACILITATION ORDER

Option exchange term. It signifies an order for the proprietary account of a broker/dealer. It is called a facilitation order because it is to be executed in whole or in part as part of a cross with that firm's public customer. Example: A customer wants to sell 100,000 shares. The broker/dealer has a "natural" for 25,000 shares—that is, buy orders from customers. The broker/dealer may enter a facilitation order for the remaining 75,000 shares. The order ticket must be marked as such: "facilitation order."

FACTORING

1. The sale of accounts receivable owned by a company to another company. The sale is made at a discount to provide cash flow to the seller and a source of profit to the buyer.
2. In the securities industry, factoring refers to the financing of security positions. Example: A dealer borrows against securities in inventory, or a customer borrows against portfolio securities in a margin account.

FADED

Term used to designate that previously given prices have either been withdrawn or have been revised downward. Example: The market for ABC has faded.

FAIL

Any securities contract that has not been honored or completed. See also FAIL TO RECEIVE and FAIL TO DELIVER (WWS).

FAIR MARKET VALUE

Price at which a buyer and seller are willing to exchange an asset. Generally synonymous with current market value determined by the competitive forces of supply and demand operating in a free and open marketplace. Endeavors to rig the price to favor the buyer or seller are manipulative and violate federal laws.

NASD also defines it in terms of swaps against syndicate offerings: the price that a dealer normally would pay for the security in the ordinary course of business if there were no swap involved.

FAQS

Acronym: Firm Access Query System. A computerized service provided by the NASD to its members. Through FAQS, members may access the NASD database of pending securities registrations, and may schedule qualification examinations and review the results thereof.

FARMER'S HOME ADMINISTRATION
Acronym: FHDA. FHDA, an agency of the Department of Agriculture, grants loans for farms, homes, and community facilities in rural areas of the United States.

FASCISM
General term for a socioeconomic system in which the government dominates production and distribution of goods and services by the control of private industry.

Term is pejorative. It infers that such domination is primarily intended to promote national esteem rather than the good of the populace.

Often called "the right," as distinguished from the left, another term for Communism.

F/C
1. First call date—that is, the earliest date at which the issuer of a debt security or preferred stock may call the security for premature redemption.
2. First coupon date—that is, the first interest payment that the issuer will make to holders of a bond. The term is not used unless the first interest payment will be less than, or more than, the regular six months between interest payments.

FCM
See FUTURES COMMISSION MERCHANT.

FCOP
See FOREIGN CURRENCY OPTIONS PARTICIPANT.

FEDERAL CREDIT AGENCIES
General term for U.S. government-sponsored agencies that supply financial aid to specific institutions, classes of individuals, or economic segments of society. Example: There are federal credit agencies that supply credit to farmers, farm cooperatives, students, exporters, small businesses, and savings and loan associations.

FEDERAL FINANCING BANK
Acronym: FFB. A government bank, supervised by the Treasury Department, established to consolidate and reduce

financing costs of those federal agencies whose obligations are guaranteed by the federal government. Examples of such agencies: Export-Import Bank, the U.S. Postal Service, and the Tennessee Valley Authority.

FEDERAL FUNDS
Excess reserves of member banks of the Federal Reserve System. These excess funds can be loaned to other member banks, usually on an overnight basis, at the federal funds rate.

Term also used of any immediately usable funds that can be used to pay for government securities transactions. In this sense, the term includes cleared credit balances in client accounts, in special miscellaneous accounts (SMAs) in margin accounts, checks drawn by a member bank of the Fed on its account with the Fed, and—with the increased popularity of money market funds—transfers from these funds to the client's cash or margin account.

FEDERAL RESERVE WIRE NETWORK
See FED WIRE.

FED WIRE
Abbreviation: Federal Reserve Wire Network. The FED Wire is a communication facility operated by the Federal Reserve Banking System to transfer funds and book-entry securities between subscribers to the wire.

There are approximately 30 member banks and U.S. government security dealers who are primary subscribers to the wire. These are called "primary money market dealers."

FEEMAIL
Disparaging slang for the legal fees charged by attorneys to settle stockholder suits that attempt to bar management from ransoming shares held by prospective corporate raiders.

For further information about the repurchase of shares from corporate raiders, see GREENMAIL.

FELONY
In law, a more serious crime than a misdemeanor. Root of word is Scottish and means a wicked person. Generally, a felony is punished by jail sentences of more than one year. The law defines which crimes are considered felonies.

In the securities industry, certain violations of securities law are defined as felonies. Adjudication of guilt in such cases is reserved to the federal courts and is not part of the administrative decisions of the SEC.

FENCE SITTER
Slang: a retail customer or portfolio manager who is unable to come to a decision about the merits of an investment opportunity.

FF
Also: FrF. Initials used to designate the French franc, the primary currency unit in France.

FFB
See FEDERAL FINANCING BANK.

FGIC
Acronym: Financial Guaranty Insurance Company. FGIC is a consortium of financial institutions and brokerage firms that insures municipal securities and municipal unit investment trusts against default.

The fee is paid by the issuer, or the UIT, and the insurance covers both interest and principal payments on the bonds covered. FGIC is similar in function to AMBAC and MBIA.

FHA
See also FEDERAL HOUSING ADMINISTRATION (WWS).

FHDA
See FARMER'S HOME ADMINISTRATION.

FHLB
See also FEDERAL HOME LOAN BANKS (WWS).

FHLMC
See also FEDERAL HOME LOAN MORTGAGE CORPORATION (WWS).

FICB
See also FEDERAL INTERMEDIATE CREDIT BANKS (WWS).

FICTITIOUS ORDER
Buy or sell instructions given to a broker by a person, or persons, attempting to manipulate the price of a security. Such orders are called fictitious because, as a general rule, these persons do not intend to honor their commitment; instead, they

seek only to create the illusion of activity in the security and thus influence its market price.

See also FICTITIOUS CREDIT (WWS).

FIDUCIARY

Person entrusted with the control of assets for the benefit of others. Most states have laws governing the conduct of fiduciaries.

Fiduciaries are generally court-appointed: executors of wills, administrators of estates, receivers-in-bankruptcy, and committees for incompetents. Trustees also are considered fiduciaries. The document of appointment usually limits the power of fiduciaries and sets guidelines for their activities.

Custodians under Uniform Gifts to Minors Acts are fiduciaries in the sense that they may not alienate assets for their own benefit. They are not, however, directly governed by a written court-approved document governing the conduct of such accounts.

FIELD GOAL

Industry slang for U.S. Fidelity & Guaranty Corporation. Its trading symbol, FG, is the same as that employed in football for a field goal.

FIGS

Acronym: Future Income Growth Securities. A Paine Webber municipal product patterned after the GAINS originated by Goldman Sachs.

Concept: The bond is issued at a discount; then, after a number of years, it pays a fixed rate of interest based on a par value of $1,000. Example: The bond sells at $500; in eight years it becomes a $1,000 face value bond paying 9% annual interest until its maturity.

FINAL DIVIDEND

English financial term: the final cash dividend paid to shareholders in a particular year. English custom requires a final dividend to be approved by the stockholders. A final dividend is descriptive only and does not imply that other dividends were paid in the same year.

FINANCE PAPER

Commercial paper issued by companies engaged primarily in extending credit to customers of their firms. Well-known issuers of finance paper include General Motors Acceptance Corporation,

Ford Motor Credit Corporation, Household Finance Corporation, and CIT Financial Corporation.

The term also is used of registered debt offerings of such corporations with maturities greater than 270 days.

FINANCIAL FUTURE

Futures contract for interest-sensitive securities: T-bills, T-notes, T-bonds, CDs, and GNMA pass-throughs.

Trading is governed by the Commodities Futures Trading Commission (CFTC) and requires special registration.

Trend of financial futures trading is often an indicator of interest rates, but interpretation of trend requires sophisticated assessment of the basis, which is the difference between cash and futures price.

FINANCIAL GUARANTY INSURANCE COMPANY

See FGIC.

FINOP

Acronym: financial and operations principal.

Under MSRB and NASD rules, persons responsible for the maintenance of financial records or the approval of financial reports must qualify as a FINOP through a qualification examination.

Each member must have at least one such designated principal.

See also MUNICIPAL SECURITIES RULEMAKING BOARD and NATIONAL ASSOCIATION OF SECURITIES DEALERS (WWS).

FIP

Acronym: Fixed Income Security Options Permit.

FIP is a license that may be purchased from the ASE. It permits licensees to trade in interest rate options for their own account on the floor of the American Stock Exchange.

FIRM ACCESS QUERY SYSTEM

See FAQS.

FIRM COMMITMENT

The underwriter, either through negotiation or competition, agrees to buy the securities to be issued. The underwriter, therefore, owns the securities. If the securities are sold at the public offering price, the underwriter usually makes a profit. If the securities are not sold at the public offering price, the underwriter may have a diminished profit or a loss.

In no case can the underwriter make a profit from a sale above the public offering price (unless the securities are exempt) because federal law requires that a bona fide public offering be made.

Also called "firm commitment underwriting."

FIRM QUOTE

Also: firm market. A quotation made by a dealer who is prepared to buy or sell immediately at least the minimum quantity associated with trades in that security.

Generally, the minimum quantities are 100 shares of stock. In the block markets for stocks, the minimum quantities are higher. Secondary market Treasury quotes generally are firm for $100,000 face amount. In the secondary markets for corporate and municipal bonds, unless such quotes are given AON (all or none) the minimums are for 5 and 25 bonds, respectively.

FIRST COUPON

Used only of newly issued bonds if the first interest payment will be less than, or more than, six months from the issue date. Example: the LMN 11s of '95, dated 5-1-85, F/C 1-1-86.

After an irregular first coupon, all subsequent coupon payments are made on a semiannual basis until maturity.

See F/C.

FIRST SINKING FUND DATE

Also: FSF. The earliest date at which the issuer of a debt security obligates itself to begin sinking fund payments. The bond indenture designates the methods that may be used, either by the issuer or the bond trustee, for the early retirement of the bonds. Such methods include calling the security for redemption or making open market purchases.

FIRST-YEAR REPUBLICAN JINX THEORY

A lighthearted market indicator: The market will go down in the first year of incumbency of any Republican president, even of a second term. The theory is waggish and has not been proved in practice.

FISCAL POLICY

Economic term used to designate actions by either the president or Congress that affect spending practices by the government. Fiscal policy is used to differentiate such practices from monetary policy—that is, actions by the Federal Reserve Board that affect the money supply in the United States.

FISH

Slang: an endeavor by a dealer to find out the buyer or seller when another broker/dealer wants to trade a significant quantity of a security. Generally, such information is confidential. However, federal law requires self-disclosure in certain situations; and the rules of the NASD, if the contraparty is acting as agent, require the revelation of the other side of the trade if this is demanded. This rule is to prevent certain conflicts of interest, hot-issue problems, insider trading, and the like.

FIVE & TEN

Industry jargon used to identify the F.W. Woolworth Company, a major retailer and a stock included in the Dow Jones Industrial Average.

FIXED–DOLLAR SECURITY

A nonnegotiable debt instrument that can be redeemed at the holder's option for a dollar value set forth in a schedule of fixed prices. Example: Series EE Savings Bonds are fixed-dollar securities. The redemption value is set monthly and varies with the prevailing established interest rate and the time that it has been held by the owner.

FIXED–INCOME SECURITY OPTIONS PERMIT

See FIP.

FIXED LIABILITY

Balance sheet terminology for corporate debt obligations that will mature in more than one year. The time to maturity is the governing factor; thus bonds, notes, and debentures will be included.

On the balance sheet of municipalities, fixed liabilities are called "bonded debt."

FIXED–RATE LOAN

A loan with a preset rate of interest. Of itself, the term does not state whether payments will be self-amortizing—that is, include interest and a partial repayment of principal, or interest only.

Term is used to distinguish from floating-rate loan—that is, a loan whose rate of interest will be periodically adjusted to prevailing rates.

FLAT YIELD

English term: the annual interest paid divided by the current market price. Thus, it is the equivalent of current yield as this is measured in the United States.

As with current yield, the measurement does not take into account possible gain or loss that will arise if the instrument is held to maturity.

FLB

See FEDERAL LAND BANKS (WWS).

FLEX REPO

Abbreviation: flexible repurchase agreement.

A flex repo is a long-term master contract between a borrower and a lender with securities pledged as collateral. At some time in the future, the borrower must repurchase the collateral. In the meantime, the principal amount may be expanded or contracted, and the interest rate will be adjusted to market conditions.

FLIGHT TO QUALITY

Term used to describe the changes in portfolio management policies during adverse economic conditions. Although the general use of the term refers to the sale of lower-rated bonds and the purchase of higher-rated bonds, it also refers to the sale of speculative stocks and the purchase of investment grade (blue-chip) stocks.

Barron's Confidence Index, by measuring yield spreads of higher versus lower rated bonds, is an endeavor to anticipate stock market movements based on the increase or decrease of investor confidence shown by the flight to quality, or the opposite.

FLIPPER

Jargon for the shares of the FPL Group, Inc. The nickname is derived from the NYSE symbol, FPL, for the company formerly known as Florida Power & Light Company.

FLIP–OVER PROVISION

A provision introduced into the charter of a target company on the occasion of an unfriendly takeover attempt. Under this provision, preferred shares are granted the privilege of conversion into the common stock of that company, or into common shares of an acquiring company that is forcing the merger. Such a conversion makes takeover much less attractive, because it increases the number of shares that will have to be acquired, or dilutes the percentage of ownership.

See POISON PILL.

FLOAT
1. The number of shares in the hands of the public; thus, it gives insight into the number of shares available for trading. Example: "ABC has a small float."
2. Float also is the time lag in the check-clearing process. Float may be advantageous to the checkwriter, or disadvantageous to the check depositor, depending on the number of days it takes for a check written to appear as a debit, or a check deposited to appear as a credit.

FLOATING SUPPLY
Term most commonly used of the dollar value of municipal bonds offered in the Blue List. For example, the floating supply is about $2.5 billion.

Also used of individual securities to designate quantity of an issue in the hands of persons willing to sell at current levels. Example: "We estimate that the floating supply is no more than 50,000 shares."

FLOOR TICKET
Industry terminology for the written summary of customer instructions contained on the original order ticket. The format and content of floor tickets are prescribed by the exchanges where they are received.

A floor ticket may not be given verbally from one member to another; instead, the physical piece of paper must be so transferred that responsibility is established and the duplication of order executions is prevented.

FMAN
Acronym: February, May, August, and November.

Designation of the months for the quarterly expiration of option series assigned to some classes of listed options. Current practice is to offer a maximum of three expiration months at one time.

FOB

In the securities industry, a frequently used abbreviation on corporate and municipal bond calendars to designate First Boston Corporation, a major underwriter.

FOCUS REPORT

Acronym for Financial and Operational Combined Uniform Single report. Broker/dealers must make such reports to SROs (self-regulatory organizations) on a monthly and quarterly basis. Reports detail capital, earnings, trade flow, and other pertinent information.

FOOTSIE

Slang for: FT-SE. This is the Financial Times–Stock Exchange Index. This index of the 100 largest publicly owned stocks traded on the London Stock Exchange is as popular in England as the Dow Jones or the Standard & Poor's are in the United States.

FORCE MAJEURE

Legal term: a disruptive event that may excuse one or both parties to a contract from completion of the contract.

Such disruptive events may include acts of God; for example, earthquakes, floods, and the like, or catastrophic social events, such as war, revolution, nationalization of property, and so on. Often such events are included in the terms of the contract; at other times, they may be defined in the law.

FORECAST

1. The act of predicting, either short or long term, the course of financial events, such as the stock or bond market, trends in the economy, interest rates, or the fortunes of individual companies. Generally, the term *analyst* is used of persons who forecast based on measurable present and past events.
2. The written or spoken statement that evidences the act of forecasting.

FORECLOSURE

The legal procedure brought by the holder of a mortgage (creditor) or the representative of a deed of trust (trustee) for the purpose of claiming deeded property in satisfaction of a defaulted debt. Example: When XYZ Company failed to make its interest payments, the trustee moved to foreclose under the provisions of the deed of trust (indenture).

FOREIGN CURRENCY OPTION
Acronym: FCO. Put or call options for packages of individual foreign currencies traded on the Philadelphia Stock Exchange. The packages, which are traded separately, are for: 62,500 deutsche marks; 62,500 Swiss francs; 50,000 Canadian dollars; 12,500 British pounds; 6,250,000 Japanese yen; and 125,000 French francs.

FOREIGN CURRENCY OPTIONS PARTICIPANT
Acronym: FCOP. A licensee of the Philadelphia Stock Exchange who, in exchange for a one-time fee, is authorized to conduct a principal or customer business in selected foreign currency options on the floor of the exchange.

FORM S-1
A comprehensive form for the registration of securities with the SEC prior to a public sale. The form includes detailed information about the issuer, the security, and the method whereby the offering will be made.

FORM S-2
A form of securities registration that is less detailed than Form S-1. Public companies with a three-year history of reporting to the SEC under the provisions of the Securities and Exchange Act of 1934 may use Form S-2. This shortened form permits the detailed information required in Form S-1 to be included by reference to the company's latest annual and quarterly reports. Purchasers of the securities will receive these reports together with the shortened prospectus.

FORM S-3
An abbreviated SEC securities registration form that can be used by corporate officials and control persons to sell personally owned stock at various times and at prevailing market prices.
Form S-3 also can be used by highly capitalized and widely held corporations with good credit ratings to make offerings over a two-year period.
Also called "shelf registration."

FORTRAN
Acronym: Formula Translation System. The most complex of the computer languages. The other popular computer languages are BASIC and COBOL.

FORWARD PURCHASE UNDERWRITING

An underwriting technique whereby a corporation can raise capital by issuing stock at a price that is higher than prevailing levels if the company is willing to defer receipt of the proceeds until a later date.

FORWARD RATE

The dollar price at which payment versus delivery will be made on a specific future date for a commodity, currency, or certain types of debt instruments. It is a completed contract and not a futures or an option. Example: On the day of writing, the forward rate on Swiss francs for 90-day forward delivery was .3839—that is, 38.39 cents per franc.

FRAGMENTATION

SEC-coined term to describe the fact that order flow for a particular security is dispersed among many market centers. As a result, it is impossible to determine which is the principal market for the security.

FREIT

Acronym: (pronounced: free it) Finite Life Real Estate Investment Trust. An investment trust whose underlying assets are restricted to real property, such as raw land, commercial real estate, residential housing, developmental or mortgage financing, or any combination thereof. It differs from a typical REIT in that these assets must be liquidated at a predetermined time in the future. The proceeds are then distributed to the unit holders who, individually, bear the tax consequences.

FRIVOLITY THEORY

A lighthearted market indicator with a lead-in time of about one year. Using figures published annually in *The World Almanac,* the dollars spent on household operations are compared with the dollars spent on restaurant meals and drinking. If the latter frivolous expenditures go above 36%, or below 33%, people are too frivolous, or not frivolous enough, and the market is expected to decline.

FROZEN ASSET

An item of value which, by law or other restriction, may not be liquidated or otherwise disposed of during a fixed time period.

FSF

See FIRST SINKING FUND DATE.

FTD

Past-due contract between brokers where the seller has not presented the security to the buyer for payment.

See also FAIL TO DELIVER (WWS).

FTR

A past-due contract between brokers where the buyer has not made payment because seller's broker has not yet made delivery.

See also FAIL TO RECEIVE (WWS).

FT-SE

See FOOTSIE.

FULL

See HANDLE.

FULL TRADING AUTHORIZATION

Industry term for the document whereby the owner of an account gives full power of attorney to an employee of a broker/dealer to make buy/sell transactions for the client.

See also TRADING AUTHORIZATION (WWS).

FULLY MODIFIED PASS-THROUGH SECURITIES

Pass-through securities are debt issues with fractional claims upon a specific multimortgage portfolio. The issuer, for a fee, distributes funds received, either principal or interest, to the holder.

Such a security is said to be "modified" or "fully modified"—both expressions mean the same thing—if the distributions are to be made whether or not they are received. Thus, the distributions are guaranteed. In practice, this guarantee is made by the Government National Mortgage Association.

FULLY TAX–EXEMPT SECURITY

A municipal obligation whose interest payments to holders is not subject to federal, state, or local taxation. Generally, this exemption applies to holders who are domiciled in the same state as the issuer of the security. Some states, however, distinguish between individual and corporate holders in the application of this exemption.

Often called "triple tax exempt."

FUNDED DEBT
Balance sheet terminology for those corporate liabilities with maturities of more than five years.

The exact meaning of the term can only be determined from the context. Thus, fixed liabilities (bonds with a maturity of more than one year) and funded debt are often used interchangeably.

See FIXED LIABILITY.

FUNDS
1. Any accumulation of usable money.
2. Popular name for both mutual funds and unit investment trusts.
3. In England, the debt securities issued by the government of the United Kingdom. Commonly: the funds.

FUNDS RATE
Negotiated interest rate charged by a bank that lends excess reserves to a bank that needs to increase its reserves or to a government securities dealer who needs it to settle transactions. The funds are usually loaned overnight, at the "federal" rate.

See also FEDERAL FUNDS RATE (WWS) and FEDERAL FUNDS.

FUNNEL SINKING FUND
Term used of the sinking fund provision for a number of an issuer's outstanding debts. Under the funnel provision, the issuer may combine sinking fund payments from several issues. In this way, the monies can be used to retire the most expensive of the issues. Example: A corporation has two bonds outstanding, one with a 12% coupon, the other with a 14½% coupon. Under a funnel sinking fund, the monies that would be set aside to retire both issues, can be combined to retire the 14½% bonds.

FUTURE INCOME GROWTH SECURITIES
See FIGS.

FUTURES COMMISSION MERCHANT
Acronym: FCM. Any business entity that solicits or accepts orders for the purchase or sale of commodities futures contracts or exchange-traded commodity options.

Such organizations must register with the Commodities Futures Trading Commission (CFTC) and are regulated by the National Futures Association (NFA).

FUTURES CONTRACT
Completed, but transferable, agreement to make or take delivery of the object of the contract at a specified time at a specified price. The most common futures contracts center on commodities and financial instruments.

A futures contract should not be confused with an option contract. An option contract is not completed and leaves with the buyer of the option the choice of requiring or not requiring the completion of the contract.

FX
Abbreviation for foreign exchange—that is, the rate at which foreign currencies may be exchanged for U.S. currency and vice versa.

FY
Any consecutive 12-month period of financial accountability for a corporation or other governmental agency.

See also FISCAL YEAR (WWS).

FYI
The commonly used annotation to notes or copies of correspondence; meaning: for your information.

G

G
Annotation occasionally used in the newspaper reports of securities transactions. Generally used lowercase, the g means that the dividend is paid in Canadian funds although the prices quoted are U.S. dollars.

GAINS
Acronym: Growth and Income Securities. This is a type of tax-exempt issue created by Goldman Sachs. Concept: The security is issued originally at a deep discount and pays no interest for a fixed number of years. At this time, it becomes a regular bond with a fixed par value and pays a predetermined semiannual interest. Example: The bond is issued at $500. In nine years, it becomes a $1,000 face value bond paying 8% interest.

GCO

Acronym: GNMA Collateralized Obligation.
See COLLATERALIZED MORTGAGE OBLIGATION.

GEM

Acronym for: growing equity mortgage.

A home real estate mortgage whose initial payments of principal and interest are based on 25 years. However, the annual payments are increased 4% each year. Because the increase will be applied totally to the reduction of the principal amount, equity is increased and the mortgage will be amortized in 15 years.

GENERAL MOTORS BELLWETHER

Popular market theory. It holds that General Motors common stock signals general market direction for the four-month period following a new high, or low, of GM stock. If GM does not, within that time frame, set another new high or low, the market will reverse direction.

GENERAL SERVICES ADMINISTRATION

Acronym: GSA. Government agency created to construct, purchase, and manage government properties. GSA also is empowered to sell such facilities. The stockpiling of strategic materials and their distribution also is part of the mandate of GSA.

GSA may issue participation certificates. These debts are guaranteed by the United States; thus, interest is exempt from state and local taxation, although it is subject to federal taxes.

GENSAKI RATE

Rate associated with repurchase agreements for Japanese bonds traded in yen. The rate is comparable to the yen CD market, but there are adaptations made for Japanese and international investors.

Gensaki agreements may not be offered publicly in the United States.

GG

Abbreviation: government guaranteed. GG often is used in the footnotes of statistical tables or other listings of debt securities to designate issues that are guaranteed either by the U.S. government or the foreign government in which the securities were issued.

GIC

An investment contract sold by insurance companies to pension and to profit-sharing plans.

See also GUARANTEED INCOME CONTRACT (WWS).

GIFT TAX

A federal tax levied on the donor of a gift in excess of $10,000 to any one individual in one year. The limit is $20,000 if the donor is married and the spouse concurs in the gift.

The tax is graduated according to the amount in excess of $10,000; however, the tax is integrated with the estate tax of the individual.

Legal advice is needed. There is no federal tax on gifts between spouses, but many states have such taxes or legislate a different threshold.

GILT

English slang: an obligation of the United Kingdom.

American slang: blue chip investment.

GILT-EDGED

Technically, the edges of a book that has been gilted; that is, covered with gold leaf. By implication, anything of the highest quality or value. Example: You would have to look long and hard to find securities that are more gilt-edged than these.

GINNIE MAE II

A form of Ginnie Mae pass-through serviced by Chemical Bank. Concept: The pass-through is based on a number of mortgage pools with differing interest rates and maturities. It is hoped that Ginnie Mae II, by including pools from various areas of the United States and with varying interest rates, will tend to standardize the paydown of these pass-through securities. Unwanted paydown of Ginnie Maes is one of the negative features of these securities.

GINNIE MAE PASS-THROUGH

A security that represents a proportional interest in a pool of mortgages. The security is called a pass-through because homeowners send monthly mortgage payments to a bank, which passes through the security holder's share of the payment after deducting a service charge.

Timely payment of interest and principal is guaranteed by the Government National Mortgage Association (GNMA or Ginnie

Mae). Original principal amount is stated on the security certificate, but remaining unpaid principal is reduced monthly.

Technical name for these securities is GNMA Modified Pass-Through, because the coupon rate or production rate on the certificates is modified by the deduction of ½% from the loan rate of the mortgage pool. This deduction pays for the sponsoring bank's services. The principal is passed through without deduction.

GINZY

Commonly: the ginzy. Used as a noun. Example: "I arranged the ginzy."

This slang expression designates a transaction in a futures contract at a price that is unfavorable to the executing broker. The hope: the broker will do more business with the customer at prices that are beneficial.

This practice, which we would call a loss leader in other marketing efforts, violates the Commodity Exchange Act.

GIT

See GUARANTEED INSURANCE TRUST.

GIVE ME A LOOK AT

Industry slang used by traders, particularly on exchanges, when they want a current quotation and size for the market in a particular security. Example: "Give me a look at Bare Ass." Translation: "I would like the quote and size for Boeing Corporation." Fortunately, there is no listed corporation called Moon Industries.

GLAMOUR STOCK

Popular term for an equity security that is highly recommended for growth and that is currently favored by portfolio managers seeking aggressive growth.

Concept: glamour is what is in vogue.

GLOBAL CERTIFICATE

In foreign debt security offerings, it is customary to represent the total debt by one certificate; hence, the term *global.*

After 90 days, the global certificate is broken up into definitive pieces, each represented by individual certificates that are distributed to the subscribers according to their individual purchases.

GLOW WORM

Street slang for the stock of Corning Glass, derived from its symbol: GLW.

More common: Glass Works. This is derived from the official name: Corning Glass Works Corporation.

GNMA

Government-owned corporation—nicknamed Ginnie Mae—that facilitates financing in the primary mortgage market by (1) purchasing mortgages from private lenders to encourage construction and (2) guaranteeing the timely payment of principal and interest on certain pools of mortgages.

See also GOVERNMENT NATIONAL MORTGAGE ASSO-CIATION (WWS).

GNMA II

See GINNIE MAE II.

GNMA MORTGAGE–BACKED SECURITIES DEALERS ASSOCIATION

An industry-sponsored group of dealers devoted to furthering member interests.

The group is dedicated to education, trading, and operations. It also advises, through lobbying, anyone interested in these securities.

GNMA STANDBY

A put option on GNMA securities.

This negotiated option to sell at a fixed price hedges the originator of the pool of mortgages during the period between the assembly of the pool and its sale to a dealer from dramatic rises in the production rate; that is, the rate at which GNMA will guarantee the mortgages.

The premium (fee) is usually ¼% of the face value, although it may be higher. Unlike other put options, the buyer of the standby must give the writer 30 days notice before exercise.

GNOME

Industry jargon for anyone who is a technical analyst.

In practice, the plural form (gnomes) has been popularized by the television program "Wall $treet Week" to mean the net buy/sell recommendation of seven widely followed technical indications of market trend. Example: "This week our gnomes are 2 up, 3 down, and 2 neutral, for a net minus 1."

Origin is Greek: an opinion. Taken into Germanic lore as the shriveled person who delivers the opinion; for example, the gnomes of Zurich.

GOING AWAY

Also: going away order.

The term is from municipal bond underwriting. Concept: The buyer is going to hold the bonds to maturity; thus, there will be no immediate effect on the remainder of this underwriting nor on the secondary market for the bonds. Example: A sale to other dealers may quickly provide competition in the secondary market, whereas a sale going away gives an ultimate noncompetitive buyer. For this reason, the syndicate manager will give priority to the confirmation of orders that are "going away."

GOING PRIVATE

Corporations whose common shares are owned by 500 or more persons are said to be public. They continue to be public as long as 300 or more persons own such stock.

To go private means to repurchase shares in such a way that there are less than 300 owners. Corporations with less than 300 owners of any class of equity security are nonreporting corporations under the 34 Act, and are said to be private.

See GO PRIVATE.

GOING PUBLIC

Initial public offering of the common shares of an issuer.

Concept: Previously, either the company had sold no shares, or such shares as existed were traded privately between the company and its owners.

See GOING PRIVATE and GO PUBLIC.

GOLDEN PARACHUTE

One uses a parachute in the event of an air disaster to descend to the ground safely.

Analogy: A company anticipates a takeover or other financial adversity that may "ground" present executives. Thus, the executives vote themselves termination or other retirement benefits that will—no matter what the fortunes of the company—provide them a safe passage to financial security.

GOOD MONEY

Street slang: federal funds—that is, money that may be used immediately without passing through the clearing process.

In practice, good money is represented by: cash, cleared credit balances in a member firm client's account, a check drawn by a member bank of the Federal Reserve on its Federal Reserve account, and funds transferred by the Fed Wire.

Checks that must pass through clearing, and the proceeds of securities sales that do not settle on the same day, are not good money.

GOOD NAME BROKER

Industry term for a contrabroker suggested by SIAC (Securities Industry Automated Clearing) if there is a "break" on the contract sheet.

Concept: A break is a mismatch between the buying and selling broker. Thus, both brokers will DK—that is, don't know the transaction. SIAC will volunteer the name of another mismatch. In this way, a few calls between mismatched brokers will quickly establish the correct matches and settlement/delivery can be established.

GOOFBALL

Colorful industry slang for the shares of Wilson Pharmaceutical Corporation, a manufacturer of ethical drugs among which are included some psychoactive and mind-altering drugs. The expression builds on popular slang for tranquilizers.

GOOSE JOB

This vulgar expression refers to the influence of a trader who, in the face of a limited supply of a stock, increases the demand for a stock.

In practice, industry rules prohibit an industry professional from purchasing stocks in such a way that prices are forced up. Thus, industry professionals may buy at present prices or below; but as buyers they may not push prices for a security up.

GO PRIVATE

A small but well-organized group purchases all of the outstanding shares of a corporation. If the number of shareholders falls below 300, the corporation ceases to be a reporting corporation and no longer needs to be registered with the SEC. In this fashion, the issuer does not need to make quarterly reports and may function without public scrutiny of its activities.

Often a leveraged buyout has as its goal going private.

GO PUBLIC

A sale of equity securities by a corporation, following an effective registration with the SEC, to more than 500 persons. Such corporations are a reporting corporation and, under the provisions of the Securities and Exchange Act of 1934, must make public both quarterly and annual reports of their financial activities.

Corporations with less than 500 shareholders may elect to conform to the regulations for reporting corporations.

GORILLA

Street slang for the shares of General Instrument Corporation derived from its NYSE symbol: GRL.

GOVERNMENTS

General term for the negotiable and marketable securities issued by the U.S. Treasury.

The term does not include nonnegotiable securities of the U.S. government, currency, or securities of government agencies.

GPM

Acronym: graduated payment mortgage. A real estate mortgage loan with a fixed interest rate. Monthly payments, however, rise during the first 10 years, then level off. The end result, since the additional payments reduce principal, is to reduce the effective life of the mortgage.

Also see GEM for a similar concept for the life of the mortgage to decrease the principal balance over a shorter time.

GRANDFATHERING

Industry jargon for the recognition of continued professional work over a defined time period in such a way that the incumbent of a job does not have to pass a new qualification examination. Example: There will be a new industry examination for financial advisers, but persons who have served as registered representatives for the previous five years will be grandfathered.

GRANNY BOND

English term: a government-sponsored savings bond which may be purchased only by those in retirement or who are receiving governmental income payments. The interest is indexed to the British consumer price index, but the floor is a 4% minimum.

GRAY MARKET

1. The purchase of open-end mutual fund shares by a broker/dealer at a price above the net asset value for resale to its customers. This practice is unethical if the broker/dealer has signed a sales agreement with the underwriter of the fund.
2. In England, "if and when issued" secondary market sales made during the period when a security is in the hands of its underwriters and before the actual distribution. English law, unlike that of the United States, does not forbid such sales.

GREED INDEX

This 10-factor index, each of which is graded 1 to 10, gives an insight into the personal habits of portfolio managers. With a high of 100, scores below 30 are bullish; scores above 60 are bearish. A form of contrarian analysis—that is, managers, on balance, tend to buy at the top and sell at the bottom. Thus, low ratings are good and high ratings are bad.

Here is a list of the 10 factors:

1. Buy new money management vehicles.
2. Expected rate of return on equities.
3. Prefer stocks to bonds.
4. Are fully invested—that is, cash is low.
5. Invest for aggressive growth.
6. Acceptance of new ideas.
7. Ratios of positive commentary.
8. Institutional activity.
9. New-issue interest.
10. Money manager personal investments.

GREENMAIL

Slang: used in conjunction with takeover bids, tender offers, or unfriendly proxy fights. The concept is similar to blackmail.

Greenmail involves the purchase of a significant block of stock for one of two purposes: either to sell the block to a corporate raider, or to tender it to the company for a premium price. Because the sale of the block to a raider would threaten the continuity of management, management feels impelled to buy the shares at a premium, rather than have the shares sold to an unfriendly corporate raider.

GREEN SHOE

Provision in an underwriting agreement that permits the syndicate to purchase additional shares at the same price as the original offering. In this way, the underwriting group can cover shares sold short without financial risk.

Also called "the green shoe clause."

GRESHAM'S LAW

This postulate was made in the 16th century by Sir Thomas Gresham, an English economist. The law states that, if a country has two forms of currency, hoarding will take the currency with the higher intrinsic value out of circulation. Example: When the United States in 1964 began to circulate copper-clad coins, it quickly caused the hoarding of the silver coins then in circulation.

GROSS UNDERWRITING SPREAD

The dollar difference between the public offering price of a new issue of securities and the proceeds to the issuer.

See also UNDERWRITING SPREAD (WWS).

GROSS YIELD

The yield to maturity on a bond purchased at a discount. Because the cash flow does not take into consideration the tax consequences of the tax on interest income or the tax on capital gains, it is gross before taxes.

Because of taxes, many bond offering sheets also will include the effective yield for corporations in the highest tax bracket so the buyer may measure the actual return on invested dollars.

GROWING EQUITY MORTGAGE

See GEM.

GROWTH AND INCOME SECURITIES

See GAINS.

GS

When used on corporate and municipal bond calendars, these initials stand for Goldman Sachs & Company, a major underwriter of securities.

GSA

See GENERAL SERVICES ADMINISTRATION.

GTC

Acronym: good-till-canceled.

An order to buy or sell securities that remains valid until the order is either executed or canceled. Cancellation may be made by the entering client, but the accepting firm or the exchanges also may cancel the order.

Theoretically, a GTC market order could be entered; but in practice, GTC orders are limit orders or, if permitted, stop orders.

Antonym: day order.

GUAN

An infrequently used abbreviation for a stock or bond that is guaranteed.

Concept: A *guaranteed stock* is a preferred stock whose dividend payments are guaranteed by someone other than the issuer. A *guaranteed bond* is a bond whose interest and principal payments are guaranteed by someone other than the issuer. Example: The bonds of ARCO Pipeline, a subsidiary of Atlantic Richfield Corporation, are guaranteed by the parent corporation.

GUARANTEED ACCOUNT

An account of one customer that is guaranteed by another customer. The guarantee involves the payment of margin debits, or performance on option contracts. Such accounts require that the guarantor provide full and specific assurances in writing.

GUARANTEED INSURANCE TRUST

Acronym: GIT. A hybrid product that combines some features of a UIT with some features of a guaranteed income contract issued by an insurance company. GITs are designed to appeal to small and medium-sized nontaxable retirement funds. In practice, a broker/dealer will pool several GITs to form a unit trust with the GITs as the principal assets. Then, participation units having face values as low as $1,000 are offered to interested buyers.

Generally, the broker/dealer will maintain a secondary market, although most units are bought and held.

GUARANTEED SPREAD

A proposal by a broker/dealer to a customer in conjunction with a swap. Concept: In return for the customer's commitment to buy a new security at a price that will be determined, the broker/dealer agrees to buy from the customer those securities held by the customer at a predetermined spread between the two prices.

The guarantee is illegal if corporate securities are involved. It may be fraudulent if exempt securities are involved and the guarantee creates a contract value that is fictitious.

GUERILLA GROUP

A municipal underwriting term. Concept: The underwriting group is composed of only a few members, who thereby assume large capital risks.

In practice, municipal accounts attempt to minimize the individual risks of the participants by including a large number of underwriters in the account.

GYP-EM

A jocular term used to describe graduated mortgage payments. See GPM for a description of such mortgages.

H

HANDLE

Also called "the handle," or "the full."

Concept: Only the 8ths, 16ths, or 32nds of the bid and asked prices are quoted. The presumption is that industry professionals know the "handle," or the percentage amount that is involved.

Example: A quote of a government at 16–20 omits the handle. The full quote could be—to those acquainted with the current market for the security—$98^{16}/_{32}$ bid and $98^{20}/_{32}$ offered.

HANGNAIL

A cute nickname for Houston Natural Gas Corporation. Hangnail is based on the NYSE ticker symbol: HNG.

HANG SENG INDEX

An index that measures the price change movements of 33 stocks traded on the Hong Kong Stock Exchange.

It is similar in concept to the Dow Jones Average of Industrial Stocks. However, the Hang Seng Index represents about 70% of the market value of all stocks traded on the Hong Kong Exchange. The Dow Jones Average represents only 25%, approximately, of the stocks traded on the NYSE.

HART–SCOTT–RODINO ACT

A short-name title for Section 7A of the Clayton Antitrust Act.

In practice, this section requires a prior screening by the Federal Trade Commission and the Justice Department of possible federal antitrust violations.

Specifically, a 15 to 30 day waiting period is mandated for this screening if a prospective purchaser would hold $15 million or more of the acquired company's assets and 15% or more of that company's voting stock.

HEAVY

Industry term that designates a preponderance of offers in the market for a particular security. A heavy market for a security, or the market in general, implies a probable decline in the security, or market. Example: The unfavorable balance of trade report issued last week has tended to make a heavy market.

HEDGE

Used both as a verb and a noun to indicate reduced risk.

A hedge involves an offsetting securities position that limits loss. A hedge that eliminates the possibility of future gain or loss is a perfect hedge.

Example of a perfect hedge: A client holds appreciated stock and sells short against the box.

Example of an imperfect hedge: Buy a stock and sell a call. Client is hedged against loss by the amount of the premium received.

HEDGED TENDER

SEC Rule 10b-4 prohibits the tender of borrowed stock. However, if long stock has been tendered and the tenderer antici-pates that not all of the tendered stock will be accepted, the tenderer may want to sell some of the stock short. In this way, the tenderer will hedge against a possible decline of the stock following the partial acceptance. Such a short sale is called "a hedged tender."

HEMLINE THEORY

A lighthearted approach to the direction of general market prices. Concept: As women's hemlines go up, so will market prices. And, if hemlines go down, the general market will follow.

The concept anticipates that the hemlines will serve as a leading indicator by about six months.

HIGH–INCOME TRUST SECURITIES

See HIT.

HIT

1. Slang: an identified dollar loss. Example: "We took a $500,000 hit."

2. Slang: a capital penalty against a balance sheet asset that is judged ineligible for consideration under the SEC rule for the computation of net capital by a broker. Example: "We computed our net capital, but we had to take a hit on the value of stock exchange memberships."

HITS
Acronym: High-Income Trust Securities. This is a unit investment trust sponsored by Drexel Burnham Lambert. The trust features high-yield, lower-quality bonds—popularly known as junk bonds—and thereby diversifies the risk that may come from an individual investment in any of the bonds.

HOLDER IN DUE COURSE
Legal term: a person who, in good faith, purchases an asset before the determination that it was defective, stolen, or that title was tainted.

Generally, the holder in due course is considered immune from claim or criminal prosecution. As a result, claims are made against the original purchaser for failure to apply due diligence to ascertain ownership if the item was stolen, or against the original seller if the item is defective.

HOLDER OF RECORD
Official title of the person whose name is on the books of a corporation at the close of business on an assigned day as the registered owner of an asset. Dividends, in the case of stock—and interest, in the case of bonds—will be paid to holders of record on the assigned day.

Holder of record is an identifiable event. Member firms, through the use of due bills, justify inequities that result because securities transaction were not completed in time to make buyers the holders of record in line with contract provisions.

HOME
In usage: a home. Slang for a seller looking for a buyer in a difficult market. The buyer is referred to a home. Example: "We're looking for a home for 100,000 shares."

The term is used when no evident buyer is available, or if buyers are making an unrealistic bid, or if the quantity bid falls far short of the amount of the security available for sale.

HOOK ORDERS
See CAP ORDERS.

HORIZONTAL COMBINATION

A merger of two companies that produce substantially the same products. Thus, the merger produces economies of scale by eliminating duplicative management and support personnel. Example: a merger of two large steel companies.

Note: Do not confuse with horizontal spread as used in option terminology. A *horizontal spread* is the purchase and sale of options of the same class with the same strike price, but with different expiration months. Example: "Sell an April 50 call and buy a July call on the same security."

HOT ISSUE

NASD term for an SEC-registered public offering with an over-the-counter bid that is higher than the fixed public offering price on the day the security is offered for sale. Example: A syndicate offers an issue at $31 per share. At the end of the trading day, the OTC bid is $32 per share. This is a hot issue and special rules apply to the syndicate's distribution of the security.

HOT PANTS

A nickname for the common shares of Helmerich & Payne Corporation, a contract driller of oil and gas wells. The nickname is derived from the NYSE ticker symbol: HP.

HUMPTY DUMPTY FUND

In late 1983, the details of the AT&T breakup were known: The holder of 10 AT&T shares would receive 10 shares of the new AT&T and 1 share of each of the 7 "spun-off" operating companies. As a result, any holder of the old AT&T that did not hold a multiple of 10 would become partially disinvested because cash would be given in lieu of fractional shares of the operating companies.

A unit investment trust was formed. Any holder of AT&T stock could deposit any number of shares. The depositor would receive a fractional interest in the fund. As a result, the fund did what the nursery rhyme could not do: It "put Humpty Dumpty together again."

HYPOTHECATION AGREEMENT

Written agreement between customer and broker/dealer that details the rules under which the account is opened and carried. Principal parts of the agreement: securities purchased on margin are held by the broker/dealer; these securities may be repledged by the broker/dealer to finance the account; the broker/dealer may sell the pledged securities, if needed, to protect its financial interest in the account.

Also called "customer agreement" or "margin agreement."

I

IADB
See INTER–AMERICAN DEVELOPMENT BANK.

IB
1. Commodity trading abbreviation for: introducing broker. An introducing broker is a futures commission merchant who is a member of the National Futures Association who gives up customer execution and clearance to another member.
2. A sometimes-used abbreviation for the World Bank. The technical abbreviation is IBRD: International Bank for Reconstruction and Development.

IBIS
Acronym: International Banking and Investment Services. IBIS is a computerized currency trade system located in Valley Forge, Pennsylvania.

The service prepares confirmations, arranges settlement, gives up-to-date currency positions, and gives credit exposure to its customers throughout the world.

IBRD
See WORLD BANK.

I BUY
Commonly used expression in the over-the-counter markets by traders who are buying for their own accounts. The expression acknowledges transactions, avoids human error, and emphasizes the dealer role of the trader.

The expression is particularly important for recordkeeping by the trader. Example: If the customer of a member is selling, the trader for the same firm is buying. Thus, accurate terminology is required to maintain inventory positions.

ICC
See INTERSTATE COMMERCE COMMISSION.

IC/VC
See INVESTMENT COMPANY AND VARIABLE CONTRACT PRODUCTS.

ID
See INSTITUTIONAL DELIVERY SYSTEM.

IDR
See INTERNATIONAL DEPOSITORY RECEIPT.

IF COME ORDER
Customer order to purchase a specific bond issue from a broker/dealer if that firm can find and buy these securities from a current holder of that security.

IFX OPTIONS
Fungible foreign currency options tradable on either the Philadelphia or the London Stock Exchanges that are cleared by the Options Clearing Corporation (OCC). This intercontinental linkage of exchanges and contracts was pioneered in early 1986, and these instruments are often referred to as "international options."

INACTIVE STOCK/BOND
A particular security that trades infrequently or trades in relatively low quantities.

Caution: The term is relative both to trading and to volume available. Example: Many 10-share traders on the New York Stock Exchange—usually preferred shares—trade in large blocks in the OTC market. Thus, they are inactive in one marketplace and active in another.

IN–AND–OUT TRANSACTION
Slang for a purchase and sale of a security completed within a brief time, often on the same day. The technique is used by traders, specialists, and marketmakers able to trade with low transaction costs and minimum capital risk. Some full-service brokers and most discount brokers provide speculators with lower commission charges on the in and out transactions completed the same day.

INCOME COMPANY
An investment company whose principal objective is to provide investors with current income higher than that usually

obtainable from other securities. Thus, a diversified portfolio of utility common stocks assembled by a mutual fund normally would be designated as an income company (fund).

INCOME STATEMENT
Commonly used term for the numeric description of the income, expenses, interest and taxes paid, and the net profit of a company during a specific accounting period. Except for mutual funds that issue semiannual income statements, publicly traded corporations issue both quarterly and annual statements of income.

Also called "profit-and-loss statement."

IN COMPO
Contraction for: in competition.

Most frequent use: an invitation to a buyer or seller to submit a bid or offer that will compete with bids or offers from others.

IN CONCERT
Two or more persons, together or through an agent, try to achieve an investment goal. There are restrictions against such efforts.

See also ACTING IN CONCERT (WWS).

INDEX CALL
A feature written into the indenture of a bond issue. Under an index call, the issuer may call—that is, retire the bond issue at a price keyed to prevailing government bond rates, rather than at a fixed-dollar price.

The index call is rarely used.

INDEX PROGRAM
A method of portfolio management, both in terms of securities chosen and number of shares, so the market performance of the assembled shares will "track" the performance of a chosen index: Dow Jones, Standard & Poor's, Value Line, and the like. The concept: The client is "buying" the index without the investment of the dollars required to duplicate the index.

Index options are based on this principle. An index program actually assembles shares to provide similar performance.

INDICATED MARKET
Numbers quoted for price ideas only. The market maker or specialist has no actual bids or offers at the stated prices and

seeks prospective orders at those levels.

See also SUBJECT MARKET (WWS).

INDICATED ORDER

Technically, this is not an order. Rather, it is an indication of interest in a purchase or sale. It permits that broker to seek a contra order, but validation from the client is needed before a binding order can be executed.

INDIVIDUAL IDENTIFICATION

As a general rule, brokers must segregate fully paid and excess-margined securities.

Bulk segregation is the most commonly used method of segregation—that is, all street-name securities that fall into either of these categories are held in a special vault and individual certificates are not identified.

Some brokers choose individual identification of the securities in their vaults. This can be done by registering the securities in the client's name or by using identification marks. Example: a penciled inscription of the client account number on the certificate.

INDIVIDUAL PROPRIETORSHIP

Term used to describe a one-man business, or what we would call "a mom-and-pop business."

Such business enterprises are easy to establish—often requiring no more than the public statement that there is a business—but such businesses lack permanence, often find raising capital difficult, and are frequently subject to interruption because of sickness.

Individual proprietors represent business expenses on a separate tax form; otherwise the taxation of an individual proprietorship is the same as that of a person earning personal service income. This is an additional problem with this form of business enterprise.

INDUSTRY GROUP

General term for different companies within the same business area. Example: A group of international oil companies would include Exxon, Royal Dutch, Texaco, Mobil, Shell.

Although the individual business fortunes will vary among the competitors, general economic trends will tend to be favorable or unfavorable for the group. Hence, the term *group rotation*—that is, market activity will tend to center now on one industry group, now on another. Many market analysts base their recommendations on group rotation.

INFLATION

An economic condition characterized by persistent increases in the amount of money in circulation and continuously rising prices for goods and services. As a result, the purchasing power of individual dollars deteriorates as their value is cheapened.

IN FOR A BID (OR OFFER)

Equity block trading term used to describe an institutional client's request for a bid/offer from a broker/dealer's proprietary account for a significant amount of stock. Once negotiated, the request results in a binding capital commitment, subject to that firm's ability to transact at that price on the floor of an exchange.

IN HAND

Term used by salespersons and traders for orders given to them for execution during a limited time such as a morning, a day, an hour, and so on.

Used in contradistinction to "indicated" or "in-touch" orders. These orders are not official instructions to buy or sell; "in hand" orders are.

INITIAL MARGIN REQUIREMENT

The minimum amount of equity a customer must deposit when initiating transactions in a margin account. The requirement, by class of security, is set forth in Regulations T, G, and U of the Federal Reserve Board.

INJUNCTION

Court order directed at a person or group of persons to prohibit a specific activity or to require the performance of a specific action in conformity with federal securities laws. The SEC often will petition for an injunction against parties who are the subject of an inquiry, thereby preventing a continuation of a questionable practice until the case is concluded.

IN–LINE BUYER/SELLER

A buyer/seller of a significant quantity of a security who is willing to deal at prevailing price levels. The designation means that the buyer/seller is seeking a contra offer/bid that will provide the size satisfactory to meet its requirement.

INSIDE INFORMATION

Legal and industry term for material information that (1) would influence the purchase or sale of a company's security and (2) has not been publicized in a widely used medium. Example: A company suffered a dramatic loss and this fact has not yet been announced publicly.

INSOLVENCY

1. A debtor who is unable to meet obligations as they come due and payable in the normal course of business.
2. Any corporation or individual who has liabilities exceeding assets at any given time.

Insolvency generally leads to a court petition resulting in bankruptcy proceedings under federal law.

INSTALLMENT SALE

A sale in which the seller agrees to defer receipt of the proceeds until a later date and, perhaps, in more than one payment. Under IRS rules, the seller is accountable for the federal tax on the transaction upon receipt of the proceeds, and in the same proportion of profit or loss, as the payments are received. Generally used to defer the payment of taxes.

INSTITUTIONAL DELIVERY SYSTEM

Acronym: ID. A trade notification and settlement system developed and maintained by the Depository Trust Company (DTC). ID facilitates payment and delivery between broker/dealers for securities transactions made by their institutional-type customers. Basically a book-entry system, ID facilitates transfers between the institutions' custodian banks and the broker/dealer.

INSTITUTIONAL INVESTOR

Industry term for an investor who, because of the size or frequency of transactions, is eligible for preferential commissions and other special transaction services. The term is often used of banks, mutual funds, insurance companies, and large corporate investment accounts, although definition will vary from one brokerage firm to another.

INSUBSTANTIAL QUANTITY

The NASD places certain restrictions on broker/dealers in their allocations of "hot issues." Exception: the allocation of an insubstantial quantity to certain purchasers.

In its interpretation of this rule, the NASD has said that an allocation of 2,000 or fewer shares, or $25,000 face value of bonds, is an insubstantial quantity.

This interpretation applies to the entire group given below:

1. The managing underwriter's finder for this offering, its accountants, attorneys, financial consultants, or members of such persons' immediate family.
2. Senior officers, securities department employees, or persons influencing securities activities in the following:
    a. A domestic commercial bank or trust company.
    b. A domestic savings bank or savings and loan association.
    c. An insurance company.
    d. A registered investment company.

Total sales to persons in these groups in excess of the parameters given would violate the rules on "hot issues."

INTANGIBLE ASSET

1. Items of value owned by a corporation whose true worth is difficult and, at times, impossible to determine. Examples: patents, copyrights, and trade or service marks.
2. Goodwill also is an intangible asset. In a merger/acquisition, the dollar difference between the purchase price of the acquired company and its net tangible asset value is called "goodwill." IRS rules permit goodwill to be listed as an intangible asset and to be amortized, on a consolidated balance sheet, over a 40-year period.

INTEGRATED MARKETMAKING

Also known as "side-by-side" trading. The term identifies an NASD member who makes continuous bids and offers in an equity security and makes bids and offers in over-the-counter options on the underlying securities. Although the practice is not illegal, it could open the door to manipulative price abuse.

INTER ALIA

Latin: among other things.

The term often appears in complaints filed against broker/dealers or its representatives, or both. The term highlights several specific charges, but includes by inference other charges. Example: "We charge ABC, inter alia, with unauthorized trading and churning." The idea: These are but two of the unethical practices with which the broker/dealer is charged.

INTER–AMERICAN DEVELOPMENT BANK

Acronym: IADB. A bank organized to promote and advance the economic and social development of member countries located in Latin America. The bank is owned by the governments of various countries in the Western Hemisphere.

INTERBANK MARKET

General name for spot and forward currency transactions. International banks and multinational corporations are the principal participants in this market.

Foreign currency options listed and traded on the Philadelphia Stock Exchange are based on the interbank market.

INTERBANK RATE

The percentage of interest at which commercial banks are willing to buy and sell excess reserves among themselves. The term is similar to federal funds; however, federal funds may be bought and sold both by banks and nonbanks.

INTEREST ON INTEREST

A frequently used synonym for compound interest.

Compound interest is not based on the original principal; instead, during each period of compounding, the rate is applied to the accumulated principal and accrued interest. Thus, the interest will increase over time because the base (principal plus accrued interest) is constantly increasing.

Antonym: simple interest.

INTEREST–RATE OPTION

Acronym: IRO. A put or call in which the underlying is specific bills, notes, or bonds issued by the U.S. Treasury, or certificates of deposit with a specified face value. Because the premiums on these nonequity options are especially sensitive to interest-rate trends, they are called "interest-rate options."

INTERIM DIVIDEND

English term: the periodic cash distributions made to shareholders. Example: The company made three interim dividends of 50p and a final dividend of 75p.

See FINAL DIVIDEND.

INTERMARKET

1. Of stocks: trades of the same security made on different exchanges.

2. Of bonds: the sale of one type of bond and the purchase of another type of bond. Example: A sale of Treasuries and a purchase of corporate bonds would be an intermarket trade.
3. In corporate finance: the sale of one asset and the acquisition of another. Example: IBM sold Satellite Business Systems and bought an 18% stake in MCI Communications.

See also INTERMARKET TRADING SYSTEM and CONSOLIDATED TAPE (WWS).

INTERMEDIARY
A person or organization helping an investor to make, or to implement, investment decisions (i.e., persons who permit the investor to buy into a portfolio of securities). Example: An insurance company, a bank, or a mutual fund are called portfolio intermediaries. Persons who assist an investor with the execution of orders to buy or sell, or who provide investment advice, are called marketing intermediaries.

INTERMOUNTAIN POWER AGENCY
Acronym: IPA. A legal entity and political subdivision of the state of Utah, organized in 1977, to own, acquire, construct, and operate electric power facilities within the state. IPA finances its activities through the issuance of municipal revenue bonds.

INTERNALIZATION
SEC term for a practice of broker/dealers making over-the-counter markets for listed securities. Specifically, internalization means executing customer orders as principal without exposing to the customer the possibility of a better execution that may be available in different market centers.

INTERNAL RATE OF RETURN
Acronym: IRR. A finance term from real estate investing. It endeavors to recognize the fact that, in real estate investing, shifting values caused by interest and depreciation make the computation of return difficult. Generally, IRR is computed by dividing actual dollars invested by net rents and the residual value of the property minus interest paid on the mortgage during its lifetime. In effect, therefore, IRR is an endeavor to compute the time value of money in the investment.

INTERNATIONAL BANK FOR RECONSTRUCTION AND DEVELOPMENT
Acronym: IBRD.
See WORLD BANK.

INTERNATIONAL BANKING AND INVESTMENT SERVICES
See IBIS.

INTERNATIONAL DEPOSITORY RECEIPT
Acronym: IDR. A negotiable equity instrument issued by a commercial bank to represent a specific number of shares in a corporation that is not domiciled in that bank's native country. The bank holds the underlying shares. Transfer of the depository receipt is effected by the bank on its own records. Similar to the ADR, EDR, JDR in concept, although the IDR is more flexible because it can accommodate domestic trading in all international securities.

INTERNATIONAL OPTIONS
See IFX OPTIONS.

INTERPOSITIONING
A potentially unethical practice whereby a broker employs a second broker to complete a transaction between a customer and a market maker. The customer, therefore, pays for two agency transactions. The customer pays more or receives less than he would have if the original broker had dealt directly with the market maker.

INTERSTATE COMMERCE COMMISSION
Acronym: ICC. A federal agency that has jurisdiction over common carriers doing business across state boundaries. Offerings of equipment trust certificates fall under its jurisdiction. Other debt securities and equity issues of these same issuers are under the jurisdiction of the SEC.

INTESTATE
Legal term for a person who dies without leaving a valid will to direct the disposition of assets in the estate.

IN TOUCH WITH
Industry jargon used by salespersons to signify that they know a customer who has an interest in buying or selling a particular security but who has not entered a specific order to do so. The expression is used to try to locate a contra party who will complete the transaction.

INVENTORY TURNOVER

Also called "inventory turnover ratio."

Used in financial statement analysis as one measurement of the efficient use of assets; here, the ability to manufacture and sell, thereby generating income and profits. The most popular formula is:

$$\frac{\text{Cost of goods sold}}{\text{Year-end inventory}}$$

Average inventory also is used as the divisor.

Net sales divided by year-end inventory is also used, but it is a less accurate measurement of inventory turnover.

INVERTED MARKET

See BACKWARDIZATION.

INVERTED SCALE

The scale is the schedule of offering prices for bonds with serial maturities.

The scale is said to be inverted if the net yields for shorter maturities are greater than the yields on longer maturity bonds.

INVERTED YIELD CURVE

Term describing the graph of yields on similar debt securities if short-term yields are higher than long-term yields. Example: "The yield curve on AA utility issues is inverted."

See YIELD CURVE.

INVESTMENT ADVISER

Acronym: IA. A person who, for a fee, gives counsel to others regarding the purchase, sale, or holding of securities and other financial investments. Such persons are subject to the Investment Advisors Act of 1940 and must register with the SEC.

There are many exceptions to registration (e.g., general circulation newspapers, broker/dealers, persons who give advice to a limited number of persons); as a result, the category of IA is more important under state law. Legal advice should be sought by anyone who intends to sell investment advice for a fee.

INVESTMENT ASSETS

Technical term used by the regulators of the suitability of securities option activity in a client account. Investment assets include cash, stocks, bonds, and other assets and investments used to produce income or capital appreciation.

Concept: The regulators will not sanction the use of more than 15 to 20% of such investment assets in the purchase of put and call options. Reason: Long puts and calls are "wasting assets," with an expiration date at which they become worthless.

INVESTMENT BANKER

General term for a broker/dealer who assists corporations with the distribution of securities or with other money management or public relations services.

Investment bankers do not take time and demand deposits and, as a general rule, do not make short-term loans to corporations, as do commercial banks. In many other respects, however, commercial and investment banks compete for government and municipal securities business.

Also called "an underwriter."

INVESTMENT COMPANY

A corporation engaged primarily in the business of investing and trading in securities. The definition includes face-amount certificate companies, unit investment trusts, and management companies.

The definition excludes holding companies, banks, broker/dealers, and insurance companies.

INVESTMENT COMPANY AND VARIABLE CONTRACT PRODUCTS

Acronym: IC/VC. NASD term for a form of limited registration, either as principal or representative, that qualifies an individual to sell (representative) or manage the sale of (principal) investment company shares or variable annuity contracts.

Qualification is by an examination. Persons so qualified are limited to the sale of such products.

Antonym: General Securities Representative Examination, which qualifies for the sale of all securities products.

INVESTMENT GRADE

Term used of the top four ratings made by a national bond-rating service. Such ratings give an insight into the credit risk—that is, of the risk of bankruptcy, of the issuer of a bond or other debt instrument.

Popular designations: Standard & Poor's, or Fitch, both of which use AAA, AA, A, BBB. Moody's uses Aaa, AA, A, Baa. Moody's also uses MIG-1, 2, 3, 4 for investment-grade municipal notes.

Bonds rated BB (Moody's: Ba) or below are considered speculative and are popularly called "junk bonds."

INVESTMENT LETTER

The written agreement between a seller and a buyer in a private placement of securities.

In the investment letter, the buyer states that he or she is acquiring the security as an investment and does not intend to reoffer the securities publicly.

Because the sale is accompanied by an investment letter, the securities purchased are often referred to as "letter stock" or "letter bonds."

INVESTMENT SKELETON

Industry slang. It refers to speculative securities that are worthless or were purchased contrary to one's general investment objectives, or which failed to meet expectations.

The concept is a pun: "Everyone has an (investment) skeleton in their closet."

INVOLUNTARY UNDERWRITER

See STATUTORY UNDERWRITER (WWS).

IOC

Acronym: immediate or cancel (order).

An order that restricts the time of execution but does not restrict the size.

Example: Buy 2,500 LMN 52 IOC. The customer instruction says: I want to buy 2,500 shares at a limit price of 52 right now. Buy all 2,500 if you can. If you cannot, buy 2,400, or 2,300, and so on. Whatever portion of the order cannot be filled should be canceled.

Antonyms: FOK (fill or kill)—buy/sell all of the order right now, or cancel the entire order. Also, AON (all or none)—buy/sell whenever you can, but I will accept only a complete trade at my price.

IPA

See INTERMOUNTAIN POWER AGENCY.

IPO

Acronym: initial public offering. Often used as an abbreviation in the designation of an issue of securities.

In practice, the expression is used only of equity securities.

In general, the interstate sale of securities worth more than $1.5 million to more than 35 persons by a nonexempt issuer requires that the issuer register the securities with the SEC.

IRB

Acronym: industrial revenue bond.

An IRB is a debt security issued by a municipality. The proceeds are used to build a commercial facility. The net lease payments received from the renting company will be used to amortize the bond debt service. Because of the contract between the issuer and the renter, the rating on such bonds will tend to reflect the creditworthiness of the renter.

Pollution control bonds are the most common form of IRB. There is a statutory limit on the dollar amount of IRBs that may be issued for nonpublic use.

IRISH DIVIDEND

A derogatory expression for a reverse split—that is, a stock split that results in fewer shares outstanding.

See SCOTTISH DIVIDEND.

IRO

See INTEREST–RATE OPTION.

IRR

See INTERNAL RATE OF RETURN.

IRS

Acronym: Internal Revenue Service. The IRS is a federal agency that is responsible for the collection of individual and corporate taxes and for the surveillance and enforcement of U.S. tax laws.

The IRS may not assess criminal penalties. It may, under the guidance of the tax laws, assess civil penalties.

ISLAND REVERSAL

Term used by technical analysts.

Concept: There is a reversal from down to up or up to down. However, between the two trends there are a number of trades marked on both sides by a gap both on the up and the down side.

Example: Stock moves regularly from 35 to 50. Stock gaps to 51 and trades over a time period to 52. Then, following a gap to 50½, the stock trades down to 40. The trades from 51 down to 50½ form an island, and the technicians call it "an island reversal."

ISO

Acronym: incentive stock option.

A form of permitted executive compensation. If the executive exercises the option, no tax is due at the time of exercise. If the stock is held more than one year and then sold, any profit is considered a long-term capital gain.

Note: This is an exception from the six-month holding period generally required to receive preferential long-term capital gains treatment.

ISSUER

A corporation, trust, or association legally empowered to distribute its own securities.

Definition also includes governments, governmental agencies, municipalities, and political subdivisions thereof if these latter are empowered to distribute their own securities.

ITC

This is a tax credit permitted to the purchaser of certain tangible assets in the year when the purchase is made. The typical credit is 10% of the cost.

See also INVESTMENT TAX CREDIT (WWS).

ITS

The electronic system that links the floors of the American, Boston, Midwest, Pacific, Philadelphia, and New York stock exchanges.

See also INTERMARKET TRADING SYSTEM and CONSOLIDATED TAPE.

J

JAMES BOND

Slang: U.S. Treasury bonds that mature in 2007. Allusion is to the fictional hero who uses the pseudonym "Agent 007."

JDR

Abbreviation for Japanese Depository Receipt. Similar to an ADR, these registered receipts represent ownership of a specific number of shares in a non-Japanese corporation. Upon sale, the receipts are transferred by the depository to the new owner only on its own records. The underlying securities remain on deposit.

JELLY ROLL SPREAD

Colorful terminology occasionally used by professional traders in index options. The jelly roll spread combines long and short positions in the same index option, but with different classes, that is, put and call, and for different expiration months. A typical jelly roll OEX spread might combine the following:

LONG OEX NOV 190 Call
SHORT OEX DEC 190 Call
LONG OEX NOV 190 Put
SHORT OEX DEC 190 Put

In equity options parlance, this would be a put and a call time (horizontal) spread.

JENNY TEL

Wall Street abbreviation and identifier for General Telephone & Electronics Corporation.

JOBBER

English securities term for a marketmaker on the London stock exchange. The term is analogous to that of the specialists on U.S. exchanges, with this exception: The jobber acts only as a principal. His contra parties are brokers for the public and other jobbers.

JOBBER'S TURN

English securities term for the spread—that is, the difference between the bid and asked prices—of the quote given by a jobber. Example: In a quote of 170 p bid and 190 p offered, the jobber's turn is 20 p.

JOINTLY AND SEVERALLY

Expression used in Eastern accounts for municipal underwritings. Such accounts are undivided and the entire account is responsible for the entire offering. Thus, an account member with 3% of the participation who sold 3% of the offering would still be responsible proportionately for any unsold bonds in the offering.

JOINT TENANTS IN COMMON

Frequently used abbreviations: TIC, or Ten. in Com. In this form of joint ownership, two or more persons maintain a collective securities/commodities account with a broker/dealer, each having a fractional financial interest in the assets in the account. At death, the decedent's estate shares in the percentage of value attributable to that party's participation in the account.

JOINT TENANTS BY THE ENTIRETIES

Abbreviation: Ten. by Ent. A form of joint ownership recognized and legally used in only a few states. Such tenancy is restricted to husband and wife. It is similar to joint tenant with right of survivorship, but there are nuances in terms of disposition, assessment, and the like that require legal advice.

JOINT TENANTS WITH RIGHT OF SURVIVORSHIP

Two or more persons who maintain a collective account with a broker, but there is no specific fractional financial interest. Upon the death of one party, his ownership passes immediately to the other party. There is no probate, but there could be estate taxes if the decedent's portion, except in the case of a spouse, exceeds estate tax exemptions.

JOINT VENTURE TENDER

Term used to describe two or more companies that pool capital to take over another company. If successful, the victors either will jointly own the venture or divide up the assets of the acquired company. Example: In 1983, Martin Marietta and United Technology unsuccessfully tried a joint venture tender for Bendix Corporation.

JUNK BOND

Industry expression for bonds with a credit rating of BB or lower. Such bonds have speculative overtones.

K

K

Greek: *chilion* (pronounced: kill-e-on), meaning a thousand. Hence such words as kilometer, kilogram, and the like.

K is used as an abbreviation, following an arabic number, to designate that the number is to be multiplied by 1,000. Examples: $20K, 231K, and so on.

K is not used in the securities industry. Instead, the Latin M (1,000) is used, as in 20M and 10M. This abbreviation is used to give buy/sell instructions for bonds to designate the face value of the bonds.

KEEP IN MIND

Acronym: KIM. A customer or salesperson memorandum to a marketmaker that gives the price or size, or both, at which they would be buyers or sellers of a particular security. It is a nonbinding indication of interest.

KEEPWELL AGREEMENT

Also: keep well. A contract between a parent company and a third party in which the parent company agrees to cause a subsidiary to maintain certain minimum financial ratios or net worth. This arrangement arises to protect the integrity of a prospective financial deal between the subsidiary and the third party.

KEOP

Acronym: Key Indicator Operational Report. A weekly report mandated by the NYSE from member organizations who carry or clear customer accounts. Purpose: to enable the NYSE to quickly identify any member firms that are experiencing operational difficulties in the processing of their business, which difficulties, in turn, could jeopardize the quantity or quality of the firm's net capital.

KEYNESIAN THEORY

Also simply: Keynesian. An economic theory, named after the late John Maynard Keynes (pronounced to rhyme with canes), a prominent English economist. This theory is based on the belief that liberal government spending programs are needed to stim-ulate and maintain continuing economic growth in a country's gross national product. This theory, in times of depression and recession with elevated unemployment rates, would make the government the employer of last resort to revive the economy.

KILL

Slang: cancel. Examples: kill the bid, kill the offer, fill or kill.

KILLER BEES
Jargon for a law firm, proxy solicitor, public relations firm, and a bank to provide credit. These are held on retainer by a corporation as a continuing defense against a hostile takeover through tender offers or a proxy contest. This team of specialists is in the hive and, as "killer bees," are ready to protect the company from all unfriendly outsiders.

KIM
See KEEP IN MIND.

KIND ARBITRAGE
The near-simultaneous profitable purchase and sale of substantially identical securities in the same marketplace, based on price differences which prevail in their separate trading values.

KITING
The unwise and flighty practice of sustaining credit or of raising money by causing prices to soar.
See also CHECK KITING (WWS).

KIWIS
Slang for a five-year floating rate note marketed by the Student Loan Marketing Association (Sallie Mae) in the United States. The interest rate is denominated and payable in New Zealand dollars. The variable rate is set at $1\frac{3}{4}$ percentage points less than the New Zealand bill rate. This rate was chosen because, at the time of issuance, the rate was higher than comparable rates available on U.S. securities.

KNIFE
Word derived from the phonemes of NYFE.
See also NEW YORK FUTURES EXCHANGE (WWS).

KNOCKOUT
Colorful name used for the shares of Coca-Cola Company, Incorporated. The term is derived from the company's NYSE ticker symbol: KO.

KP
When used on corporate and municipal bond calendars, these initials identify Kidder, Peabody & Company, a major underwriter of securities.

L

L

Latin: Libra, a pair of balances, whence also the sign of the zodiac. Used as the symbol for pound sterling, the primary currency of Great Britain.

LAISSEZ–FAIRE CAPITALISM

French: let (it) act. A theory of capitalism which holds that the economy works best when market forces (i.e., supply and demand) are permitted to operate without intervention. Thus, the theory would have the government eschew all intervention in the economic order, or keep such intervention at a minimum. In practice, laissez-faire capitalism has not worked and has resulted in revolution wherever it has been absolutely implemented. Some governmental control of business forces is always required.

LANDOWNER ROYALTY

This is a share of the gross production of an oil or gas well—usually ⅛th percent—paid to the owner of the land from which the oil or gas is removed. The landowner royalty is paid without any financial contribution to the development of the well on the part of the owner.

LAPPING

A fraudulent scheme, also known as a Ponzi scheme, which takes money stolen from current participants in the scheme to repay persons who were victimized earlier. Theoretically, such a scheme will continue indefinitely until no new persons can be bunkoed into the ever-widening circle of victims.

LAUNDER MONEY

To transfer money through several financial institutions to conceal its illegal source.

See SEC RULE 17a-8, which is designed to prevent the laundering of money through an account with a broker/dealer.

LAY UP

Slang term derived from the sport of basketball to designate an easy execution of an order to buy or sell a security. Example: In today's market, 10,000 shares should be a lay up.

LBO

This is the purchase of a controlling interest in a company through the use of borrowed money.

See also LEVERAGED BUYOUT (WWS).

LEASE UP

The act of filling a commercial building with rent-paying tenants for periods specified in a contract known as a lease agreement. Broker/dealers often own or occupy such buildings and the lease agreement is often critical to that firm's profitability.

LEFT–HAND FINANCING

Colloquial term used to describe borrowing collateralized by assets which, in double-entry bookkeeping, are listed on the left-hand side of a corporate balance sheet. Concept: Asset-rich companies, by using these assets, can obtain capital at lower than usual costs.

LEG

Describes one or the other side of a transaction that partially offsets an existing position without closing out the position. For example, a client buys a call at 50. To turn this into a call spread, the client could add a leg by selling a call at 60.

You will also see the term to "take off a leg" if one side of a spread is closed, leaving the other side as either long or short.

LEG INTO A HEDGE, TO

A hedge is any offsetting security position.

To leg into a hedge, as this term is used by securities traders, describes the intention to create an offsetting position in a security by executing one side now and waiting until some later time to execute the other side of the trade. They hope that the subsequent position can be effected at a better price than the one now prevailing.

See LEG.

LEGAL

Also: legal item, or legal transfer. Commonly used as a noun. Example: It's a legal.

Term is used of a certificate registered in the name of a corporation, trust, or deceased person. The transfer agent will not effect transfer unless the certificate is accompanied by supporting documentation. As a result, buying brokers are not required to accept legals; instead, the selling broker must first have the security transferred to street name. It is then delivered to the buying broker.

LEHMAN INVESTMENT OPPORTUNITY NOTES
See LION.

LENDER OF LAST RESORT
Colloquial term for the Federal Reserve System. In regional or national emergencies, the Federal Reserve, through its 12 district banks, stands ready to extend credit to member banks. Such borrowing is covered by stringent regulations, and for this reason is said to be the "last resort."

LENDING FLAT
Term used of the borrowing of securities collateralized by cash if no fee is paid by the borrower nor interest paid by the lender. Term refers to short sales.

Antonym: lending at a premium—that is, interest paid by the lender who has the use of the cash collateral. Lending at a rate—that is, a fee paid by the borrower for the use of the certificate.

LESS A...
Term used to designate a concession granted to a member who helps in the distribution of a security. Examples: "Less a buck"—that is, the selling dealer will be permitted to buy a security at $1 under the public offering price, thereby making a profit when it is resold at the public offering price. "Less a quarter," which means the concession, on a bond sale, would be a quarter point (i.e., $2.50).

LESSEE
The person who enters into a contractual agreement to rent an asset from someone for a fixed time in return for the periodic payment of a fixed sum of money. The terms of the contract will determine whether the lessee or the lessor is responsible for maintenance and insurance.

Synonym: renter, although in context the word may be deceptive.

Antonym: lessor.

LESSEE MEMBER
An individual who has leased the use of a membership (seat) on a national securities exchange from a regular member. Such

leases are for a set time period and under qualifications set forth by the exchange.

LESSOR
The person who enters into a contractual agreement to rent to someone an asset for a fixed time in return for the periodic payment of a fixed sum of money. In addition to the payments received by the lessor, current tax laws permit the lessor to depreciate the value of residential and commercial property and, in the case of newly purchased qualifying equipment, to be eligible for investment tax credits.
Antonym: lessee.

LETTER BONDS
Bonds sold privately with ability for transfer or resale subject to terms of an investment letter.

LETTER OF CREDIT
A document issued by a commercial bank to a broker/dealer enabling that firm to borrow money as needed to meet its obligations and contractual commitments. The broker/dealer pays an annual percentage fee to the bank for this privilege, even if the letter of credit is not used to borrow funds.

LETTER OF FREE CREDIT
A written statement from one broker/dealer to another on behalf of a purchasing customer. The letter of free credit attests to the availability of funds to fully pay for securities that are to be delivered versus payment. Regulation T mandates this procedure if the purchasing customer regularly instructs that payments are to be made COD (cash on delivery) or POD (payment on delivery). Such letters are used only with institutional accounts.

LETTER OF INDEMNIFICATION
An agreement stating that one party to a business contract will compensate one or more other parties for losses incurred as a result of the venture. This agreement is fairly common in corporate finance activities involving mergers, acquisitions, and private placements. In public offerings, such agreements generally are limited to prospective litigation costs or penalties.

LETTERS OF ADMINISTRATION
A court-issued certificate that empowers a court-appointed

administrator to settle the estate of a decedent who left no will.

Securities in such an estate cannot be sold or reregistered unless this court certificate, dated within the past six months, is submitted to the transfer agent for inspection and acceptance.

See INTESTATE.

LETTERS TESTAMENTARY

A court-issued certificate that empowers the executor of an estate to settle the decedent's affairs as quickly as possible under the terms of the recognized will.

Securities in this estate cannot be sold or reregistered unless this court certificate, dated within the past six months, is submitted to the transfer agent for inspection and acceptance.

LEVEL

1. Noun: often used synonymously for the price or yield at which a security may be bought or sold, or at which a customer may be interested in a purchase or sale. Example: "I'd be interested in those bonds at the 8.50 level."
2. Verb: price or yield area where activity in a security will tend to remain for a time period. Price or yield may be higher or lower than present prices. Example: "We expect the market to level at 1350 until the last quarter of the year."

LEVERAGE

In finance, the term *leverage* is applied to:

1. The control of a large amount of money by a small amount of money. For example, a warrant or a long call controls a large amount of money with a small amount.
2. The use of borrowed money at a fixed rate of interest to achieve a greater rate of return. For example, a client buys on margin or a company borrows money.

LEVERAGE TRANSACTION MERCHANT

This is a futures commission merchant (FCM), registered with the CFTC, who is permitted by exemption to deal in selected over-the-counter futures instruments. As a general rule, such off-exchange futures trading is prohibited. However, those FCMs who were already in the business before June 1, 1978, can be grandfathered from current rule compliance with the authorization of the CFTC.

LEVERAGED BUYOUT

Acronym: LBO. Jargon for the purchase of a controlling interest in a corporation through the use of borrowed money. The concept includes the idea that the resulting consolidated balance sheet will contain debts that are to be paid off from assets currently on the balance sheet of the acquired company, or from cash flows generated by that company. Insurance companies, commercial banks, or venture capital organizations are often the sources of such borrowed funds.

LEVERAGED LEASE TRANSACTION

An equipment lease contract in which the cost of the equipment is substantially financed by a nonrecourse loan. The lessee gains use of the equipment for its business uses without a substantial outlay of capital. The lessor, who remains the owner, obtains depreciation benefits and the investment tax credit, and retains the residual value of the asset when the contract expires.

LF

Initials used on corporate and municipal bond calendars to designate Lazard Freres & Company, a major underwriter of securities.

LFR

Initials used on corporate and municipal bond calendars to designate L.F. Rothchild, Unterberg, Towbin, a major underwriter of securities.

LIBID

Acronym: London Inter-Bank Bid Rate. The bid in a quotation representing the rate of interest at which U.S. dollar deposits retraded within the English banking community.

The offer side of this quotation is called LIBOR (offered rate).

LIFFE

Pronounced: life.

See LONDON INTERNATIONAL FINANCIAL FUTURES EXCHANGE.

LIFTING A LEG

Expression used when an investor with a hedged investment removes one or the other part of the hedge. Example: A client with a long call and a long put (i.e., a straddle) makes a closing sale of the long call. This leaves the client with a long put outstanding. The client has lifted a leg.

LIFTING A SHORT
Term used by traders in commodities futures. Lifting a short describes the closing of a short position—that is, the obligation to deliver, by purchasing futures contracts for the same commodity in the same delivery month. On the records of the clearing house, the customer has a zero net position.

LIGHT BID/OFFER
Expression used by equity traders to indicate that their bid or offer is not equal to or better than the best prevailing bid or offer. The expression indicates institutional interest if and when the market moves up or down from present levels. Example: "I'm not buying, but I've got a couple of light bids if prices fall."

LILCO
Acronym and short name identifier for: Long Island Lighting Company, a large public utility whose shares are listed on the NYSE. LILCO also is used as the company's commercial logo.

LIMITED ACCESS TO BOOKS AND RECORDS
Generally, the right of a shareholder to inspect certain records of a corporation.

Specifically, of companies registered with the SEC, the requirement that shareholders be given an annual report, regular quarterly announcements, plus—as required—interim reports of significant activities as and if they occur. In most cases, shareholders receive such interim reports through newspaper press releases.

LIMITED EXERCISE OPTION
Term coined by the CBOE to describe an option contract which may not be exercised prior to the fifth business day before the expiration of the contract. In this way, a limited exercise option is similar to European options for debt and equity securities.

At the time of writing, there are no limited exercise options traded.

LIMIT ORDER SYSTEM
Short form: LMT. Part of the NYSE Designated Order Turnaround System (DOT) that accepts, stores, and executes limit orders. After execution, LMT generates a report to the member

firm that entered the order.

At the time of writing, DOT is being superseded by Super-dot. Thus, the quantity that will be stored by LMT depends on the underlying security and whether the order is entered before the market opens or after the opening.

LION

Acronym: Lehman Investment Opportunity Notes. This is a trademarked product marketed by Lehman Brothers Kuhn Loeb, Inc., now a subsidiary of American Express.

LIONs are similar to TIGRs and CATS in that they represent ownership interest in future principal and interest payments of selected U.S. government securities.

LIQUID YIELD OPTION NOTES

See LYON.

LITIGATION

A lawsuit or legal proceeding involving at least two disputants. In general, the term *litigation* is limited to civil suits.

Because controversies between broker and customer generally involve entitlements to money or securities, the industry provides arbitration facilities to reduce the number of judicial cases that must be opened.

LMT

1. Abbreviation used on security orders to buy or sell that also set a maximum price (buy limit) or a minimum price (sell limit) at which a customer will accept an execution.
2. See LIMIT ORDER SYSTEM.

LOBSTER TRAP

A defense mechanism used by a company that has convertible securities outstanding to prevent an unfriendly takeover. The mechanism prohibits conversion into common shares by any holder of the convertible if the holder owns, or would own, 10% or more of the voting shares.

This colorful analogy is derived from the design of real lobster traps—they catch and hold large lobsters, but they permit small lobsters to escape.

LOCKED MARKET

A temporary situation in a highly competitive market signifying that the bid and offer prices are the same. Once the offsetting buys and sells are completed, the market will unlock.

LOCK UP

1. On the occasion of the preparation of a final competitive bid for an underwriting, the representatives of the syndicate are sequestered until the competitive bids are opened at the office of the issuer. In this way, the participants, except for the manager's agent, have no way of compromising the secrecy of the sealed bid.
2. A secret sales agreement between principal stockholders and someone intent on the acquisition of a company. This secret agreement often precedes the purchaser's tender offer to other public stockholders for the balance of that company's stock.
See also LOCKED IN and LOCKED MARKET (WWS).

LOLLIPOP TACTIC

A colorful slang expression used to describe a company's endeavor to thwart a hostile takeover. In this tactic, certain current shareholders are given the right to tender shares at a premium price—but only if an undesirable bidder acquires a predetermined number of the outstanding shares. Thus, the deal tastes good to everyone except the hostile suitor.

LOMBARD RATE

The German banking system's equivalent of the Federal Reserve's discount rate in the United States. It is the rate of interest the central bank of Germany charges other commercial banks when they borrow money collateralized by German government securities.

LONDON INTERNATIONAL FINANCIAL FUTURES EXCHANGE

Acronym: LIFFE. A newly organized futures exchange in England that permits speculators, hedgers, and arbitrageurs to trade selected financial instruments. All of the instruments are sensitive to interest-rate change. Contracts currently are available for Eurodollars, pound sterling CDs, and long-term UK government issues.

LONG COUPON

1. A new issue of bonds or notes on which the first coupon payment will be greater than the usual six-month coupon

158

period. Example: a bond dated April 1 with the first coupon to be paid on December 1. Normally, subsequent coupons will be at six-month intervals.

2. Interest-bearing bonds with maturities in excess of 10 years.

LONG HEDGE

Strategy used to lock in a future yield on fixed-income securities if a drop in interest rates is anticipated. Two strategies: (1) Buy a futures contract on the security. Risk: The investor can lose more than the good faith deposit on the purchase if interest rates rise dramatically. (2) Buy a call option on the security. Risk: The purchase of the call automatically makes the investor's breakeven point the execution price plus the premium paid. Thus, the call may not be profitable unless a drop in interest rates is dramatic.

LONG POSITION

1. Any security that has been purchased and not yet sold. In the case of options, the term is used of securities purchased but not yet exercised or expired.
2. A term denoting ownership of a security on the financial records of a broker/dealer. The term may designate a security either held for a customer or owned by the broker/dealer for its proprietary account.

LOOK–BACK OPTION

A put or call privilege in commodities. It enables the holder to buy or sell, as the case may be, at the most advantageous price available during the life of the option. Example: The holder of a 60-day silver call could purchase silver at the lowest price available in the cash market during the 60-day period, even if silver is currently selling at a higher price. Such look-back options usually have premiums that double those that would be paid for a fixed-price option. Look-back options were originated by Mocatta Metals Corporation, a major participant in the precious metals market.

LOUSY LOUIE

Colloquial name used to identify Louisiana Land & Exploration Company, a concern engaged in oil, gas, and mining ventures. The name is derived from its NYSE ticker symbol: LLX.

LS

Abbreviation for last sale—that is, the most recent price at which a stock, bond, or other security has traded.

LTM

See LEVERAGE TRANSACTION MERCHANT.

LYON

Acronym: Liquid Yield Option Note(s). A Merrill Lynch product that combines the capital needs of its investment banking client with the investment needs of its retail customers. LYONs are callable zero-coupon securities with a put option that becomes operative in the third year after issuance. The call price reflects a fixed rate of interest; thus, the call price increases over time. The same is true of the put feature.

In some cases, the debt security is convertible into common stock, but at an increasing conversion ratio to reflect the accrued interest on the zero-coupon bonds.

M

M1

Also: M-1. Used as an identifier of the basic component of the money supply: currency in circulation plus bank demand deposits. Because this definition lacks some precision, M-1a and M-1b (defined below) were invented in 1980.

In practice, economists regroup M-1a and M-1b back into M-1 as the kind of money supply that most immediately affects the U.S. economy.

M1a

Also: M-1a. A current gauge of the money supply that combines currency and demand deposits but excludes U.S. government, domestic, and foreign bank proprietary deposits, checks in the Federal Reserve's float, and currency held in bank vaults. Thus, it is a more stringent definition of money and demand deposits.

M1b

Also: M-1b. A broader gauge of the money supply than M-1a. It adds to M-1a the dollar amounts in checking-like deposits, such as NOW and Super-NOW accounts, at savings banks and other thrift institutions.

M2

Also: M-2. A broader definition of the money supply in that it includes all monies in M-1a and M-1b and adds overnight repurchase agreements, money market mutual fund shares, savings and small time deposits at commercial banks and thrift institutions.

M3

Also: M-3. A continued expansion of the definition of the money supply. M3 is M2 plus large time deposits ($100,000 and over) and term repurchase agreements at commercial banks and thrift institutions.

M4

Also: M-4. The last measurement of the money supply, M4 is M3 plus other liquid assets, such as U.S. savings bonds, commercial paper, and bankers' acceptances.

As a general rule, newspaper reports of the money supply do not include M4, although it is given in the Federal Reserve's reports, because it is not part of the target area expansion set by the Federal Reserve.

M&A

Acronym: mergers and acquisitions. A special unit within a broker/dealer's corporate finance department. This special unit attempts to find business enterprises suited for purchase by, or amalgamation with, its investment banking clients. M&A also advises companies that are the subject of a takeover attempt.

MAC

See MUNICIPAL ASSISTANCE CORPORATION FOR THE CITY OF NEW YORK.

MAD DOG

Nickname for the common shares of McDonnell Douglas Corporation, a large defense industry contractor. The nickname is derived from its NYSE ticker symbol: MD.

MAE WEST SPREAD

Named after the popular life preserver used by pilots, the Mae West spread can return profits during periods of market stagnation. The spread combines a short straddle and a long strangle.

See STRANGLE.

The strategy involves a credit in the account that results from a short, at the money, straddle. There is a small debit from the long strangle. The end result is, in most cases, a profit on the expiration of the positions.

MAJOR-BRACKET UNDERWRITER

An investment banking organization that consistently subscribes to the largest portion of security distributions and whose name, therefore, appears near the top of tombstone advertisements and on the front page of the prospectus.

Associated terms for underwriters who are *not* major-bracket underwriters: mezzanine, second tier, third tier.

MAJORITY CONTROL

Ownership by a person, or a group of persons working in concert, of 50% or more of the voting stocks of a corporation constitutes majority control.

In practice, effective control often can be exercised by persons with less than 50% of the voting stock.

MAKE A MARKET

A broker/dealer who habitually maintains competitive quotations for one or more specific issues, and who stands ready to buy and sell at those stated prices.

Noun: marketmaker.

MANAGING UNDERWRITER

The investment banker who represents one or more similar organizations in its dealings with an issuer of securities. As managing underwriter, this investment banker works with the issuer, organizes the syndicate, arranges for a selling group, maintains the syndicate books, and stabilizes the security's price during the distribution. In return for these services, the managing underwriter receives an extra financial benefit from the gross profit of the other underwriters.

MANNY HANNY

An endearing term for the Manufacturers Hanover Trust Company, a large commercial bank headquartered in New York and a member of the Federal Reserve Banking System.

MAPLELEAF SERIES

Nickname for a product created and offered exclusively to non-U.S. customers of Merrill Lynch Capital Markets, Inc. It is a Euro-Canadian warrant to purchase a specific amount of a specific issue of Canadian government bonds. Example: Series I permits the holder to buy the Government of Canada $10\frac{1}{4}\%$ bonds due in 2004 at a price of Can$ $87\frac{1}{2}$.

MAPS

Acronym: market auction preferred stock. A variable-rate preferred issue whose dividend rate is reset every 49 days by a Dutch auction. Holders who are dissatisfied with the new rate can redeem their shares at face value.

MAPS are immediately callable by the issuer if the dividend rate ever exceeds the CD equivalent rate of 60-day AA-rated commercial paper.

MARITAL DEDUCTION

Also: unlimited marital deduction. Under present tax laws, a decedent may leave to a spouse all, or any part, of an estate without the payment of estate taxes.

This unlimited marital deduction does not avoid estate taxes, it simply postpones them until the death of the surviving spouse. As a result, proper estate planning for estates in excess of $400,000 (1985), $500,000 (1986), or $600,000 (1987) require legal advice.

MARKETABLE LIMIT ORDER

An instruction to buy or sell that has a maximum (buy) or minimum (sell) price established by the customer. However, because of present market conditions, the customer's limit prices better the current market; hence, the order can be executed immediately. This concept is of particular importance in the opening or reopening of the market.

MARKET AUCTION PREFERRED STOCK

See MAPS.

MARKET AVERAGE

An indicator of general stock price movements based on the sum of the market values for a selected sample of stocks, divided either by the number of stocks or by a divisor adjusted for stock splits or other changes in capitalization. The Dow Jones Industrial, Transportation, and Utility averages are classic examples of market averages.

MARKET BASKET
See BASKET TRADING.

MARKET–IF–TOUCHED ORDER
Acronym: MIT. An instruction permitted only on some exchanges. But MIT orders are entered below the market and are to be executed at the market if the issue trades at or below the established price. Sell MIT orders are to be executed at the market if the issue trades at or above the established price. Thus, in terms of market dynamics, MIT orders are exactly the opposite of buy and sell stop orders.

MIT orders are used extensively in commodity futures trading.

MARKET MULTIPLE
The multiple is another name for the price-earnings ratio. The comparison of the multiple for an individual security with the multiple for a group of stocks. For example, the S&P Index is called the "market multiple." The market multiple will give an indication whether a stock is overpriced or underpriced. As a general rule, such market multiples are better indicators if the comparison is made between one company and other companies in the same industry. Example: A company selling at a multiple of 9 while other companies in the same industry are selling at 12 may be an indication that the first company is undervalued.

MARKET–ON–CLOSE ORDER
Acronym: MOC. An instruction given to a stock exchange floor broker to buy or sell at the best available price during the 30-second period that designates the close of trading. The customer has no assurance that the order will be executed or, if executed, that the price will be the final trading price of the day.

MARKET ORDER SYSTEM OF TRADING
See MOST.

MARKET OUT CLAUSE
A feature found in most underwriting agreements. Under this market out feature, the investment banker (underwriter) can terminate its firm commitment to the issuer before the formal closing of the contract if certain material events occur that

impair the investment quality of the securities about to be offered.

MARKET OVERSIGHT SURVEILLANCE SYSTEM
Acronym: MOSS. A computerized market monitoring system, operated by the SEC, which incorporates the monitoring systems of the self-regulatory organizations into a single database. Purpose: to facilitate analysis of unusual market activity in a security or group of securities that could indicate manipulation, insider leaks, and the like.

MARKET RAID
See PREMIUM RAID.

MARKING
A manipulative action by a trader or investor involving the execution of an option contract at the close that does not represent the fair value of the contract and that results in a net improved equity position in the client's account.

MAT
Abbreviation often used for maturity—that is, the date the principal amount of a debt security must be repaid to creditors.
Also: Mat and M/D or MD.

MATCHED BOOK
Broker/dealer term that describes an equal borrowing and loan situation. The broker/dealer can make a profit if the borrowings are made at one rate of interest and the loans at a higher rate. Repurchase agreements (repos) and reverse repurchase agreements are used to achieve a matched book and thus finance the dealer's security inventory.

MATCH FUND, TO
Used as a verb: the act of borrowing money with a repayment date that is the same as the date on which the same amount of money will be due to you from a different borrower. Example: "$100,000 is due to me on April 23. If I borrow $100,000 that also must be repaid on April 23, I can be said to match fund."
Banks, through the sale of CDs, and broker/dealers, through repurchase agreements, match fund extensively. It is quite profitable if the interest rates favor the person who is match-funding.

MATRIX TRADING

Traditionally there are yield spread differences between fixed-income securities of the same class with different ratings, or between fixed-income securities of different classes. When these spreads diverge from traditional ranges, astute traders can profit by buying and selling the right securities if the ranges subsequently return to traditional patterns.

Matrix trading is a form of bond swapping.

MAX

Acronym: Midwest Stock Exchange Automated Execution System. This is an electronic linkage between the Midwest exchange and the Intermarket Trading System (ITS).

MAX permits the MSE to accept and automatically execute up to 1,099 shares of any dually listed issue at a price that equals the best price represented in the ITS system.

MBCS

Acronym: Municipal Bond Comparison System. MBCS is sponsored by the NASD through the National Securities Clearing Corporation (NSCC).

MBCS will accept daily municipal trade data from Municipal Securities Rulemaking Board (MSRB) members and will clear these transactions by (1) gaining contra party acceptance of the trade terms and (2) facilitating settlement by book entry debits and credits where this is possible.

MBIA

See also MUNICIPAL BOND INSURANCE ASSOCIATION (WWS).

MBS

Commonly used acronym: mortgage backed security. An MBS is any debt instrument whose underlying collateral is the pledge of a specific pool of real estate loans. The pool may have fixed or adjustable rates, even balloon maturities, and may be based on multiple, single-family, or mobile homes. However, all mortgages in any given pool will have a single set of characteristics.

MBSCC

Acronym: Mortgage Bond Securities Clearing Corporation. This is an industry-sponsored entity that facilitates ownership transfer between participants in the various mortgage-backed securities and pass-throughs. MBSCC is patterned after the Depository

Trust Company, in that it permits trade comparisons and the transfer of monies and securities by book entry debits and credits.

McFADDEN ACT
Federal law, passed in 1927, that gave to the states the authority to regulate commercial banks within their borders. The effect of this law was to restrict—and, in some cases, to prohibit—branch banking within those states.

MDS
Acronym: Market Data System. MDS is a communications device that automatically captures and continuously displays in summary form the trade and volume statistics generated by activities on the NYSE's trading floors.

MEDIUM BOND
Term sometimes used to identify a bond with a maturity ranging from 2 to 10 years.

More commonly: intermediate-term bond.

MEMBER CORPORATION
A term used to signify that a broker/dealer organization has purchased a seat on a stock exchange in the name of a corporate entity.

MERCHANT BANK
A British term for the rough equivalent of commercial bank in the United States: a bank that takes demand and time deposits. There is, however, a difference: Merchant banks in England may underwrite new issues of corporate securities. The underwriting of corporate securities is not permitted under the banking laws of the United States.

MESSAGE SWITCHING
Also called "message switching unit." An automated communication procedure that links sales, operations, and trading locales by means of a computer. The MSU of the NYSE routes orders, stores information, and relays execution prices to subscribing member firms.

MEZZANINE FINANCING
Term used in conjunction with leveraged buyouts. As opposed to pure debt financing, the term refers to financing a takeover by preferred stock or convertible subordinated debentures. In this

way, the resulting company's equity capital is expanded, rather than its debt, and it satisfies important creditors that the new owners will have a larger financial commitment to the merged corporations.

MIDGETS

Slang for mortgage pools of GNMA securities with a 15- rather than the usual 30-year maturity. The presumed prepayment period is 8 years on midget pools; it is 12 years on 30-year pools. Only the original maturity period differs; midget pools, like the regular GNMA pools, have a minimum principal amount of $1 million in underlying mortgages.

MIDWEST STOCK EXCHANGE AUTOMATED EXECUTION SYSTEM

See MAX.

MINIMUM LENDING RATE

Acronym: MLR. The interest rate charged to banks in Great Britain when they borrow from the Bank of England. It is comparable to the discount rate charged by the Federal Reserve to its member banks.

MINIMUM PRICE CHANGES OMITTED

An announcement that appears on the consolidated NYSE and ASE tapes if reports of trades are more than 10 minutes late. Following this announcement, only trades that fluctuate by more than ⅛ point from the preceding report on that security are printed on the tape.

When the lag time is substantially reduced, normal reporting continues.

MINT

See MUNICIPAL INSURED NATIONAL TRUST.

MIP

1. Acronym: monthly investment plan. A generic term for the periodic investment of small sums in the shares of a given company. MIP customers could purchase full and fractional shares. The term is not used of periodic purchases of mutual funds; instead, dollar cost averaging is used.
2. Acronym: mortgage insurance premium. An annual fee paid to the FHA or to a private insurance company to protect grantors

of mortgages against loss due to defaults by borrowers or from losses due to natural hazards to the underlying property.

MISCELLANEOUS LIABILITIES
Entry on corporate financial statements to designate liabilities whose payment date is not yet determined. Adverse legal judgments under appeal, deferred taxes under adjudication, and other similar indeterminate liabilities would be included under this heading.

MISDEMEANOR
Under federal securities law, an action that is considered to be a minor violation of the law. Generally, misdemeanors will result in a fine, rather than imprisonment.
Antonym: felony.

MJSD
Initials for: March, June, September, and December, which are the expiration months for certain stock and debt options traded on option exchanges. As a general rule, no more than three of the expiration months are traded at any one time.
Index options also offer three expiration months for trading, but the months are successive rather than in three-month intervals.

MKT
Abbreviation for the word *market.* Its most prevalent use is on customer order instructions to buy or sell at the best available price at the time the order reaches the trading area.

ML
Abbreviation used on corporate and municipal bond calendars to identify Merrill Lynch & Company, a major underwriter of securities.

MLR
See MINIMUM LENDING RATE.

MM
1. Abbreviation frequently used to designate a dealer who acts as a marketmaker.
2. When following a whole number, the initials stand for 1 million. Example: 1MM means 1 million, 2MM means 2 million.

As a general rule, MYN is a more frequently used designation than MM.

MMA
Industry abbreviation for: money market account.
See MONEY MARKET ACCOUNT.

MMC
See MONEY MARKET CERTIFICATE.

MMID
Acronym: marketmaker identifier. This is a four-letter identifying code assigned by the NASD to broker/dealers who enter quotations into the NASDAQ trading system. Examples: The code for Merrill Lynch & Co. is MOTC (Merrill Over the Counter), and the code for Salomon Brothers Inc is SALB.

MMMF
Acronym: money market mutual fund. Popular name for open-end investment shares that invest in short-term money market securities in an endeavor to provide investors with (1) relatively risk-free investments that (2) give a daily payment of competitive short-term interest rates.

MMP
See MONEY MARKET PREFERRED.

MO
Frequently used symbol in newspaper summary earnings reports. When used following the name of the company, it signifies that the principal marketplace for the shares of the security is the Montreal Stock Exchange.

MOC
See MARKET–ON–CLOSE ORDER.

MONETARIST
An economic theory holding that economic recession and boom is primarily a function of the control of the money supply rather than a function of governmental fiscal policy. Example: In a recession, a monetarist would moderate the recession by controlling the money supply; a Keynesian economist would

increase governmental spending. Supply-side economics is a variation of monetarist economics.

MONETARY AGGREGATES

Formal name for the money supply. It is measured in various ways, generally by decreasing liquidity.

See M1, M2, M3, and M4.

MONEY MARKET ACCOUNT

Acronym: MMA. A special bank savings account that provides an interest rate higher than the usual $5\frac{1}{4}\%$ given to time savings accounts. Generally, a minimum account balance is required, such as $2,500 or more. The interest rates on MMAs are generally competitive with that earned by money market mutual funds.

MONEY MARKET CENTER BANK

Any large bank located in a major city that plays an active role in the issuance and trading of short-term financial instruments. These instruments include bankers' acceptances, commercial paper, and certificates of deposit.

MONEY MARKET CERTIFICATE

Acronym: MMC. A savings instrument offered by many thrift institutions. Generally, an MMC has a $10,000 minimum face value and a maturity of 26 weeks. The percentage of interest is guaranteed and is tied to the prevailing six-month Treasury bill rate at the time of issuance. There is a cash penalty, both in principal and interest, for the premature redemption of an MMC.

MONEY MARKET PREFERRED

Acronym: MMF. A class of equity security whose dividend is payable every 49 days. At that time, the rate is recalculated to reflect current market rates for the next dividend period. Holders who are dissatisfied with the calculated rate may sell their shares in a special auction. If there are insufficient buyers to take care of dissatisfied sellers, the rate is recalculated at 110% of the commercial paper rate then obtainable for AA-rated companies.

MONEY MULTIPLIER SECURITY

Also called "Zerials." Initiated by Salomon Brothers, these securities are zero-coupon offerings of the same issuer, but with a choice of different maturities. Because the longer-term obligations are sold at a lower price than shorter-term obligations, but all are redeemed at par at maturity, the investor can double, triple, or quadruple his or her money by choosing the appropriate maturity date.

MONEY RATE OF RETURN
Annual yield expressed as a percentage of invested asset value. The calculation involves dividing annual dollars received by the value of assets employed to receive it.

MONKEY WARD
Colloquial name used of the shares of Montgomery Ward Corporation before it was acquired by Mobil Oil Company. This colorful name undoubtedly will be revived if Mobil Oil, as it has announced, spins off Montgomery Ward as an independent corporation.

MONTHLY INVESTMENT PLAN
See MIP.

MOODY'S
A registered investment adviser. Moody's is best known for its company reports, which appear periodically in bound form for: Governments and Municipals, Industrial, and Utility Corporations.

Its bond ratings also are extensively used to qualify the credit ratings of corporate and municipal issuers and to determine whether the security is investment (bank) grade. The principal investment grade ratings are: Aaa, Aa, A, and Baa.

MOPS
See MULTIPLE OPTION PUT SECURITIES.

MORRE
Acronym: Montreal Exchange Registered Representative Order Routing and Execution System. This mouthful is an electronic system that connects the MSE and the Boston Stock Exchanges. The system enables traders and investors to execute orders in selected issues in U.S. dollars on the Boston Exchange if that price is more favorable than the price available on the MSE. MORRE will accept market orders for execution at the best bid or offer price in amounts from 100 to 1,299 shares.

MORTGAGE BACKED SECURITY
See MBS.

MORTGAGE BANKER
General name for the middleman between the originator of a mortgage (e.g., a bank or credit union) and the investor who assumes the mortgage risk by purchasing the mortgage. This gives liquidity to the original lender and passes the mortgage risk, with its reward, to the investor.

MORTGAGE BOND SECURITIES CLEARING CORPORATION
See MBSCC.

MORTGAGE BROKER
An agent who, for a commission, arranges real estate loans for purchasers of property.

Unlike mortgage bankers, mortgage brokers do not service the loan after the financing is completed.

MORTGAGE CORPORATION, THE
A U.S. government-sponsored corporation that was created in 1970 to purchase qualifying conventional residential mortgages from members of the corporation—FHLMC, or Freddy Mac—which it then packages under its own name and assurances and resells to the public.

See also FEDERAL HOME LOAN MORTGAGE CORPORATION (WWS).

MORTGAGE CREDIT CERTIFICATES
Acronym: MCC. Sanctioned by the Deficit Reduction Act of 1984, these are annual credits that can be issued by state and local governments. The MCC then are applied against that mortgage subscriber's federal tax liabilities. In effect, MCCs enable the local governments to subsidize mortgage payments at federal government expense. In this way, public housing projects are encouraged.

MORTGAGE POOL ORIGINATOR
Descriptive title for any mortgage banker, either commercial or thrift, that assembles real estate loans on similar classes of property, then issues a new security representing a fractional interest in that multimortgage portfolio, and distributes monthly to certificate holders the monthly interest and principal payments

of the mortgagees. A fee is charged for this latter service.

The securities are said to be mortgage backed; the monthly distribution is called "a pass-through"; and if the pool is guaranteed the securities are said to be modified. Hence: Ginnie Mae Modified Pass-Throughs.

MOSS
See MARKET OVERSIGHT SURVEILLANCE SYSTEM.

MOST
Acronym: Market Order System of Trading. This is an electronic linkage between the Toronto Stock Exchange and the American Stock Exchange. MOST, which works in tandem with PER, the ASE's order system, permits an order flow for dually listed stocks so the order can be executed automatically on the market that gives the best price.

MOTORS
Common trading nickname for the common shares of General Motors Corporation, the largest manufacturer of automobiles in the United States.

The nickname is not used of the new Class E or Class H shares of General Motors.

MS
Abbreviation used on municipal and corporate bond calendars for Morgan Stanley & Company, a principal underwriter of securities.

MSE
1. Midwest Stock Exchange, Inc., located in Chicago. MSE trades many local issues as well as many of the securities listed on the NYSE and ASE.
2. Montreal Stock Exchange. MSE trades shares of many Canadian companies and options on these shares. MSE is subject to the regulatory jurisdiction of the Quebec Securities Commission.

MULTICURRENCY CLAUSE
A paragraph found in a typical Eurocurrency loan that permits the borrower to repay in another currency when the loan comes due and if a new loan is to be created immediately.

The borrower may be able to profit if repayment can be made by using a depreciated currency.

MULTIPLE OPTION PUT SECURITY

Acronym: MOPS. Term coined by E.F. Hutton to identify municipal bonds with 30-year maturities, but with 2-, 3-, and 5-year put options attached to the certificates. As a result, it is a long-term security that has an effective price floor because of the put options. In effect, the original bond will trade near par as though it were a short- to intermediate-term bond.

MULTIPLIER EFFECT

Term used to describe the expansion of credit in the U.S. banking system. The multiplier effect arises from the reserve requirement imposed on member banks by the Federal Reserve. Theoretically, the expansion of credit is the reciprocal of the reserve requirement. Example: A 20% reserve requirement will multiply credit five times if money is deposited in a commercial bank. In practice, many banks have excess reserves; thus, the full multiplier effect is not achieved.

MUNI

Popular contraction for any municipal security. In terms of the issuer, securities issued by any state, political subdivision thereof, or agency thereof. In terms of taxation, any security whose interest payments are exempt from federal income tax liability.

Plural: munis.

MUNICIPAL ASSISTANCE CORPORATION FOR THE CITY OF NEW YORK

Also known as: MAC or Big MAC. MAC is a state governmental agency, organized as a public benefit corporation, to provide financing assistance and fiscal oversight for New York City. It was organized in 1975 by the New York State legislature and is empowered to incur debt, refund and redeem New York City obligations, and, in general, to oversee the financial affairs of New York City.

MUNICIPAL BOND COMPARISON SYSTEM

See MBCS.

MUNICIPAL INSURED NATIONAL TRUST

Acronym: MINT. A service mark of Moseley, Hallgarten, Estabrook, and Weeden for a tax-free bond fund. MHEW acts as the trust's sponsor.

MINT is a municipal investment trust that features monthly

net investment income payments derived from a diversified portfolio of municipal securities.

MUNICIPAL OPTION

In the parlance of municipal securities trading, this is an offering of bonds to another dealer at a fixed price for a limited period. Within that time frame, the offering firm must honor the original terms if the dealer decides to exercise the privileges of purchase.

Note: Do not confuse with municipal bonds with a put option privilege. This privilege accompanies ownership and is granted by the issuer.

N

NAKED OPTION

Industry jargon for:
1. The writer of a call who does not own the underlying security, a convertible security, or a long call at a strike (execution) price equal to or lower than the strike price of the call that was written and that does not expire before the call that was written.
2. The writer of a put who is not short the underlying security, or who does not own a long put with a strike price equal to or higher than the strike price of the put that was written and that does not expire before the put that was written.

NASAA

See NORTH AMERICAN SECURITIES ADMINISTRATORS ASSOCIATION.

NASDAQ OPTIONS AUTOMATED EXECUTION SYSTEM

Acronym: NOAES. A computer-assisted process designed to facilitate NASD-member trades in over-the-counter put and call options. By means of CRT terminals, members may automatically trade up to three contracts in specific option series if a marketmaker shows the best bid or offer. The transaction is executed and automatically compared between the parties. The transaction also is reported immediately to the OPRA (options ticker tape) system.

NATIONAL FUTURES ASSOCIATION

Acronym: NFA. A commodities industry regulatory organization to which futures exchange members, commodity pool operators (CPOs), and commodity trading advisers (CTAs) must belong. NFA is responsible to the CFTC (Commodity Futures Trading Commission) for futures industry registrations, rule formulations, and recordkeeping examinations within member offices.

NATIONAL MARKET SYSTEM

Congress, in the 1975 amendments to the Securities and Exchange Act of 1934, mandated a national market system. The amendments did not say how such a system was to be implemented; thus the system is more theory than fact at present.

In practice, the system envisions a nationwide electronic linkage of the various marketplaces for securities so all bid and asked prices are publicly displayed on a CRT so everyone has access to the best available prices. The Intermarket Trading System (ITS) is such a system, although trades cannot be completed electronically. Thus it remains an information system.

NATIONAL PARTNERSHIP EXCHANGE

Acronym: NPE. This is a computer-based marketplace, located in St. Petersburg, Florida, for units of public limited partnerships.

Only SEC-registered partnerships are eligible for such secondary market trading.

NATIONAL SECURITY TRADERS' ASSOCIATION

Acronym: NSTA. The lobbying arm of professional salespersons and traders who deal in over-the-counter securities. The association is composed of affiliated membership groups located in many places where brokers and dealers are centrally based. The association has approximately 4,600 members and they hold both instructional and social meetings.

NATURAL SELLER

Term used to identify the offerer of a security currently held in an investment portfolio. By definition, a natural seller is long, not short, the underlying security. The term is not used of proprietary or block trading accounts.

The term *natural*, used alone, often identifies a trade involving a natural seller and a contra party other than the member firm.

Thus, the firm had no inventory risk. Example: That 100,000 share trade was a natural.

NEAR MONEY

Accounting term used to describe noncash assets that can be quickly liquidated at a reasonable value. Near money items include marketable securities, government savings bonds, bank accounts, and the cash value of certain insurance policies.

In practice, accounts receivable are treated as near money in the computation of net quick assets and the asset test ratio. Actually, such accounts are not near money because they must be factored—that is, sold at a discount, to produce ready cash.

NEGATIVE YIELD CURVE

Term used of fixed-income securities if interest rates for shorter-term securities are greater than rates for longer-term securities of the same class and rating. Term derives from the graph which depicts yields on the y-axis against times to maturity on the x-axis.

Also called "yield curve with a descending slope."

NELLIE MAE

See NEW ENGLAND EDUCATIONAL LOAN MARKETING CORPORATION.

NET ASSET VALUE

Acronym: NAV. Used by investment companies to identify the net tangible asset value per share. Typically, the NAV forms the bid price in the quotation for an open-end management company. NAV also is used for closed-end management companies shares to determine the premium or discount reflected by the market price.

Calculation: value of portfolio securities minus management group fees and all other liabilities divided by the number of shares outstanding. NAV is calculated each business day, generally at the time that securities trading ceases on the NYSE.

NET CAPITAL REQUIREMENT

Popular term for SEC Rule 15c3-1 that mandates the ratio of net capital, that is, cash and other assets readily turned into cash, and aggregate indebtedness, which is customer-related indebtedness that must be maintained by a broker/dealer.

The rule is complex, and various measurement standards can be used. In general, however, it can be said that aggregate indebtedness may not exceed net capital of a broker/dealer by more than 1500%.

NET DOWN

Also: netdown. Used as a verb: term describes the process whereby a taxpayer offsets short-term gains against short-term losses, and long-term gains against long-term losses to achieve a final figure in both columns. If there is a net loss in one column and a net gain in the other, the client must net down once more for the final tax consequences.

Note: In some cases, tax advice is needed to determine what is, or is not, a capital loss.

NET INTEREST COST

Acronym: NIC. In conjunction with municipal and corporate underwritings, NIC identifies the issuer's rate of interest expense over the life of its debt security. NIC often is computed as an interest rate for the average life of a bond issue.

The term is important in competitive underwritings because the net proceeds to the issuer and the NIC will determine which competing syndicate will be sold the issue.

NET SHARES MARKET

Term used of the trading of U.S. equity securities in European marketplaces. In Europe, most U.S. securities are traded in dealer markets. Thus, the trades are made by banks and brokers as principals—that is, net of commissions.

NEUTRAL SPREAD

A vertical call spread with a long call at a lower price, and two short calls at a higher price. Thus, it is the same as a ratio write for the holder of the underlying shares.

Term is used when the market for the underlying shares is calm—that is, the underlying is trading in a fairly narrow range. Term is not used in other circumstances.

NEW ENGLAND EDUCATION LOAN MARKETING CORPORATION

Nickname: Nellie Mae. A Massachusetts private, nonprofit corporation organized for the sole purpose of acquiring student loan notes incurred under the federal Higher Education Act of 1965.

Nellie Mae offers tax-exempt bonds to the public. The proceeds are used to purchase qualified education-related loans from eligible lenders. In this way, the lenders are made liquid, and they are in a position to make new student loans.

NEW YORK CASH EXCHANGE

Acronym: NYCE. A network of commercial banks in the northeastern United States that is connected by computer to provide their customers with a common automated teller service. Customers of these banks may make account inquiries and cash withdrawals at any of the group's teller machines.

NEW YORK INTERBANK OFFERED RATE

Acronym: NIBOR. The interest rate at which U.S. financial center bank deposits trade in the U.S. marketplace. NIBOR is comparable to LIBOR (London Interbank Offered Rate) and is often preferable because it is set in the same time frame and regulatory environment (principally, the reserve requirement) in which they operate.

NFA

See NATIONAL FUTURES ASSOCIATION.

NG

Popularly used initials for: not good.

Although used of checks that are returned for insufficient funds, NG also is used popularly in the brokerage industry for defective or returned securities deliveries.

NH

See DRT.

NICKEL

1. Popular identifier for the shares of INCO, a Canadian corporation formerly called International Nickel Company, Ltd.
2. Street slang for a movement, plus or minus, of five basis points (+/− .05%) in the yield of a debt security. Example: Since yesterday, the bonds have moved down a nickel.

NIF

See NOTE ISSUANCE FACILITIES.

NIPPER

Slang for the shares of Northern Indiana Public Service Company. The nickname is derived from the NYSE stock ticker symbol: NI.

NITWIT
Slang for the common shares of Northwest Industries, Inc., now known as Farley Northwest Corp., a large conglomerate involved in consumer and industrial businesses. Term is derived from its former NYSE symbol: NWT.

NMS
See NATIONAL MARKET SYSTEM.

NO-ACTION LETTER
Often it is difficult to determine whether an activity is prohibited under the securities laws of the United States. In such a case, the party contemplating the action may write to the SEC for a specific opinion. A no-action letter from the SEC means that it will undertake neither civil nor criminal action if the activity occurs as indicated. No-action letters are specific to the inquirer and are applicable only to the circumstances outlined in the inquiry.

NOAES
See NASDAQ OPTIONS AUTOMATED EXECUTION SYSTEM.

NOMINEE
1. The name inscribed on a stock/bond certificate if it is different from that of the beneficial owner.
2. Also: nominee name. Term is used to describe securities registered in the name of a partnership specifically formed to facilitate transfer or sale on behalf of the actual owner. Example, CEDE is a partnership organized by the Depository Trust Company, Inc. to facilitate transfer of securities it holds for the actual owners.

Synonyms: in nominee name, in the name of a nominee, held by the nominee, and the like.

NONBORROWED RESERVES
A weekly statistical indicator issued by the Federal Reserve. It states the total of member bank reserves minus their borrowings through the discount window. As such, nonborrowed reserves is a factual dollar amount; it may or may not reflect the Federal Reserve's willingness to supply or absorb reserves from the commercial banking system.

We use the term *moral suasion* to indicate whether the Federal

Reserve, through personal contact with its member banks, would like to see this number increase or decrease.

NONCUMULATIVE PREFERRED

A class of preferred stock that imposes no future obligation on the issuer if a dividend payment is omitted.

Noncumulative preferred stock is extremely rare. Almost all preferred issues with a stated dividend are cumulative.

NONDIVERSIFIED MANAGEMENT COMPANY

A management investment company that declares that it does not intend to be bound by the definition of a diversified company. This declaration, made to the SEC, also is included in its prospectus.

A nondiversified management company is not subject to the asset allocation limitations outlined in the Investment Company Act of 1940, but it loses the privileges accorded to registered and diversified management companies accorded by the Internal Revenue Code. In practice, therefore, it loses a tax exemption. This loss can be justified only by the prospect of extraordinary long-term capital gains.

NONPURPOSE LOAN

A loan made, using collateralized securities, in which the borrower attests that the money will not be used to purchase, carry, or trade in securities subject to Federal Reserve Board credit regulations or limitations. Example: "I went to my bank to borrow $50,000. I brought along listed securities worth $80,000. My banker said that the bank could not lend the money unless I made it a nonpurpose loan." (Reason: A $50,000 loan on $80,000 of securities collateral exceeds the percentage amount permitted under Federal Reserve credit regulations if the money is to be used to buy securities.)

NONRESIDENT AFFIDAVIT

Term formerly used when opening a brokerage account. It refers to a form that attests that the account holder—an individual, joint, or partner—is *not* a resident of New York State. By definition, all corporations were residents.

This attestation exempted the owner from resident stock transfer taxes, although nonresident stock transfer taxes were applicable.

The stock transfer tax, while still on the books, is subject to a

100% rebate. Thus, no tax is paid and the form need not be supplied.

NONRESIDENT–OWNED INVESTMENT CORPORATION

Acronym: NRO. Term used in Canada of a company whose shares and funded indebtedness are exclusively owned by nonresidents of Canada.

An NRO can qualify, if it meets certain other requirements concerning sources of revenue, for a preferential tax rate of 25% on taxable income.

Status as an NRO obviously encourages foreign investment in Canada.

NO–REVIEW OFFERING

Slang for an accelerated public offering of securities under an S-16 registration statement.

Substantial-sized issuers, up-to-date in their SEC reports and with publicly held securities already outstanding, can file this registration statement, receive a no-review commentary from the SEC, and make an underwritten public offering within 48 to 72 hours (in most cases).

NORMAL EXERCISE OPTION

CBOE term for an option that may be exercised at any time prior to its expiration date. All CBOE options are normal exercise options within the limits set for the exercise of options of the same class during a period of five business days.

Antonym: limited exercise options. Limited exercise options, a British term, permits exercise only within the five business days preceding expiration.

NORTH AMERICAN SECURITIES ADMINISTRATOR ASSOCIATION

Acronym: NASAA. A trade organization comprised of state securities administrators of the United States, Mexico, and the Canadian provinces. Purpose: to provide a medium for co-operation and coordination of state and international securities regulations.

NOTE ISSUANCE FACILITIES

Acronym: NIF. General term for the underwriting facilities associated with offerings of offshore Eurodollar notes and Eurodollar certificates of deposit.

Frequent synonym: revolving underwriting facilities.

NOT HELD

Acronym: NH. A qualifier sometimes added to a customer's market order sent to a securities exchange.

This qualifier permits a floor broker, but not a specialist, to use personal judgment about the time and price of the execution of an order. Not held means: not held to the tape; in other words, "I the order enterer will not hold you liable for missing the market if you as you use your best judgment to get me the best price."

NOVATION

The substitution of one debt for another by the payment of a dollar difference. Many synonyms could be used: restructuring, postponing, and the like.

Here is a frequent example of novation: A GNMA forward contract is canceled, another contract is substituted, and either the buyer or the seller makes a cash settlement to the other, depending on market conditions and the conditions of the new contract.

Novation is not considered to be a capital transaction by the Internal Revenue Service; therefore, gains are ordinary income gains and losses are ordinary income losses.

NSTA

See NATIONAL SECURITY TRADERS' ASSOCIATION.

NUCLEAR WAR

Corporate finance term for a situation where two or more companies compete for the acquisition of another corporation.

The expression reflects the fears of any nuclear confrontation: The situation is mutually destructive for all concerned.

NYCE

See NEW YORK CASH EXCHANGE.

NYFE

See also NEW YORK FUTURES EXCHANGE (WWS).

NYME

Acronym: New York Mercantile Exchange. NYME provides a marketplace for the trading of futures contracts in several metals, currencies, petroleum, and agricultural by-products.

NYSE

Acronym: New York Stock Exchange. Founded in 1792, the NYSE is a not-for-profit membership organization. It provides space and facilities for the trading of securities issued by many of America's largest and most prestigious corporations.

Often called the "Big Board," the NYSE is the largest of the nation's securities trading organizations for stocks. The dollar value of shares listed exceeds $1.25 trillion, a dollar value that represents over 60% of the top 5,000 publicly traded corporations in the United States.

O

OCD

See OTHER CHECKABLE DEPOSITS.

OCT

Acronym: order confirmation transaction. OCT permits NASD members to directly negotiate OTC option transactions for more than three contracts, yet use the NOAES facility. Once contract terms have been agreed upon, the completed transaction can be entered into the NOAES system and will appear on OPRA (the options ticker tape) system.

OFF BOARD

Although the term may be used of any over-the-counter transaction, the most prevalent usage is of a transaction in a listed security that is completed either in the OTC market or is completed within the member firm itself. For example, if a member firm receives a sell order for a listed security that is transacted OTC, or that it buys for its own account, the transaction is off board.

OFF–BUDGET AGENCY

A government-sponsored enterprise whose activities do not appear in the federal budget, although these agencies are within the discipline of the federal budget because of guarantees, both legal and moral. Typical of such off-budget agencies are: the U.S. Postal Service, the Student Loan Marketing Association, and the Federal Home Loan Mortgage Association.

OFFICIAL STATEMENT

Abbreviation: OS. This is the counterpart in the municipal securities industry of a prospectus in the corporate securities field.

Technically, municipals are exempt securities and need not register with the SEC. Issuers are, however, required to avoid "fraud and manipulation." To avoid any semblance of selling securities without making the full facts known to the buyer, many municipal issuers prepare an official statement, quite similar in appearance to a prospectus, for distribution to the initial purchasers.

OFFSET

General term for a transaction that:
1. Eliminates a commitment in a futures or forward contract by means of an equal and opposite transaction in an identical commodity or security. Example: A long contract for $1 million GNMA 9% of September 1983 can be offset by the sale of a forward contract for the same amount, coupon, and date.
2. Hedges, partially or fully, a present position in a security or commodity. Example: A client with a long-term paper profit in a security sells an equal number of shares short against the box.

OFF THE CURVE

The yield curve is a graph of the yields to maturity of various U.S. Treasury securities listed according to time to maturity.

Corporate debt securities are said to be "off the curve" if the Treasury yield curve is used as a benchmark in the pricing of the corporate debt securities.

OFF–THE–RUN ISSUE

Slang used by OTC marketmakers for equity securities that are not regularly included in the pink sheets.

Such securities are off the run because there is little trading or interest in the security. Thus, such securities do not merit the effort needed to update prices until an enquiry is received.

ONE–MAN PICTURE

A trader's description of a quotation that is obtained from only one marketmaker. This single source may represent a somewhat slanted view of the market; hence, it is a one-man picture.

ONE PERCENT BROKER

An agent who arranges for the borrowing and lending of securities between dealers and institutional investors. The fee for this service is 1% of the interest rate paid by the certificate lender for the receipt and use of the cash deposited by the borrower as collateral for the loan.

ONE–SIDED MARKET

A trader who is willing to deal only on one side of the market (i.e., the trader is willing to buy or sell but not both).

Also known as a one-way market.

ON–FLOOR ORDER

NYSE term for an order originated by a member either on the trading floor or on the adjacent premises, including the members' luncheon room on the seventh floor of the exchange. The designation is important because it affects the trading tactics that may be used and limits the priority that may be ascribed to such an order.

ON THE HOOK ORDERS

See CAP ORDERS.

OPEN INTEREST

The aggregate number of exercisable contracts, for either an option series or a commodity future, that are currently existing on the records of a clearing corporation. An open interest of one means that there is a buyer and seller with the same contract specification. Example: a writer of an LMN Apr 50 call and a holder of an LMN Apr 50 call that has neither been exercised nor expired.

OPPORTUNITY COST

Expression that compares current yields on a fixed number of dollars. Example: A customer can invest $10,000 at 10% with little risk of loss. Instead, the customer invests at 5% because the second investment, which gives only 5%, presents an opportunity for substantial gain. The customer takes a known decrease in yield for the unknown opportunity to make substantial profits. The known decrease in yield is the opportunity cost.

OPPOSMS

Acronym: Options to Purchase or Sell Specified Mortgage Securities (pronounced: o-pahs'-ems). This packaged product was created by Merrill Lynch Mortgage Capital Corporation. In response to customer demand, Merrill Lynch creates conventional puts and calls on Ginnie Mae, Fannie Mae, and other mortgage-backed securities and customizes them by issue, coupon, exercise price, and expiration date to suit the needs of the client.

OPTION PREMIUM
The price of a put or call option paid by the purchaser to the seller of that contract. Newspaper reports of the option premium are stated in dollars and fractions per share.

Also known simply as the premium.

OPTION SPREAD STRATEGY
Here is a schematic diagram of bull and bear spreads:

		Bull Spread	Bear Spread
Call	long leg:	lower strike	higher strike
	short leg:	higher strike	lower strike
Put	long leg:	higher strike	lower strike
	short leg:	lower strike	higher strike

Technically, bull and bear are correctly used only of vertical spreads.

See also BEAR SPREAD and BULL SPREAD.

OPTIONS TO PURCHASE OR SELL SPECIFIED MORTGAGE SECURITIES
See OPPOSMS.

OPTION TENDER BONDS
Acronym: OTB. Term coined by Kidder Peabody & Company to identify certain variable- (floating-) rate tax-exempt bonds with a put option included in the indenture. The interest rate is reset semiannually. If the bondholder is dissatisfied with the newly set rate, the option permits the holder to tender the bonds at year end for the full principal amount plus accrued interest.

OPTION TRADING RIGHT HOLDER
Acronym: OTRH. A nonmember of the NYSE who has purchased a license from the exchange. The license permits floor access and trading privileges but only for use in listed NYSE index options.

OR BETTER

Common abbreviation: OB. These words, sometimes written but always understood, form a supplemental instruction for all limit orders. In effect, the executing broker is instructed whenever possible to try to improve on the customer's limit price.

Generally, OB will be added to the order ticket when a buy limit order is entered above prevailing prices, or vice versa on a sell limit order. Thus, OB prevents confusion about the customer's intent to buy or sell.

ORD

British abbreviation for: ordinary shares.
See ORDINARY SHARES.

ORDER CONFIRMATION TRANSACTION

See OCT.

ORDER DEPARTMENT

Also known as: the order room or the wire room. A work area within a broker/dealer organization that is responsible for the routing of buy and sell instructions to the trading floors of the various stock exchanges. The order department also is responsible for the execution of over-the-counter transactions for customer and firm trading accounts.

ORDINARY SHARES

In British terminology, the equivalent of what is here called "common stock" (i.e., certificates representing residual ownership in a corporation).

ORIGINATION FEE

A service fee charged to the party that initiates the processing of a mortgage loan. Popularly known as "points," each point is 1% of the face value of the loan. Example: If the origination fee is 2 points (2%) on a loan of $100,000, the fee will be $2,000.

Current IRS rulings consider origination fees paid as interest; thus, the fee is a deductible item in the year paid.

OS

See OFFICIAL STATEMENT.

OTB

See OPTION TENDER BONDS.

OTHER CHECKABLE DEPOSITS
Federal Reserve Board terminology for one of the components used in the calculation of M-1. Other checkable deposits consist of negotiable orders of withdrawal (NOW), automatic transfer service accounts at depository institutions, credit union share draft accounts, and demand deposits at mutual savings banks.

OTRH
See OPTION TRADING RIGHT HOLDER.

OUT FOR A BID
Terminology used when a dealer offers municipal bonds to a broker who, in turn, will solicit bids for the bonds. The broker's fee is contingent on the sale of the bonds. Usually the broker will solicit competing bids without revealing the underlying source of the offering.

OVERBOUGHT
Term used by technical analysts of the level of security or market prices if they believe that vigorous buying has left prices too high and thus prone to an imminent decline. The term infers that a price rise was expected but prices rose too rapidly to be sustainable at present levels. Example: Following last week's sharp rise of 40 points, the market appears to be overbought.
Antonym: oversold.

OVERLAPPING DEBT
Term used of municipal securities if (1) there are co-issuers of a security, or (2) if a higher-ranking municipality and a lower-ranking municipality share responsibility for an issue.

Thus, if two townships were to issue a common security, or if a township and a village in the township were to issue a security, we would have an example of overlapping debt.

Do not confuse overlapping debt with the term *double barreled,* which states that a revenue bond is backed by a tax-collecting municipality if revenues are not sufficient for bond debt service.

OVERNIGHT REPO
A repurchase agreement with expiration set for the following business day. The interest rate associated with such short-term borrowings is lower than that for term or open repurchase agreements because the risk is lower.

In an overnight repo, the seller agrees to repurchase a security at an increment over the original purchase price. The agreement may require that the purchase be made at 100.00 and the repurchase at 100.04. Thus, .04% of a $1 million par value would be an overnight interest of $400. Annualized, $400 as overnight interest on $1 million is approximately 14.6%.

OVER THE COUNTER
1. General term for any marketplace—or marketing method—that does not involve the use of a securities exchange. Common abbreviation: OTC. Example: Most new issues of securities are sold over the counter.

    See also NATIONAL ASSOCIATION OF SECURITIES DEALERS for the self-regulation of OTC markets (WWS).
2. Term used by security analysts for pharmaceutical products that do not require a prescription.

    Both terms are used with and without hyphens.

OVERTRADING
An NASD term for this situation: A dealer, who is also an underwriter, offers a client a higher price than is justified for a security if the customer will purchase a portion of a new issue. The spread on the new issue offsets the special price set for the client's shares. Thus, if a client is offered ½ point more than is justified, provided he buys a new issue with a spread of 1 point, the underwriter will come out ahead on the combined transactions.

OVERWRITING
1. The sale of a call or put option whose premium is considered overvalued in relation to the market price of the underlying stock. In effect, the contract is not likely to be exercised. The sale may be covered or uncovered.
2. Of index options: the sale by an institution of index options as a partial hedge of a diversified portfolio of stocks. The premium received enhances the return on the portfolio and provides some downside protection against a temporary market decline.

OW
Acronym: offer wanted. Designation used by securities dealers to advise other professionals that it wants to buy a specific issue and is willing to negotiate a reasonable trade price with prospective sellers.

OXY

Industry slang for the shares of Occidental Petroleum Corporation, an international producer and marketer of crude oil. Term is derived from NYSE ticker symbol: OXY.

P

PACE

Acronym: Philadelphia Stock Exchange Automated Communication and Execution System. This is an electronic linkage between the specialists on the PHLX and the Intermarket Trading System (ITS) and the Computer Assisted Execution System (CAES).

See also ITS and CAES.

PACE permits the automatic execution of agency orders up to 599 shares at the best available price in the three marketplaces.

PAC–MAN DEFENSE

Named for the Atari video game, owned by Warner Communication Corporation, to designate a financial maneuver that is used to thwart an unfriendly merger. Under Pac-Man defense, the reluctant target tries to purchase control of the raider before the raider can exercise controlling influence over that party.

PACS

Acronym: Principal Appreciation Conversion Securities. This is a Smith Barney version of Goldman Sachs GAINS.

See GAINS for a full explanation.

PAMM

Acronym: performance appointment marketmaker. This is a CBOE term for an exchange member obliged to maintain two-sided markets in designated classes of CBOE-traded options. PAMMs must maintain quotes and must trade in illiquid as well as popular option series. PAMMs thereby provide market depth and supplement the activities of registered competitive market-makers. In exchange for this service, PAMMs are accorded certain economic advantages by the CBOE.

PARITY

Used of convertible securities if the value of the underlying common stock is equal to the market value of the convertible security. Example: If a bond is convertible into 50 shares of common stock, parity exists if the bond is priced at $700 and the stock is priced at $14 per share.

PARKING
A term used to cover illegal practices. Parking occurs if:
1. A dealer sells a security to another dealer to reduce its net capital requirement. Later, when a customer is found, the dealer buys back the security at a price that repays the other dealer for his cost of carrying the security.
2. An employer's transferring the registration of an employee to another employer so, at a later date, the former employee can be rehired without the need for a new registration examination.

PARTIALLY PAID BONDS
Term used to describe certain initial public offerings of dollar-denominated bonds sold to foreign investors. The name derives from the fact that the purchasers deposit only 20 to 30% of the cost and agree to pay the balance at some specified time in the future. Such payments are legal if they are completed outside the United States and thus away from the jurisdiction of the Federal Reserve Board's credit restrictions.

PARTICIPATING INCENTIVE PREFERRED STOCK
Acronym: PIPS. An equity security issuable by a prospective takeover target. Its purpose is to deter the acquiror intent on 100% ownership because it is sold to, and provides voting power to, the business constituencies of the target company. It is designed to protect the financial interests of those constituencies. PIPS is convertible, participating, and nontransferrable.

PARTS
Acronym: periodically adjustable rate trust securities. PARTS are a pass-through mortgage trust composed of municipal loans; thus, interest payments are exempt from federal taxes.

PARTS have a put feature and rates periodically are adjusted to reflect early calls and ordinary mortgage redemptions. In effect, interest rates may vary, but the holder, because of the put option, is protected against loss of principal.

PARTY IN INTEREST
Term used in the Employee Retirement Income Security Act (ERISA) to identify a person who provides a service to a pension or other employee benefit plan. Service includes investment

advice to a retirement plan; it also includes broker/dealers who make purchases, sales, leases, underwriting, or credit transactions for or with a retirement plan.

PAYDOWN
1. Used of a refunding of one debt by another if the new debt is smaller than the originally outstanding debt. Example: A company borrows $8 million to refund bonds with a face value of $10 million.
2. Used of Ginnie Mae modified pass-through pools if the experienced reduction in the unpaid principal balance is greater than the anticipated reduction. Example: a GNMA pool, after eight years, should have a factor of .8532456; its experienced factor is .7894321.

P–COAST
Slang for the Pacific Stock Exchange.

PEFCO
See PRIVATE EXPORT FUNDING CORPORATION.

PEGGY
Industry nickname for the shares of Public Service Electric and Gas Company, a large utility operating in the state of New Jersey. The term is derived from the NYSE ticker symbol: PEG.

PENNY
Industry nickname for the shares of J.C. Penney, Inc., a large retail department store.

PENTAPHILIA THEORY
One of the many theories ascribed to by technical analysts. In this case, the theory holds that the market always moves higher in calendar years ending in, or divisible by, five. Example: 1975, 1980, 1985. Thus, our next certain moves will be in 1990, 1995, 2000.

As with most of such technical theories, they are jocular.

PEP
Acronym: program execution processing. An NYSE-endorsed plan designed to facilitate executions of orders in multiple issues entered simultaneously as part of an institutional investor's index-based portfolio program. PEP is tied into the exchange's

Super-DOT program and, at the time of writing, may involve as many as 30,099 shares of certain stocks if such orders are entered before the opening.

PERCENT
Also: per centum. Abbreviation: pct. A ratio stated as a part of the base 100 so capitalizations, dividend and interest yields, and other numbers may be directly compared. Example: There is currently a spread of 7% between the yields on stocks and bonds. Or, AJAX Corporation has a bond ratio in excess of 35%.

PERFORMANCE APPOINTMENT MARKETMAKER
See PAMM.

PERIODICALLY ADJUSTABLE RATE TRUST SECURITIES
See PARTS.

PERMANENT MORTGAGE REIT
A form of real estate investment trust that lends long-term monies to builders and developers of commercial and residential projects. Such long-term loans often run up to 40 years.

PESO
The primary unit of currency in Spain and many other nations that were originally colonized by that nation, such as Mexico, Argentina, the Philippines.

PFD
Abbreviation: preferred (stock).

PFX OPTIONS
Any foreign currency option traded on the Philadelphia Stock Exchange.

PG
Acronym: parent guaranteed. Used in descriptions and statistical tables of certain debt securities that are issued by a subsidiary corporation and whose interest and principal payments are guaranteed by the parent corporation.

PHANTOM SHELF
See CONVENIENCE SHELF.

PHANTOM STOCK PLAN

A work-compensation incentive given to officers of a corporation. Under this plan, future bonus compensations are tied to the dollar value increase of the company's common stock. Thus, the bonus compensation will be computed as though the officers held a fixed number of the underlying shares; hence, the word *phantom* and the term *phantom stock.*

PHILADELPHIA STOCK EXCHANGE AUTOMATED COMMUNICATION AND EXECUTION SYSTEM

See PACE.

PHYSICAL ACCESS MEMBER

An individual who, for a special fee paid annually, has purchased from the NYSE the right to use the trading floor facilities to buy and sell securities. Such a member has no voting privileges in exchange affairs and has no liquidation rights in the event of the exchange's dissolution.

PI

Acronym: principal and interest. Term used by bond traders in discussing the typical payments made by bond issuers to their creditors.

PICKUP

Term used of a swap of bonds with similar coupon rates and similar maturities at a basis price that is advantageous to the swapper. For example, a client sells 8½% bonds of 2000 at a basis of 10.30% and buys 8½% bonds of 2001 at a basis of 10.70%. The client has picked up 40 basis points of yield.

Pickup implies that the monetary adjustment between the purchase and sale prices is relatively small.

PICKUP BONDS

Term used of bonds with a relatively high coupon and a relatively short callable date. If interest rates drop, the issuer usually will call the bonds at their premium price. The investor, therefore, will receive a return that is higher than anticipated because of the premium received when the bond is called.

PIE IN THE SKY

Colorful nickname for the common shares of Piedmont Aviation, a regional commercial air carrier. The nickname is derived from the NYSE ticker symbol: PIE.

PIGGYBACK EXCEPTION

This is a colloquial term that stems from a 1984 amendment to SEC Rule 15c2-11.

The rule makes an important presumption. Generally, factual information must be filed with the SEC—and this rule continues in force. However, the amendment presumes that regular and frequent quotations in an actively traded market are an appropriate substitute for information. The SEC's point of view: The market will not trade if they sense any reticence by the company to provide up-to-date information, both positive and negative.

PIPS

See also PARTICIPATING INCENTIVE PREFERRED STOCK.

PIT BOSS

A member of the CBOE appointed by the exchange to assist regular floor officials. Although this is a junior position, a pit boss is nevertheless authorized to: (1) resolve disputes unrelated to rule violations; (2) oversee the quality and accuracy of quotation information, as well as opening and closing prices; and (3) act as a preliminary contact between trading crowds and the exchange's regulatory staff.

PITI

Acronym: principal, interest, taxes, and insurance. Since PITI basically put the mortgage holder at risk, it is common to incorporate such factors into the contract associated with a mortgage loan when made by a bank. In this way, the principal remains fixed, but there are adjustments that can be made to raise the mortgage payments—usually on an annual basis—so the lender is protected against increased taxes, mortgage insurance, and the like.

PLAIN VANILLA

Street lingo used to designate a simple solution to a problem. Most often used in conjunction with a corporate financing to signify that a security offering is routine and traditional and thus without gimmicks or special features to enhance or promote it.

PLUS

Often written as a mathematical sign: +.
1. A fractional variation to designate a quote in 64ths; for example, 85.16+ means 85 and $33/64$th of par. The numerator is 2 times 16 plus 1; 64 is the denominator.

2. A designator for a transaction above the previous regular way transaction. Example: On the Quotron system, 45+ means that the last trade at 45 is higher than the previous trade.
3. In the stock column of the newspaper, a + in the change column means that the closing price of listed securities was higher by the stated amount over the previous day's close. For mutual funds and OTC securities, the change is measured from the previous day's bid price.
4. Used of the difference, if a positive number, between a closed-end investment company's offer price and the net asset value of the underlying share assets.

POES
Acronym: Public Order Exposure System. This is a soon-to-be-developed industry procedure to make sure that customer orders are not crossed in-house before they have an opportunity to get a better price in the public marketplace.

POINTS
See COMMITMENT FEE.

POISON PILL
Slang for a corporate finance tactic to defend against unfriendly takeovers. Generally, the "poison pill" is an issue of convertible preferred stock distributed as a stock dividend to current stockholders. The preferred stock is convertible into a number of common shares equal to or greater than the present number of outstanding shares. However, because of dividend adjustments, there is little incentive to convert unless there is a takeover. The takeover attempt, therefore, becomes its own poison because it will vastly increase the price that will have to be paid for the company.

POLISH DIVIDEND
See SCOTTISH DIVIDEND.

PONZI SCHEME
Popular name for any scam that bilks people by promising high returns for money invested but that can only do so by using funds received from new investors to pay earlier depositors. The scheme is doomed to failure because its pyramid effect requires ever-increasing sums of money "borrowed from Peter to pay Paul." Charles Ponzi, after whom the scheme is named, cost investors millions of dollars with such fraudulent practices in the 1920s.

POOL

Commonly used expression if a group of debt instruments is gathered together and an undivided interest in the securities is represented by another security. Example: A bank issues mortgages on 50 homes with a $20,000 mortgage on each home. If the bank were to issue a security with a face value of $1 million, the security would represent a pool of mortgages.

POOLING OF INTEREST

Balance sheet term for the accounting procedure used if one corporation acquires another through merger or acquisition.

Principal concepts: (1) all assets and liabilities are merged; (2) if there is a difference between the cost of acquisition and the net tangible value of the acquired corporation, it is entered on the acquiring corporation's balance sheet as "goodwill." Present IRS rules permits this entry to be amortized over 40 years.

POPULARIZING

An NYSE term applied to certain promotional activities by exchange specialists in options on stock issues in which they make markets. These activities may be advertisements, market letters, sales literature, research reports, or buy/sell recommendations made to investors to trade in the overlying options.

PORTFOLIO MANAGER

Term used to refer to the individual at an institutional investor organization who decides what securities to buy or sell on behalf of that institution.

POSITION BID (OFFER)

A bid (offer) made by a broker/dealer who is willing to buy (sell) a block of securities for his or her own account as an accommodation to an institutional customer. Generally, the bid (or offer) is slightly away from the market to provide the broker/dealer some protection against market risk, while the broker/dealer seeks to close out the resulting long or short position.

POSITIVE YIELD CURVE

Term used to describe the yield versus time graph of securities of the same issuer, or of securities with a similar credit rating, in which longer-term securities have a higher yield than shorter-term securities. Thus, if 2-year Treasury bonds yield 8% and

4-year bonds yield 9% and 15-year bonds yield 11%, there is a positive yield curve.

Also called "yield curve with an ascending slope."

POSTAL SERVICE

The successor corporation to the Post Office Department. It is a federal agency that issues debt securities to finance capital improvements and to cover deficits in operating expenses. The Postal Service pledges its own assets and revenues as collateral for these bonds, although the Postal Service could ask for and receive a U.S. government guarantee from the Secretary of the Treasury.

POST–DATED

1. Any document that is dated after the calendar date on which the agreement was signed.
2. A check, draft, or other transfer document that is dated at some future date. Although both the issuance and acceptance of a post-dated check, in many circumstances, may signal a credit problem, there is one exception. Bankers' acceptances are always post-dated checks. Any credit problem is quickly solved: the accepting bank's guaranteed performance on the loan.

POT

Slang for that portion of the shares or bonds of a corporate issue returned to the account manager, as agent, for convenient sale to institutional buyers.

If sales are made from the pot, the members of the syndicate share in the spread in proportion to their takedown of the issue. Thus, on an issue of 1 million shares with 100,000 in the pot, a member of the account with a 10% participation (takedown) will share in 10% of the sales from the pot.

POT LIABILITY

Term that refers to an underwriter's financial responsibility for unsold securities remaining in the pot when the syndicate price restrictions are lifted by the manager. Generally, each member of the syndicate is liable for unsold pot securities in direct proportion to its percentage commitment to the issuer.

POUND

As a general rule, this represents the primary unit of currency in Great Britain. Because other nations also use pound as a primary currency unit, the word is often used in a compound form: pound sterling.

PREFERENCE INCOME
Certain income items (such as the excluded portion of capital gains and excess depreciation over straight line) that are not included in the adjusted taxable income of an individual. If such excluded income items exceed a specified amount, the taxpayer is required to compute an alternate minimum tax. If the alternate minimum exceeds the tax found by using the tax schedules, this becomes the individual's tax for that year. Concept: to prevent wealthy individuals from paying a lower percentage tax than that paid by wage earners.

PREFERRED PREFERRED
Slang often used with prior preferred stock (i.e., an issue of preferred stock that takes precedence over one or more issues or preferred stock of the same corporation). This precedence may be in terms of dividend payments or the claim on assets upon dissolution of the company.

PRELIMINARY AGREEMENT
A temporary commitment between an issuing corporation and an underwriter drawn up prior to the effective date of the issuer's registration statement. The replacement of the preliminary agreement by a formal agreement hinges upon the underwriter's estimation of the success potential for the offering and the corporation's acceptance of the underwriter's terms and conditions.

PREMIUM RAID
British securities industry term to describe a quick purchase of a large percentage of a company's stock at prices above the prevailing market. Because there is little advance notice, and because the trade often is completed in 30 minutes or less, few public investors have a chance to sell their shares at these advantageous prices.

PRESCRIBED RIGHT TO INCOME AND MAXIMUM EQUITY
See PRIME.

PRESUMPTIVE UNDERWRITER
Term, by SEC interpretation, that describes any investor who acquires a relatively large amount of securities in a public offering with a view toward an early resale. In practice, the SEC

has regarded anyone who purchases 10% or more of an offering and who sells it within two years as a presumptive underwriter.

PRICE–EARNING RATIO
Abbreviations: PE or P/E. The ratio is formed by dividing the current market price of a company's shares by the current annual earnings per common share. Technically, the ratio is the quotient of this division.

Synonym: multiple. Example: The stock is currently selling at a multiple of 9.

PRIMARY MARKET
General term for any market for assets where the proceeds of the sale go to the issuer. As such, the term includes:
1. The underwriting of original issues of securities.
2. Government securities auctions.
3. Opening sales of option contracts and commodity futures contracts.
4. An exchange, or the OTC market, which is the principal market for a specific outstanding security.

PRIME
Acronym: prescribed right to income and maximum equity (i.e., one of the two component parts of an Americus Trust). The first Americus Trust was established for the common shares of AT&T.

Holders of the PRIME component receive all dividend distributions plus any asset value of the trust up to a maximum of $75 per share when it is dissolved on or before September 1988. Holders of the SCORE component receive the remainder of the capital value of the underlying shares.

See SCORE.

PRINCIPAL
1. The face amount (par value) of a debt security.
2. A person or firm that buys and sells securities for its own account and risk.
3. A person associated with an NASD member who is actively engaged in the management of that firm's investment banking or securities business, including supervision, the solicitation of account and their approval, and compliance.

PRINCIPAL APPRECIATION CONVERSION SECURITIES
See PACS.

PRIOR LIEN BOND

A debt security that gives priority to its holders over the claim of other bondholders.

The term is not used to distinguish secured bonds from unsecured bonds, for example, mortgage bonds as opposed to debentures. Instead, a prior lien bond would give priority to one secured bond over another.

Secured bonds with a prior lien over other secured bonds normally are issued by companies in financial difficulty and then only with the authorization of the holders of previously issued bonds who give their authorization to try to save the company.

PRIVATE EXPORT FUNDING CORPORATION

Acronym: PEFCO. A corporation that makes loans to foreign importers of goods and services of U.S. manufacture or origin. Its interest and principal repayment liabilities on borrowed money are guaranteed by the Export-Import Bank (Eximbank), which in turn is guaranteed by the full faith and credit of the United States.

PROBATE COURT

This is the juridical arm of local government given power over wills, intestacies, guardianships, adoptions, and—in some cases—incompetencies. Such courts are also known as surrogate courts.

Judges of probate issue letters (often called "certificates") to executors, administrators, or guardians to complete certain financial actions. Examples: manage the assets of an incompetent, settle an estate, or guard the financial affairs of a minor.

PRODUCTION RATE

The current coupon rate for issuance of pass-through securities of the Government National Mortgage Association (GNMA). It is an interest rate set 50 basis points (1/2%) below the prevailing FHA mortgage rate (i.e., the maximum interest rate at which the Federal Housing Administration will insure, and the Veterans Administration will guarantee, residential mortgages).

PROFIT TAKING

A commonly used expression to explain a sudden drop in the stock market following a long- or intermediate-term rise in the market.

As a matter of fact, the expression means that the pundits have no accurate reading of the cause for the drop. The drop may have been caused by selling—a reasonable cause for a drop—or by a lack of interest of buyers. Thus, the reader may substitute his or her own reason for the drop. In practice, the reason is unknown.

PRO FORMA
Latin: according to form or custom. In practice, the expression is used:
1. If a financial statement is currently unaudited but is sufficiently representative of the corporation's financial condition to be a reasonable and fair disclosure of the company's balance sheet.
2. If an action, done with due diligence and proper authorization, awaits only official approval. Example: The shareholders of a corporation have approved a stock split and application has been made for a charter revision. The application is pro forma because it will be approved.

PROGRAM EXECUTION PROCESSING
See PEP.

PROGRAM TRADING
Term associated with money managers who are bound by ERISA rules as they endeavor to track the performance of a popular index or average. In this way, they avoid doing worse than the market.

In practice, program trading and basket trading are similar, although program trading is associated with market closing prices, whereas basket trading can be effected at any time during the market day.

PROPORTIONATE SHARE OF ASSETS
The right of common stockholders to the residual assets of their corporation upon its dissolution. In practice, after all liabilities have been fully satisfied, and preferred stockholders have been provided for, the common stockholders divide the remaining assets, if any, among themselves.

PROTECTIVE COVENANT
General term for agreements and promises of a municipality to protect purchasers of an issue of municipal securities. These agreements are in the bond resolution made when the security is issued.

Typical content of the covenant: a promise to service and repair the facility built with the borrowed funds, adequate insurance coverage, the maintenance of books and records, and the assessment of adequate rates or tolls to cover interest and the repayment of principal.

PROVISIONAL ALLOTMENT LETTER
In England: the means whereby corporations offer present shareholders the right to subscribe to additional shares before the general public is allowed to participate. The letter, therefore, is the English equivalent of a rights offering in the United States.

PROXY DEPARTMENT
A work area in a broker/dealer cashiering function that distributes corporate publications, including financial reports, meeting notices, and voting information to the beneficial owners of shares held by that broker/dealer. Thus, the proxy department acts as an intermediary between the issuer and these beneficial owners and casts votes on their behalf according to the instructions received from these owners.

PRUDENT MAN RULE
Rule contained in the laws of many states governing the investment activities of persons who act as fiduciaries, such as trustees, executors, and administrators.

In general, the rule precludes speculative activities by fiduciaries and legislates as a norm the kind of investment actions that a prudent man would use in the conduct of his own financial affairs.

See also LEGAL LIST (WWS).

PUBLIC UTILITY HOLDING COMPANY ACT OF 1935
The federal law requires SEC registration for all publicly owned holding companies engaged in the electric utility business or in the retail distribution of gas. The law also requires, in many circumstances, that public issues of such securities be the subject of competitive underwritings.

PURPOSE LOAN
Name of a loan, collateralized by securities, if the money borrowed will be used to purchase, carry, or trade in securities subject to Federal Reserve Board credit regulations and limitations.

PURPOSE STATEMENT
A form that must be completed by a borrower and filed with the lender if margin securities collateralize the loan. In the

statement, the borrower lists the purpose of the loan and attests that the loan is not made to purchase, carry, or trade securities subject to Federal Reserve Board restrictions.

PUSSY
A colloquial and picturesque name for the shares of Pillsbury Company, derived from its NYSE ticker symbol: PSY.

PUT A LINE THROUGH IT
English expression for a transaction that is canceled by the mutual consent of both buyer and seller. Term is derived from those somewhat easier and more informal days when trades were jotted on a pad; putting a line through it, in effect, canceled the trade.

PUT BONDS
Also: putable bonds. A feature of some debt securities that enables the holder to redeem the bonds at face value according to a schedule set forth at the time of issuance. This optional feature will prevent loss—at the time the put option is operative—if there is a general rise in interest rates.

PUT INTO PLAY
Used of a company that currently is not, but which may become, the target of an acquisition. Companies are "put into play" by means of rumors, or by block purchases of slightly less than 5% of the outstanding shares. Thus, there is no SEC Rule 13-D filing as yet. The buyer or rumormonger hopes to get others, particularly arbitrageurs, to also buy large quantities of the company. Example: "There was a lot of activity in Harmon Cross stock. No one is taking credit for the move, but it looks as though someone is trying to put the company into play."

PVT
Abbreviation: private. The abbreviation is generally followed by the word *placement* (i.e., a distribution of securities to a relatively small number of nonaccredited investors, and thus an offering that does not have an effective SEC registration statement).

Q

QUALIFIED STOCK OPTION

Term describing a stock option granted before May 21, 1981. Under it, recipient could exercise the option at the less than market price of the security. If the security was then held three or more years, the entire profit was a long-term capital gain. If sold before three years, the difference between the exercise price and the fair market value at the time of exercise was an ordinary income gain and a tax preference item. Only the amount above the fair market value and the ultimate sale price was eligible for capital gains.

QUALIFYING COUPON RATE

Used in conjunction with Ginnie Mae contracts, whether cash or forwards, if GNMAs with coupon rates below the current production rate are deliverable against the contract. There is, of course, an adjustment in the aggregate exercise price that takes into account the lowered coupon rate on the certificates delivered. Thus, current production GNMAs may be delivered at par, but GNMAs with coupons 4% below current production could only be delivered at 80% of par.

QUIET PERIOD

Term used to describe the 90-day period between an issuer's initial public offering and the earliest time its underwriters may publish and distribute original research material about the company and its business.

The purpose of this SEC rule is to enable these securities to settle into investment portfolios (as opposed to trading accounts) based on the merits set forth in the prospectus. By legislating a quiet period, the SEC wants to make sure that investors are not swayed by dealers who may have a vested interest in the success of the offering and its secondary market.

R

RACKETEER INFLUENCED AND CORRUPT ORGANIZATION ACT

See RICO.

RADAR ALERT

Industry jargon for the close monitoring of the market activity in a client's stock to determine whether an accumulation is taking place in advance of a hostile tender offer or takeover attempt. If this is perceived to be happening, corporate officials are immediately notified so they may take appropriate defensive actions.

RADIO
Industry lingo for the shares of RCA Corporation. The name is derived from its earlier corporate title: Radio Corporation of America.

RAES
Acronym: Retail Automatic Execution System. This is a computerized facility that expedites the execution of small orders in the Standard & Poor's Index Options traded on the CBOE. With RAES, customer orders for five or fewer contracts are immediately executed at a single price determined by prevailing bid/asked quotations.

RAIDER
1. Anyone who tries to buy control of a company's stock so he can install new management. Federal law places restrictions on raiders if they become control persons, that is, holders of 10% or more of a company's outstanding stock. The term *raider* is not generally used if the purchaser is buying stock as an investment.
2. Bear raider: a person who tries to sell a company's stock, either long or short, with the intent of repurchasing it at a lower price.

RANDOM WALK
An investment theory based on the supposition that stock price movements are unpredictable and without prior indication. Consequently, the advocates of this theory believe that stock selection may prove as profitable by the random throwing of darts at the financial tables in the newspaper as with any other investment philosophy or method.

RANGE FORWARD CONTRACTS
A service mark of Salomon Brothers Inc used to identify certain foreign exchange agreements that combine features of futures and option contracts. Range forward contracts are structured to limit down-side currency risk while protecting up-side profit potentials. The customer chooses either end of a currency range and the expiration date of the contract. Salomon Brothers

chooses the opposite end, based on market conditions and currency rate spreads. If the rate moves against the customer, the risk is limited to the lower end of the range. If the range at expiration is inside or above the range, the contract is exercised and the obligation offset at the spot exchange rate.

RATE COVENANT

A promise included within the bond resolution that accompanies a revenue bond. In summary, a rate covenant requires that the issuer raise, or in some cases lower, utility rates so the rate is sufficient to fund bond debt service.

Reference to the flow of funds statement is critical to determine whether, in terms of a particular bond, this covenant also includes insurance, maintenance, and repairs in addition to bond debt service.

RATE REOPENER

Term used in conjunction with long-term financing so arranged that the interest rate is renegotiated and adjusted every three to five years over the life of the loan. At the time of each reset period, the issuer generally has the option of terminating the loan at a small premium.

RATING

Judgment of creditworthiness of an issuer made by an accepted rating service, such as Moody's, Standard & Poor's, or Fitch.

The judgment, based on rater's investigation of the risk of default by the issuer, is stated in letters. Ratings of AAA, AA, A, and BBB (S&P) are considered investment grade. Ratings of BB or below have increasing risk of default. Similar ratings are given to preferred stocks.

Letter ratings for common stock pertain to firm's history of dividends and dividend coverage, but make no promise about future coverage.

RATIO BULL SPREAD

Term used to describe a call option spread position that is composed of one long call option and two short call options in the same underlying stock with the same expiration month.

It is called "ratio" because there are two short options and one long option. Technically, the strategy is neutral; but it is called "bull" because the long call has a lower strike price than the short calls.

R&D

Acronym: research and development. R&D is an expense item found in the budgets of many corporations. It designates funds set aside from operating revenues to finance the discovery and introduction of new products, thereby ensuring the corporation's future economic well-being.

REACH THROUGH

Slang for a broker's endeavor to enter a quotation in the Intermarket Trading System (ITS) that is worse than the best quotation already in the system for that issue. The endeavor to reach through is a form of carelessness on the part of the entering broker. The system will reject the new quotation.

READY TRANSFERABILITY

A feature of all publicly traded securities that gives shareholders the right to sell, give, or bequeath the security without prior consultation or consent of the corporation.

REAL ESTATE APPRECIATION NOTE

An obligation of a corporation that has pledged real estate as collateral for this loan. The loan is unique: it promises a fixed rate of interest plus a percentage of accrued appreciation of the underlying property. The percentage of appreciation often is payable annually from the fifth year until the maturity of the loan.

REBATE

1. A return of monies previously collected. Generally, such rebates are made to encourage sales. Example: In late 1985, the automobile industry engaged in extensive rebates.
2. A return of sales commission charges to the buyer or seller. Such rebates are legitimate if done by a principal; if done by an agent, they violate industry standards.
3. The term *rebate* also is used of directed payments to a third party. Example: A directed payment of part of an underwriting spread to another member of the syndicate could legitimately be called "a rebate" (although such usage is not common).

RECEIVER IN BANKRUPTCY

An impartial, court-appointed administrator of a corporation that has sought protection from creditor claims under federal bankruptcy laws. The receiver helps the court to decide whether reorganization or liquidation is the better alternative. The receiver is remunerated out of the residual assets of the corporation after wages and taxes have been paid.

RECEIVE VERSUS PAYMENT
Instruction often added to sell orders entered by institutional clients.

Concept: The buyer will pay in cash when the seller, or his agent, delivers the securities. The contract is, in effect, made COD (cash on delivery) or RAP (receive against payment). Such contracts are made to obtain immediately usable funds or because the seller is obligated, by law, to have either the security or its cash value.

It is important that both buyer and seller agree that there will be a transfer of securities for cash on the settlement date.

RECESSION
Economic term used to describe a period of reduced economic activity. Generally, a recession is marked by two successive quarterly drops in the GNP. Recessions usually are short-lived, are marked by increased unemployment, increased business inventories, and increased short-term interest rates. Although the term is usually widespread within the economy, recessions also may mark decreased production in sectors of the economy. Example: The agricultural sector has gone through a four-year recession.

RECORD DATE
Calendar date on which an issuer temporarily closes its register of holders to identify those holders who are eligible for a distribution of dividends, either cash or stock, interest or rights. The date is determined by the board of directors, and the register is closed at the end of business on that specified date.

REDUCIBLE RATE BOND
A debt instrument for which the issuer has an option of lowering the interest rate as well as its call premium. Usually, bonds have a reducible rate only if the bond is subsequently collateralized by U.S. government securities through an advanced refunding and thus becomes triple-A rated. This characteristic is not common and when found marks certain municipal obligations.

REFINANCING
Term used if an issuer sells new bonds and uses the proceeds to retire an existing issue. In this way, the issuer by borrowing at a

lower rate can substantially reduce interest charges. Many outstanding bonds limit the circumstances under which they may be refinanced.

The term *refinancing* and *refunding* are synonymous and may be used interchangeably.

REFUNDING
See REFINANCING. The two words are used as synonyms.

REGISTERED HOME OWNERSHIP SAVINGS PLAN
Acronym: RHOSP. A special type of savings account permitted in Canada. A person may deposit up to $1,000 annually of tax deductible income (total $10,000) provided the money is eventually used to purchase residential property for personal use. Only one such plan is permitted during a person's lifetime.

REGISTERED REPRESENTATIVE RAPID RESPONSE PROGRAM
Acronym: RRRR. Also known as: 4R. This is a NYSE communications system that enables salespersons in member firm offices to immediately quote execution prices to buying or selling customers without the need to wait for a trade confirmation from the exchange floor.

REGISTERED RETIREMENT SAVINGS PLANS
Acronym: RRSP. The Canadian equivalent of the Keogh plan. Under RRSP, an individual may deduct annually the lesser of $5,500 or 20% of taxable income and deposit it in a savings contract established by a bank, trust company, insurance company, or mutual fund. The maximum is $3,500 if the person also is covered by an employer-sponsored retirement plan. The plan money accumulates tax free, and at maturity (when the subscriber is 60–71 years old) the money can be used to purchase an annuity or shares in a retirement income fund.

REGISTERED SECURITY
1. Any certificate that has the name of the owner inscribed on the certificate. Example: a registered bond or a registered stock.
2. Any stock or bond or other security whose public sale was registered with the SEC at the time of sale, or that—excluding such initial registration—was subsequently sold publicly in conformity with SEC rules. Example: A security originally sold privately is subsequently included in a registered secondary or a public sale under SEC rules 144 or 145.

REGISTRAR

In the securities industry, a person who:

1. Maintains the names and addresses of the security holders of an issuer.
2. Verifies that ownership transfers have been correctly effected; thus, no more new shares have been issued than have been properly canceled.

Usually, a registrar is a commercial bank other than the transfer agent.

REGULAR SPECIALIST

A stock exchange member, so registered by the exchange, who is obliged to maintain a fair and orderly market in the specific stocks assigned to him or her. In this capacity, the specialist accepts orders from other members in these specific stocks and, as needed, buys and sells for his or her own account and risk. This latter function is highly regulated and is never in conflict or competition with public orders.

REG(ULATION) T CALL

This is a notice, mandated by the Federal Reserve Board, requesting a customer to deposit a specific amount of money following initiation of a securities transaction. The dollar amount will be the Reg T initial margin requirement minus funds available through the Special Memorandum Account.

A Reg T call must be satisfied by the seventh business day following the trade date, although industry rules require settlement by the fifth business day.

REG(ULATION) T EXCESS

A widely used term for the amount of credit a broker/dealer may extend to a margin account customer over and above the amount of credit already being utilized. The procedure for determining excess credit and the method of annotating it is set forth in Regulation T of the Federal Reserve Board.

REGULATION X

A rule of the Federal Reserve Board that governs the amount and type of credit that can be obtained and accepted by someone who purchases, carries, or trades in corporate securities. This rule regulates persons who need credit, as opposed to Regulations T, U, and G, which apply to persons who give credit.

REINTERMEDIATION

The flow of funds by the public from money market and debt securities into savings and time deposits within the banking system.

Reintermediation takes place after disintermediation has occurred. It is a return flow into the banking system as bank savings interest rates become higher than the interest on comparable debt securities.

REOPEN AN ISSUE

Used of government securities if the Treasury sells more of an issue that is already outstanding, with the same terms and conditions, at prevailing price levels. Example: Rather than auction a new issue of notes with a new coupon rate, the Treasury reopens an older issue and sells notes with the same coupon priced to compete with current prices.

REPRESENTATIONS AND WARRANTIES

"Boilerplate" used in contracts to generalize the legal opinions and guarantees of performance that are given by attorneys or the signatories to the contract. Should these representations be false, or the signatories default in their performance, they must bear responsibility for the losses sustained by the contra party to the contract.

REPRESENTATIVE BID AND ASKED PRICES

Acronym: RBA. This was the old system used on NASDAQ Level I quotes. RBAs were median bid and median offer prices.

Today, Level I quotes represent the highest bid and lowest offer prices from the inside, or interdealer, market.

REQUISITIONIST

English term for an individual or group that is intent on unseating the management of a public corporation. We would use the term *insurgent.*

RESIDUAL VALUE

1. A description of common stock. It is the residual value of a corporation after all debts are paid and preferred stockholders are satisfied.
2. In real estate finance: the difference between out-of-pocket cost for real estate and what is received for it upon disposal in 10,

20, or later years. The residual value also includes the net rentals during this period.

See INTERNAL RATE OF RETURN for a measurement of "yield" on real estate.

RESPONDEAT SUPERIOR

Latin: let the superior reply.

Concept: a complaint is brought against a broker/dealer because of an action done by one of its employees. The principle of this term means that the superior is responsible for the proper and adequate supervision of his or her employees.

RESTRICTIVE COVENANT

A term often applied to the indenture, or bond resolution, of a municipal security.

The term is descriptive—that is, it looks at the indenture in terms of actions that the municipality may not take.

RESTRICTIVE ENDORSEMENT

If the assignment on the reverse side of a registered certificate—or the stock/bond power that accompanies a certificate—designates a specific person, the endorsement is said to be restrictive. This is true whether the person named is an individual or a corporation.

As a general rule, clients who mail assigned securities are recommended to make a restrictive endorsement—that is, to appoint the brokerage firm as their attorney for the transfer of the certificate.

RETAIL AUTOMATIC EXECUTION SYSTEM

See RAES.

RETAIL REPO

A collateralized loan between a bank and a depositor—as opposed to the traditional repo between a broker/dealer and an institutional investor. In a retail repo, the bank is the borrower and the depositor is the lender. As with the traditional repo, it is a two-part transaction: the sale and the repurchase of the underlying collateral. The borrower pays interest for the use of the money upon termination of the loan.

RETENTION

That portion of an underwriter's takedown it may sell to its customers. Normally, the syndicate manager will hold back some of the takedown to facilitate both institutional sales and sales by members of the selling group. The remainder forms the retention for the individual member of the syndicate. Example: An individual syndicate member may have a takedown of 10,000 shares. The manager holds 2,000 shares for institutional sales and selling group members. The syndicate member's retention is 8,000 shares.

See TAKEDOWN.

RETRACTABLE LOAN

A debt security with a provision that enables the issuer to change the specified rate of interest periodically or at predetermined intervals. Such retractable loans are made attractive to investors by granting them the right to redeem the security at par value if the newly changed rate of interest is not to their liking. In this way, the retractable bond becomes competitive to both the borrower and the lender.

RETURN OF CAPITAL

A distribution of cash by a corporation or a trust that does not arise from net income or retained earnings. Example: A utility distributes cash that represents depreciation on certain assets, or a unit investment trust distributes cash that represents the proceeds of the sale of portfolio securities.

A return of capital is not a taxable distribution; instead, recipient must lower the cost of acquisition of the security because part of original purchase price was returned. Later capital gains or losses will be computed from this adjusted purchase price.

REVALUATION

An official change in the value of one nation's currency in terms of another's. For example, it would be a revaluation if the United States, independently of market factors, were to state that the Irish punt were now worth $1.25, rather than $1.10 as previously determined.

As a general rule, revaluation infers an upward valuation of the foreign currency. Devaluation, a downward valuation.

REVENUE INDEXED MORTGAGE BOND

A real estate backed security in which interest payments can be augmented by a specified percentage of the issuer's earnings.

REVERSE CONVERSION

1. An exchange of a customer's call option for a put option. The exchange is effected by an accommodating put and call broker.
2. An arbitrage technique used by a broker/dealer to lock in an interest-rate profit in money market securities.

Both strategies employ a similar technique by the broker/dealer: the short sale of the underlying security while, at the same time, buying a call and selling a put with an identical exercise price at or near the short sale price.

REVERSE DOLLAR ROLL

Term used of certain short-term trading practices in GNMA securities. In a reverse dollar roll, the holder of high coupon GNMA bonds sells them during a period of lower rates with the expressed agreement to reacquire them in about a month or so (a repurchase agreement). The buyer enjoys a higher than prevailing rate for the short period that he or she holds them.

REVERSE REPO

Term used to describe a reverse repurchase agreement.

In a reverse repo, the customer sells securities and agrees to repurchase at a slightly higher price. The price difference represents interest for the use of the money received.

Reverse repos generally are initiated by the Federal Reserve Board's Open Market Committee acting as the buyer—and are used to fine-tune the money supply.

REVERSE REPURCHASE AGREEMENT

A customer delivers securities to a broker/dealer, receives cash, and promises to repurchase the securities at a later date at a fixed price. The difference between the cash received by the customer and the repurchase price represents, in effect, interest for the use of the money received. Usually, only government, agency, or municipal securities are subject to repurchase and reverse repos. The Federal Reserve Banking System is a frequent user of reverse repurchase agreements to fine-tune the money supply.

REVOLVING UNDERWRITING FACILITIES

Acronym: RUF. Term is associated with medium- to long-term debt origination agreements between issuers of Eurodollar securities and investment banking consortia. Under these agreements, the underwriters offer three- to six-month obligations of the issuer at favorable short-term rates but are required to reoffer the notes again and again as preceding notes mature. The issuer pays the consortia a fee. The underwriters' risk is rate-related, and it varies with the difference between short and medium rates to long-term rates at the time of the initial agreement.

RICH

Commonly used expression to describe either a price or a yield that, in the mind of the the commentator, is too high. Example: "IBM at 155 is too rich for my blood."

The term connotes the implied belief that the securities are overpriced, or the yield is too high, and that the price or yield will drop to more acceptable levels.

RICO

Acronym: Racketeer Influenced and Corrupt Organization Act. This is a federal law that makes it a crime for any person to participate in any enterprise engaged in certain defined racketeering activities, including securities fraud.

RIGHT OF WAY

A land use privilege accorded by property owners to public utilities or transportation companies whereby these companies are enabled to serve the interests of the general public through the use of the land. Example: Property owners in Greene County granted a right of way to County Light & Power to erect transmission poles in the county.

RISK ARBITRAGE

General term for a long and short position taken in anticipation of, or upon the announcement of, a proposed merger. Normally, the speculator will buy shares of the company to be acquired and sell short the shares of the acquiring company on the speculation that the shares of the company to be acquired will go up, and the shares of the acquiring company will go down. The risk is that the merger will be canceled. In this case, there can be substantial loss as the shares go back to original price levels.

ROID

A slang abbreviation for the Polaroid Corporation, a large manufacturer of camera equipment and a developer of instant photography.

ROLLOVER

In general, the reinvestment of funds. Specifically, the term is used if:

1. Funds from a maturing bond or other debt instrument are reinvested in a similar security.
2. Funds in one qualified pension fund are reinvested in another. Example: an IRA rollover.
3. A security is sold at a profit and the funds are used to establish a new position in the same security at a new cost basis.

In practice, the term is not used if a capital loss or a negative cash flow is involved in the successive transactions.

ROLY POLY CERTIFICATES OF DEPOSIT

A series of consecutive six-month CDs issued as a package covering two or more years. Under the package, buyers (depositors) are obligated to purchase the same dollar amount of CDs as the previous CDs mature. These CDs may have a fixed rate, or a floating rate, depending on the status of interest rates.

RRM

Antonym: renegotiable rate mortgage. This is a 20–30 year real estate loan. The rates, however, are fixed for only 3–5 years. At the end of each of these periods, the loan can be rolled over (renewed) at a new rate that is indexed to an average national mortgage rate determination. Although the rate cannot vary by more than 1–2% per year, over the life of the mortgage this may amount to an up/down fluctuation of 5% or more.

RRRR

See REGISTERED REPRESENTATIVE RAPID RESPONSE PROGRAM.

RUBBER

Popular identifier used for Uniroyal, a large rubber producer and fabricator. The nickname derives from the former corporate name for the company: United States Rubber Corporation.

RUF

See REVOLVING UNDERWRITING FACILITIES.

RULE OF SEVENTY–TWO

Rule of thumb to determine the answer to this question: Given a fixed rate of compound interest, how long will it take for my money to double?

Formula: divide 72 by the fixed rate of compound interest. The quotient will be the number of years for the original investment to double. Example: At 9% compound interest—according to this rule-of-thumb formula—money will double in 8 years, and 72 divided by 9 is 8.

RULE OF TWENTY

A theory of stock market movements that holds that the annual rate of inflation in the United States plus the average price-earnings ratio of the Dow Jones industrial stocks should be equal to 20. In effect, as inflation goes up, the price-earnings ratio will go down.

RUN ON A BANK

Term used to describe a situation in which a substantial number of depositors, fearing a collapse of the bank, seek to withdraw their deposits at the same time.

S

SAFE HARBOR RULE

See SEC RULE 10b-18.

SAM

Acronym: shared appreciation mortgage. It is a fixed-rate real estate loan in which the lender has an equity interest in the value appreciation that occurs during the life of the loan. Example: In return for a fixed-rate mortgage that is significantly lower than prevailing rates, a borrower stipulates that one third of any profit realized from a sale or property appreciation during the term of the mortgage will belong to the lender.

SAMMIE BEES

Sammie Bees are pooled Small Business Administration guaranteed loans that have been securitized as unit trust certificates. Commercial banks that make such loans organized them in pools of $1 million to $25 million. The pools, backed by the SBA, then are sold to institutional investors that seek higher-than-usual yields for prime-quality debts.

SAMURAI BOND

Slang for a debt security of a non-Japanese issuer denominated in Japanese yen. Such securities are not registered with the SEC for sale in the United States and, therefore, may not be offered to U.S. persons on an initial distribution.

SAVINGS DEPOSIT

An interest-bearing account with a banking institution from which money can normally be withdrawn without prior notice. Technically, banks can require 30 to 60 days' notice for withdrawals, but few banks have chosen to require such notice. Because the deposits are uncertain in duration, banks pay a lower rate of interest for savings deposits than they do for time deposits.

SB

Used in corporate and municipal bond calendars, these initials identify Salomon Brothers Inc, a major underwriter of securities.

SCALE

1. Interest rates payable for the chronological maturities of an issuer's serial debt securities.
2. A schedule of interest rate payable for time deposits of varying maturity dates. Example: The scale varies from 9.10% to 10.50% for maturities from six months to three years. The same concept applies to commercial paper if the issuer varies the interest rates according to time to maturity.
3. Used, at the time of the initial offering of bonds with serial maturity, to designate the number of bonds, the maturity date, the coupon rate of interest, and the offering price of one of the serial maturities. Example: In an offering of $10 million of bonds maturing between 1987 and 1997, the scale for 1992 might appear:

$1,000,000 Jan. 15, 1992 10½ PAR

The term also is used collectively of all of the bonds, their maturities, coupons, and prices for the entire issue.

SCALPING

An unethical practice, which may also be illegal, whereby an investment adviser or research analyst recommends a security for purchase after buying the security for his own account. The subsequent purchases by persons who followed the recommendation pushes up the price of the security and permits the recommender to profit on the original purchase.

SCHEDULE 13D

A Securities and Exchange Commission form that must be filed within 10 business days by anyone who acquires 5% or more of an equity security registered with the SEC under the Securities Exchange Act of 1934. Purpose: to disclose the method of acquisition of the shares and the purchaser's intentions in terms of management or control of the company.

See SCHEDULE 13G.

SCHEDULE 13G

A short-form version of Schedule 13D. The short form is to be filed by a person who, at the end of a calendar year, owns 5% or more of an equity security of a company registered under Section 12 of the Securities Exchange Act of 1934. The short-form filing is permitted if the person acquired the securities in the ordinary course of business and if the owner does not intend to change or influence control of the company. Broker/dealers, banks, and investment companies are typical filers of Schedule 13G. It is due within 45 calendar days of year's end.

SCHULDSCHEIN

A securitized participation in a commercial loan offered by a German bank acting as private placement manager of an underwriting group. The initial certificate is issued in global form for the first 90 days and, even when available in definitive version thereafter, cannot be assigned to another owner more than three times before maturity.

SCORCHED EARTH TACTIC

A corporate defense tactic whereby an unwilling takeover target discourages bidders by selling off attractive assets or by entering into long-term contractual commitments. Thereby, the company makes itself less attractive to the buyer.

SCORE

Acronym: special claim on residual equity. One of the two component parts of an Americus Trust. Holders of the SCORE component of the trust receive no dividends; instead, they receive any assets above a certain agreed-upon dollar value. Example: Holders of SCORE for the Americus Trust on American Telephone & Telegraph shares will receive all assets above $75 per share when the trust is to be dissolved, September 1988.

See PRIME.

SCOREX SYSTEM

Acronym: Securities Communication, Order Routing, and Execution facility. This facility of the Pacific Stock Exchange enables members to automatically transmit and execute market orders up to 599 shares (300 on limit orders) at the best available price represented by all Intermarket Trading System (ITS) participants.

SCOTTISH DIVIDEND

Slang for a reverse split—that is, a split down so the shareholder owns fewer shares after the split than before.

Also known as: an Irish dividend or a Polish dividend.

S/D

1. When used on a customer confirmation, S/D stands for settlement date.
2. When used in a description of municipal bonds, S/D stands for school district.

SEAQ

Acronym: Stock Exchange Automated Quotations. This is the London Stock Exchange's version of NASDAQ. SEAQ permits marketmakers to give their quotes for 3,500 domestic (English) and international stocks. SEAQ entries are divided into alpha, beta, and gamma. *Alpha* stocks have firm quotes and require immediate reporting of trades. *Beta* stocks are firm, but do not require immediate reporting of trades. *Gamma* stocks are infrequently traded and quotations are subject, rather than firm.

SEASONED

Descriptive term often used of a new issue that was widely distributed to a large number of purchasers and that now trades frequently and with good liquidity in the secondary market. Example: "It is now a seasoned security."

SECONDARY FINANCING

Term used to identify borrowings that use loans subordinated to previous loans on the same collateral. Example: Second and subsequent mortgage bonds issued by corporations are forms of secondary financing.

SECONDHAND OPTION
See SPECIAL OPTION.

SEC RULES
The following rules of the Securities and Exchange Commission often are used in the jargon of the industry. The rules, with their numbers, are identified by the following entries. This identification is not meant to be an explanation of the rule. Many of these rules are so complex, and have further SEC and legal interpretations, that advice of counsel is needed.

The order of the SEC rules is by number, as opposed to the letter-by-letter order in the rest of this glossary.

SEC RULE 10b-6
It prohibits issuers, underwriters, broker/dealers, or anyone with an interest in a distribution of securities from purchasing, or inducing anyone else to purchase, the issue prior to the start of the public offering.

Underwriters, however, may accept indications of interest in such issues from prospective buyers, but no sales may be made.

SEC RULE 10b-10
It regulates the preparation and distribution of purchase or of sale confirmations by a broker/dealer to customers. The rule sets forth the minimum information required, the necessary disclosures required, and the frequency of such confirmations to customers.

SEC RULE 10b-18
Also known as the "safe harbor" rule, this rule permits issuers and their affiliated accounts to repurchase their own common stock without charges of market manipulation. The rule sets forth the conditions under which such purchases may be made.

SEC RULE 13D
This rule, which has subnumbers 1 through 7, requires the filing of certain disclosures by anyone who acquires a beneficial ownership of 5% or more in any equity security registered with the SEC.

SEC RULE 13E
This rule, which has subnumbers 1 through 4, regulates the purchases by an issuer, or an affiliate of the issuer, of its own securities in the public marketplace.

SEC RULE 15c3-1

The "net capital" rule governing the liquid capital that a broker/dealer must maintain in terms of his aggregate indebtedness to customers. The rule dictates the minimum net capital and the ratio of debt-to-equity capital of a broker/dealer; but from the viewpoint of a member firm customer, the most important aspect is the coverage that a broker/dealer's net capital provides for customer indebtedness.

Although other measurement criteria may be used, the rule of thumb is that customer-related indebtedness may not exceed net capital by more than 15 to 1.

SEC RULE 15c3-3

This rule regulates the handling of fully paid securities and money on deposit with a broker/dealer. In substance, the rule requires the proper segregation of customer securities that are fully paid and requires that, at least weekly, money on deposit be deposited in a special account for the benefit of all customers of that broker/dealer.

SEC RULE 16a-1

This rule mandates that officers, directors, and principal stockholders (10% or more) must file reports of beneficial ownership of any equity security they hold in their company, if that issue is registered. The rule also requires that additional reports must be filed each time their previous position is increased or decreased.

SEC RULES 17a-3 and 17a-4

Rules that establish the recordkeeping and maintenance requirements of broker/dealers. The rules set forth the documents that must be prepared, maintained, and preserved for regulatory enquiries.

SEC RULE 17a-8

This rule parallels the Currency Foreign Transaction Reporting Act of 1970. Under this rule, broker/dealers must report to the U.S. Treasury or the IRS: (1) receipt or transfer of U.S. currency in excess of $10,000; (2) the import or export of any country's currency in excess of $5,000; (3) a bank securities or other financial-type account in any foreign country in which a citizen or resident has an interest.

SEC RULE 17a-12

Rule that sets forth the filing requirements for broker/dealers who make markets in over-the-counter margin securities and who obtain preferential credit terms to finance these positions.

SEC RULE 17a-17

Rule that sets forth criteria by which broker/dealers can register with the SEC as block positioners and obtain preferential credit terms to finance their positions.

SEC RULE 17f-2

Rule that necessitates the taking of fingerprints of virtually every employee, partner, or officer of a broker/dealer as a condition of affiliation with that concern. The fingerprints are then submitted to the Attorney General of the United States for identification and background validation.

SEC RULE 19b-3

Rule that forbids the fixing of commissions and floor brokerage rates by any national securities exchange.

SEC RULE 134

Rule that defines the type of language that may be used by a dealer in conjunction with the sale of a registered offering. The rule provides a guideline for materials prepared about issuers, and it outlines information that is not deemed to be a prospectus subject to the stringent restrictions that apply prior to the effective date.

SEC RULE 147

Rule that defines the terms and conditions under which a resident issuer may make an intrastate public offering of a security without the need to register the sale with the SEC.

SEC RULE 415

Rule pertaining to the public offering of securities by means of a shelf registration. Under this rule, qualified issuers may register an offering to be sold at prevailing market prices over the next two years.

SECURED LOAN

Any borrowing arrangement that is collateralized by marketable securities. Example: Margin loans advanced by broker/dealers to their customers are secured loans, because the securities purchased are held by the broker/dealer as collateral. In the event the borrower defaults, the holder of the securities can sell them to recover the money loaned.

SECURITY PURCHASE CONTRACT
Acronym: SPC. A unique security that is issued as a debt instrument and that changes into an equity security of the same issuer after a predetermined period. The changeover is mandatory at that time, although the holder may exchange for equity securities at an earlier date. In the early 1980s, some large banks used this financing technique to raise equity capital although it is technically a liability for the first 10 years.

SELF–LIQUIDATING ASSET PURCHASE
Acronym: SLAP. Term used in corporate finance to identify the purchase of a company with a large cash flow by means of newly issued debt. The idea is to retire the debt as quickly as possible with the cash flow. Thus, in a few years, the purchasers will own the asset free and clear; this, in turn, will enhance the value of the common stock of the company.

SELF TENDER
An offer by the issuing company to repurchase a specific number or percentage of its outstanding shares. Using cash or other assets in exchange for these shares, companies sometimes use this tactic to equal or to top the bid made by a corporate raider that is endeavoring to take over the company.

SELL
To transfer ownership for a monetary consideration. The term is used in conjunction with the disposition of specific quantities of stocks, bonds, or other financial assets.

SELLER'S MARKET
A market condition in which prospective demand so exceeds supply that potential sellers can dictate prices and sale terms on most transactions.
Antonym: buyer's market.

SELLING THE CROWN JEWELS
Slang term used in corporate finance to describe a defense used by a takeover target opposed to a forced merger. Under it, the

target company sells certain valuable assets to make it a less attractive takeover candidate.

See SCORCHED EARTH TACTIC.

SELL SIGNAL

A term used by chartists. It means that the technical measurements of previous price movements indicate that this is the appropriate time to sell.

Generally, a sell signal occurs when the price of a security fails to break through a resistance level, or if the price breaks down through a previously established upward trend. Market volume is an important consideration.

SEQUENTIAL TRANSACTIONS

A flurry of trading activity in the same issue on a stock exchange. The transactions may be at the same or of varying prices. In the event of sequential transactions, the report on the ticker tape gives them in consecutive order by volume and price but without a repetition of the stock symbol. Example: Sequential transactions in Ford Motor Company common stock could appear on the ticker tape as:

F
    5s 57.2s 57⅛.10s 57.45s 57

SERIAL CATS

Evidences of ownership of the semiannual interest payment on a collection of U.S. Treasury notes or bonds. Because only one payment of cash will be received by the owner, serial cats are effectively zero-coupon bonds.

See CATS.

Evidences of ownership of the underlying bond, as opposed to the interest payments, are called "principal CATS."

SERVICING A MORTGAGE

The work responsibilities involved in loan analysis, bookkeeping, delinquency follow-up, and the preparation of financial statements for a pool of mortgages. When banks pool such mortgages and agree to service the mortgage, they charge a fee. This fee is subtracted from the mortgage payments made by the borrowers. The remainder of the payment is passed through to the lenders. This concept of a fee for servicing the mortgages lies beneath many mortgage-backed securities.

SFN
See SWISS FRANC NOTE.

SHARK REPELLANT
Slang used in corporation finance to designate a change in a corporation's charter designed to make that company less attractive to persons seeking to acquire control.

SHELF DISTRIBUTION
A time-to-time public offering of an SEC-registered security at prevailing market prices by the issuer or an affiliated person over a two-year period. The offering may be made by the holder/issuer, or through an identified underwriter, in amounts aggregating the quantity set forth in the registration statement.

Also see the next entry.

SHELF REGISTRATION STATEMENT
This abbreviated registration statement, also known as Form S-3, permits corporations and affiliated persons to make offerings of identified securities at prevailing market prices over a two-year period. Example: A corporation files a shelf registration for $100 million of bonds. The corporation uses dips in interest rates to offer portions of the issue at various times over a two-year period.

SHERMAN ANTI-TRUST ACT
This act, which has been amended in some ways since its original passage in 1890, addresses the problem of cartels and monopolies and their impact on the country's economy. The law attempts to restrict business combinations that lessen competition or which manipulate prices of goods.

SHINGLE THEORY
SEC jargon used to describe the ethical responsibility applicable to brokers in connection with their registration. Under this concept, a broker implicitly promises to treat customers fairly when hanging out a "shingle"—that is, advertising that he or she is available to do business with the public.

SHOGUN SECURITIES
Colloquial term for dollar-denominated securities issued by U.S. corporations for exclusive distribution in Japan. Southern California Edison became the first U.S. issuer to overcome both

the technical and legal barriers for the offering of such securities in Japan. This issue was distributed in 1985.

SHORT SWING

Term used in conjunction with profitable transactions made by directors, officers, and principal stockholders of publicly owned corporations within a period of six months. Such transactions may involve a purchase followed by a sale, or a sale followed by a repurchase, of securities of their corporation. The prohibition is made because of the presumption that they may be using inside information. Under federal securities law, such profits may be recoverable by the corporation.

SHORT-TERM INDEXED LIABILITY TRANSACTIONS

Acronym: STILTS. STILTS are a form of commercial paper that gives the issuer the ability to convert this debt into more commercial paper at a guaranteed interest spread for a series of short-term rollover periods.

SHORT-TERM TAX-EXEMPT PUT SECURITIES

A municipal security with a put option designed by Merrill Lynch. This feature enables the holder to sell the security back to Merrill Lynch during the limited lifetime of the security. The feature substantially limits the market risk to the holder if interest rates rise.
Acronym: STTEPS.

SHOWSTOPPER

Corporate finance term used to describe litigation designed to thwart the takeover attempt of an unwelcome suitor.

SIDE-BY-SIDE TRADING

See INTEGRATED MARKETMAKING.

SIGHT DRAFT

Term describing an immediately negotiable instrument used to transfer money from a buyer to a seller. When this checklike document is signed by the buyer, it also identifies the paying agent, and the seller can deposit it for personal credit and use the money.

SILENT SALES

Slang used to describe the secret sale of residential housing without notification of the municipality of the transfer of ownership, or notification of the original mortgagor. Such sales are illegal. They usually are motivated by the seller's desire to sell, or the buyer's inability to get either a new mortgage or unwillingness to pay new mortgage rates.

SILVER
Popular identifier of the shares of Insilco Corporation, formerly known as International Silver Company, a well-known manufacturer of silverware and related products.

SIMPLE MAJORITY
The agreement by holders of more than 50% of the outstanding shares of a company in a vote conducted by the company. Under most circumstances, that minimum percentage is all that is required to elect directors, to ratify independent auditors, and to carry other amendments to the charter of the corporation.

SINKING FUND
A fund of money that a corporation must set aside annually to provide for the early retirement of portions of a bond issue or, occasionally, an issue of preferred stock. Generally, these funds are used to retire bonds in the year that the funds are set aside, although the bond indenture may provide for alternate bond redemption provisions. Sinking funds, if promised in the bond indenture, are obligatory on the issuing corporation.

Many municipal revenue issues also have sinking-fund provisions; these are not obligatory, however, unless the revenues are sufficient to maintain the facility and provide for debt service.

The abbreviation SF often is used by Moody's or Standard & Poor's bond guides in the brief description of a bond issue to designate that a sinking-fund provision is applicable.

SIZED OUT
Exchange floor terminology used to explain the inability of a broker to cross stock at a block trader's specified price. Sized out means that another broker is currently bidding or offering a larger quantity at the stated price.

See BLOCKED for the same idea when caused by a competitor's price.

SJ (SUBJECT)
Initials sometimes used to qualify a quotation for a security as subject—that is, subject to further discussion and qualification about price and volume.

SK

Initials occasionally used to designate safekeeping: security measures that a broker/dealer must employ to protect customers' fully paid securities.

See also SAFEKEEPING (WWS).

SL

1. Common abbreviation for: sell.
2. As used on order instructions: an abbreviation for sell long—that is, the customer is selling securities owned by the customer and the customer intends to deliver those securities.
3. Used in corporate and municipal bond calendars, these initials identify Shearson Lehman Corp., a major underwriter of securities.

SLAP

See SELF–LIQUIDATING ASSET PURCHASE.

SLEEPER

Slang for an investment opportunity that has been overlooked by public and professional investors. Example: The return to more conservative accounting procedures has understated the value of LMN Corporation. At this time, and at this price, it must be considered a sleeper.

SLOB

An unfortunate nickname for the shares of Schlumberger Limited, a large manufacturer of oil drilling equipment. The nickname is derived from its NYSE symbol: SLB.

SLUGS

Slang for nonmarketable U.S. Treasury securities sold only to states and local governments. Municipalities use these Treasury issues to defease their own outstanding securities, depositing the slugs into an escrow account until their own bonds mature or become callable.

See DEFEASANCE.

SMALL ORDER EXECUTION SYSTEM

Acronym: SOES. An NASD pilot project used to automate customer OTC orders for 1,000 shares or less of certain eligible issues (five NASDAQ marketmakers or more) to the marketmaker with the best price. This is an immediate transaction and trade terms are automatically routed to the clearing corporation for on-line comparison between the two members.

SMALL SAVER CERTIFICATE
A time deposit savings account in a bank or thrift institution in which the money pledged remains there for at least 30 months. The money so pledged may be as little as $100. The rate of interest paid is pegged to the average yield of U.S. Treasury securities of comparable maturity.

SMB
Used on municipal and corporate bond calendars to identify Smith Barney, Harris Upham & Co., a major underwriter of securities.

SMO
Slang for the GNMA Collateralized Mortgage Obligations issued by Salomon Brothers Mortgage Securities, Inc.

Pronounced: shmow, to rhyme with show.

SNAKE
Nickname for an agreement between leading European nations to allow their currencies to float freely in the open market, intervening only if certain parameters are exceeded. The term derives from the days when their currencies were pegged to the U.S. dollar and a graph of their value fluctuations resembled the configuration of a snake.

Also, any graph whose configuration resembles the movement of a snake.

SNIF
Acronym: short-term note issuance facility. A term formerly used in international financing to describe ongoing placements of 1–5-year Eurodebt instruments.

SNIF has been replaced by RUF: revolving underwriting facilities.

SOCIALISM
1. State ownership of the means of production, especially heavy manufacturing, utilities, and transportation.
2. An economic system in which the state provides, through heavy taxation, medical and old-age care for all citizens regardless of need.
3. In Marxist theory, a transition stage between capitalism and

communism. It is a transition stage and is an imperfect application of collectivist principles.

SOES
See SMALL ORDER EXECUTION SYSTEM.

SOFT DOLLARS
Jargon for a method of payment by means of directed underwriting credits and commissions from portfolio transactions. This payment for research and other brokerage services takes the place of payment in "hard dollars" (i.e., dollars that are a direct payment from the portfolio manager). Example: "The computerized analysis of your portfolio will cost $3,000 hard dollars, or $10,000 soft dollars."

SONNIE–MAE
Also abbreviated SONY–MAE.
Acronym: State of New York Mortgage Agency.

SPACE ARBITRAGE
Slang term for the nearly simultaneous profitable purchase and sale of the same, or substantially identical, securities based on price differentials prevailing in different marketplaces.

The term is more specific than arbitrage, which may, in practice, include space arbitrage or arbitrages on the same exchange or marketplace.

SPC
See SECURITY PURCHASE CONTRACT.

SPECIAL CLAIM ON RESIDUAL EQUITY
See SCORE.

SPECIAL COMMODITY ACCOUNT
This is the title of an account at a broker/dealer in which a customer can effect and finance transactions in commodities and commodities futures contracts.

SPECIAL INSURANCE PREMIUM FUNDING ACCOUNT
This is the title of an account at a broker/dealer in which a customer can finance the premiums needed to purchase a life insurance policy with the equity in shares of a registered investment company purchased in conjunction with the policy.

SPECIALIST'S ACCOUNT

The title of an account at a broker/dealer in which stock exchange specialists and marketmakers in listed options can obtain advantageous credit to finance their dealer inventories. The special credit privileges do not extend to their long-term investment holdings.

SPECIAL OPTION

Term used of a conventional (OTC) put or call option with some remaining lifetime that is offered for resale by a broker/dealer or a customer in a secondary market transaction.

Also known as a secondhand option.

SPEQ

Acronym: Specialist Performance Evaluation Questionnaire. This is an NYSE document used to screen specialists. The questionnaire is given to floor brokers who, it is felt, have most to do with specialists. SPEQ asks floor brokers to truthfully answer questions about specialists. SPEQ is used to appoint, retain, and improve the performance of specialists.

SPIKE

Any significant aberration in the typical performance of a company or its securities, such as a sudden rise in the price of a stock followed by a just as sudden fall or a rise in corporate earnings in one quarter followed by a fall in the next.

Although the term ordinarily is used as a noun (e.g., there was a spike), there are many examples of its use as a verb. Example: The earnings of LMN spiked between 1984 and 1986.

SPLIT OFFERING

Term describing a public sale of a debt issue that is comprised of both serial and term maturity bonds and large-term maturity bonds of the same issuer. Example: an issue that is comprised of $40 million serial maturity bonds maturing between 1990 and 2000 and $100 million in term bonds maturing in 2007.

Split offerings are common in the issuance of municipal revenue bonds and some general obligation issues.

SPLIT RATING

The situation that results if one major bond rating service gives a higher or lower rating than another bond rating service to the same issue. Example: Moody's may rate a bond Aa but Standard & Poor's rates it A.

Split ratings are not uncommon for nonconvertible debt securities. They are usual for convertible securities because Moody's generally rates convertibles one grade below nonconvertible securities.

SPONSOR

For investment company securities, the sponsor is the same as the underwriter.

The terms *distributor* and *wholesaler* also are used synonymously with the term *sponsor.*

SPONSORSHIP

Term used to describe the active support of a specific stock issue by one or more interested professional investors.

These professional investors may be large institutions or broker/dealers with well-known research capabilities. Example: Among its sponsorship, that stock numbers Merrill Lynch and the Vanguard Funds.

SPOT LOAN

A mortgage granted on a case-by-case basis on single-family housing as opposed, for example, to a commitment to finance an entire housing project.

SPREAD BANKER

Common expression for a commercial banker, or in some cases an investment banker, who attempts wherever possible to match the maturities of its own borrowings to those of loans extended. In this way, it can profit from the spread in the rate at which it borrows and lends money.

See also MATCHED BOOK (WWS).

SPREAD SWAP

An arrangement, generally illegal if nonexempt securities are involved, between a customer and an underwriter of an upcoming issue of debt securities. It is an agreement to purchase a customer's securities in exchange for the new security at a fixed difference in price or yield that is determined before the new issue's registration statement becomes effective.

This is not illegal if it is done after the registration statement becomes effective if the price is related to the market for both securities.

SQUAWK BOX

An internal telephonic system used by many broker/dealers to provide two-way interoffice communication.

Such systems provide a means for marketing and other timely information to be communicated to the branch offices, and for branch office personnel to ask relevant questions.

Also called a "bitch box" because some of the questions are basically comments about home office shortcomings.

STAG

In British parlance, someone who subscribes to a new issue anticipating an immediate resale at a premium price. We have no similar word in the United States. However, an issue which should sell at an immediate premium is called a "hot issue" here.

STAGGERED BOARD

Term used to describe a corporate board of directors whose terms of office are so arranged that shareholders do not vote for an entire slate in any one year. Staggered boards often can be used to stymie a takeover attempt because new owners can only change a portion of the board in any one year.

STAGS

Acronym: Sterling Transferable Accruing Government Securities. This is the British equivalent of CATS and TIGRs. In effect, STAGS are zero-coupon bonds based on gilts—that is, sterling-denominated English Treasury bonds.

STAIRS

Acronym: Stepped Tax-Exempt Appreciation and Income Realization Securities. This is a Salomon Brothers version of the GAINS initiated by Goldman Sachs.

See GAINS for a detailed description.

STAKE–OUT INVESTMENT

Term used in conjunction with the purchase by one bank holding company of the convertible, nonvoting preferred stock of another bank holding company.

Concept: Present federal or state laws may prevent interstate banking; but if those laws are modified or repealed, the holder can convert the preferred into common stock. Thus, it has staked out its claim on the other bank.

STANDARD & POOR'S INDEX

A measurement of general market value of the common stocks of 500 companies. It is based on the price of the stocks times the number of outstanding shares; thus, it is capitalization weighted.

The 500 stocks represent 400 industrial, 20 transportation, 40 public utility, and 40 financial companies. These 500 companies are quite large and they represent over 70% of the dollar value of the top 5,000 companies whose stocks are publicly held.

STANDBY FEE

1. Used in investment banking of the fee paid to an underwriter who is willing to purchase any shares remaining from a rights offering to current shareholders.
2. A fee paid by the originator (issuer) of Ginnie Mae securities to selected institutional investors. The fee enables the originator to deliver the securities to the investors at a fixed price. In effect, the fee, which ranges from $\frac{1}{4}$ to $1\frac{1}{4}\%$ of the face amount, gives the originator a put option on the securities it is about to issue.

STANDING ROOM ONLY

Nickname for the common shares of Southland Royalty Company, a company engaged in oil and gas exploration. The nickname is derived from the NYSE ticker symbol: SRO.

STANDSTILL AGREEMENT

A corporate finance term that describes the contract between an issuer and the holder of a significant block of stock in that company. The holder, for example, agrees not to acquire more shares, nor to dispose of shares presently held, without prior consent of the issuer. Thus, the holder agrees to stand still.

STAR

Acronym: Short-Term Auction Rate. This is a money market preferred stock issued by the Lincoln National Corporation. The stock is cumulative preferred whose dividend rate is reset every 49 days by means of a Dutch auction. Dissatisfied holders may tender, and the company may redeem, this stock at any of the seven annual auction dates.

STATED PERCENTAGE ORDER

This is an order for a significant quantity of a listed stock. The instruction is to buy or sell in such a way that the amount constitutes a specified percentage of the total market volume in that security. In this way, the order will not upset the equilibrium that marks the normal price movements in the security.

STATEMENT

Term describing the periodic reports by broker/dealers to their customers that summarize account balances and list securities transactions. Federal law requires that statements of account be sent quarterly to all customers who transacted or who have a debit or credit balance or a net security position with the broker. In practice, statements are sent monthly if there was a transaction in the account or if there are option positions.

STATUTE OF LIMITATIONS

The provision in every law that fixes the time parameters within which parties must take judicial action. After the time has elapsed, enforcement is barred.

Under the securities laws of the United States, the statute of limitations is usually three years for civil actions. It may be longer for criminal actions. Legal advice should be sought.

STATUTORY UNDERWRITER

Federal law defines an underwriter as a person who purchases a security from an issuer for purpose of resale. The term *statutory underwriter* describes a person who performs such an action, albeit inadvertently, and thereby subjects himself to the penalties of the law for those who sell unregistered securities. Example: A registered representative fails to exercise proper diligence in the sale of securities by a control person. The representative and his firm could be penalized, as a statutory underwriter, for violations of the Securities Act of 1933.

STEPPED COUPON SECURITIES

A debt security in which all bonds pay the same interest rate each year. However, that rate is set to rise periodically on a pre-established schedule.

Some municipal securities have been issued with this characteristic.

STEPPED TAX–EXEMPT APPRECIATION AND INCOME REALIZATION SECURITIES

See STAIRS.

STERLING SECURITY

A corporation's debt securities that are issued in the United Kingdom or, if issued outside the United Kingdom, are denominated in pounds sterling.

STERLING TRANSFERABLE ACCRUING GOVERNMENT SECURITIES

See STAGS.

STIF

Acronym: short-term issuance facility. This practice has also been succeeded by RUF: revolving underwriter facility.

See also SNIF.

STIF FUND

Acronym: short-term investment fund. Industry term for any pool of money invested in money market instruments, generally with maturities up to 90 days. The popular money market mutual funds are STIF funds.

In practice, the term is not used frequently. Money market fund, however, is a well-known and widely used term.

STILTS

See SHORT–TERM INDEXED LIABILITY TRANSACTIONS.

STOCK APPRECIATION RIGHTS

Acronym: SAR. Privileges that are sometimes accorded to officers and directors of publicly owned corporations as a form of special compensation. SARs represent the right to receive a financial benefit based on a specific number of shares granted to the affiliate's account with the company. The difference is often that between the market value of shares on the day the right is granted and the day on which it is exercised. In this way, it is an artificial option in which the employee neither pays money nor can lose money.

STOCK CERTIFICATE

The actual piece of paper that evidences ownership in a corporation.

Industry standards prescribe paper quality, engraving, and other obstacles to forgery.

The term *bond certificate* also is used.

Antonym: book entry. In this case, there is no certificate, and journal entries are used to transfer ownership.

STOCK EXCHANGE AUTOMATED QUOTATIONS
See SEAQ.

STOCK INDEX FUTURE
This is an obligation to make or take a cash settlement, during a specific month in the future, based on the price movements that occur in the specific stock index underlying the contract. The most common stock indexes used for these contracts are Value Line, S&P, NYSE, and Dow Jones.

STOCK LOAN BUSINESS
A service industry, or part of a broker/dealer's business, that endeavors to make a profit from the lending of securities, or charges a fee to bring lenders and borrowers of securities together.

Such fees usually are based on the value of the securities borrowed, although in some cases, if interest rates are very high, the lender will be charged for the free use of the money obtained when the securities are loaned.

STOCK LOAN DEPARTMENT
A work area of a member firm that is involved in the lending and borrowing of securities. Securities are borrowed to complete short sales or to complete transactions if the broker's client is a seller and has failed to deliver the sold security.

STOP OUT RATE
Slang for the lowest rate of interest the Federal Reserve will accept from a nonbank dealer on repurchase agreements. In effect, the Federal Reserve is buying securities from nonbank dealers, providing cash for up to 15 days, and presuming that the nonbank dealers will deposit these funds into the banking system. In this way, the Federal Reserve is indirectly providing funds to the banking system.

See REVERSE REPO.

STRANGLE
Slang for a long call and a long put on the same underlying security when both options are out of the money. Example: When the underlying is at 85, a long call at 95 and a long put at 80 would be a strangle.

To be profitable, a strangle requires a highly volatile movement in underlying security. In the example given above, there would have to be a minimum swing of 15 points for both long options, at one time or another, to be "in the money."

STREET SIDE
Term that describes the relationship between buying and selling firms in a securities transaction made on behalf of their customers. Such transactions must be cleared and settled. In the typical member organization, the cashiering function handles the street side of the transaction.

Antonym: customer side—that is, the bookkeeping of the monetary relationship between the firm and its customers. The margin function handles the customer side.

In practice, street side is used both as a noun and an adjective.

STRIPPED BONDS
These are debt instruments placed in escrow. Then, evidences of ownership in either the bond principal or the interest payments are sold separately.

Stripped bonds give rise to TIGRs, CATs, COUGARs.

Term also used: stripped coupons.

See PRIME and SCORE for a similar concept in terms of equity securities.

STRIPS
Acronym: Separate Trading of Registered Interest and Principal of Securities. An innovation by the U.S. Treasury to sell principal and interest payments separately on certain selected government issues.

All STRIPS are book entry only.

STRIPS have substantially lowered the number of CATs, TIGRs, and COUGARs issued.

STTEPS
See SHORT–TERM TAX–EXEMPT PUT SECURITIES.

STUF
Acronym: short-term underwriting facility. See SNIF and RUF (revolving underwriting facilities).

SUBPOENA
Also: sub poena. (Pronounced: s'peeny.) A document issued by a court that requires an action by the person who is served to

provide information *(duces tecum)* or to appear in person at a judicial proceeding.

Failure to comply with the terms of the subpoena may result in punishment, either civil or criminal.

SUBPOENA DUCES TECUM

Latin: under penalty of law (I order you) to bring with you. . . . In effect, this court order requires that the recipient produce such records as are pertinent to a trial. Such orders may also be issued by the SEC in its investigation of violations, or allegations thereof, of the securities laws of the United States.

SUPER BOWL OMEN

A somewhat lighthearted market indicator used by forecasters. Concept: If the winner of the Super Bowl is from the old National Football League, the stock market will rise during that year. If the winner is from the old American Football League, the market will decline.

SUPER DOT

An NYSE automated order processing and trade reporting system that enables the prompt entry and execution of limited price orders. Super DOT can execute orders up to 30,099 shares if these are received before the opening of the market.

The Super DOT system has been greatly expanded in recent years.

SUPERMAJORITY

A stockholder vote in which 80% or more of the outstanding shares are voted in favor of a motion.

To thwart takeover attempts, some companies have written a requirement for a supermajority into their corporate charters in certain corporate decisions.

SUPER NOW ACCOUNT

This is an expanded version of the NOW (negotiable order of withdrawal) account. Under the Super NOW account, depositors with a minimum balance of $2,500 are permitted unlimited checking privileges and are paid prevailing money market rates, rather than the minimum interest rates.

SUPPORTING

This term describes the practice of buying stock at prices to prevent a decline in value and thus discourage the exercise of put options. The practice may be manipulative and in violation of federal securities laws.

SURROGATE COURT
See PROBATE COURT.

SURROGATE COURT CERTIFICATE
A judicial document issued by a surrogate court that recognizes the authority of someone to settle the estate of a deceased person. Such a certificate, dated within the past six months, must accompany requests for transfer of title of securities registered in the name of a decedent.

SUSHI BONDS
Obligations of Japanese entities issued and denominated in Eurodollars. By treaty, such instruments do not count against the limits on holdings of foreign securities imposed on some Japanese financial institutions.

SWAP RATE
In foreign exchange markets, the swap rate is the difference between a currency's immediate (spot) price and its contract price in futures trading.

SWING LINE
Slang for a demand line of credit extended by a bank to a customer. Under a swing line, the customer may borrow a fixed sum of money each day, as needed.

SWISS FRANC
The primary unit of currency in Switzerland. The franc is divided into 100 centimes, or rappen.

The Swiss franc is a major "hard currency" and is actively traded in the spot, forward, futures, and options markets.

You also will see the term *Swissy* as a slang expression for the Swiss franc.

SWISS FRANC NOTE
Acronym: SFN. A Eurodebt security denominated in Swiss francs. The usual maturity is 5–10 years. Generally, an SFN is issued in the form of a global note held by a Swiss bank that arranges the loan for the entire life of the borrowing.

SYNTHETIC PUT

Also known as: synthetic put option. An over-the-counter put option issued by a broker/dealer to accommodate a customer's request for a put option. The expression "synthetic" and the need for this type of contract arose in the period between 1977 and 1980 when, due to a moratorium imposed by the SEC, there was a large disparity between the number of call options available and the number of put options.

T

TAIL

1. In a U.S. Treasury auction: the difference between the average bid and the lowest bid price accepted.
2. In a competitive underwriting: the decimals that follow the point bid. Example: In a bid of 98.7542 for a bond, .7542 is the tail. There is no limit on the number of decimals that can be used.
3. In Ginnie Mae terminology: a certificate that, when issued, does not bear a round-dollar face value. Example: a certificate with an original face value of $52,431.56.

See GNMA (GOVERNMENT NATIONAL MORTGAGE ASSOCIATION).

TAKE DOWN

1. As one word: takedown is the dollar discount given by the manager of a municipal syndicate to syndicate members when they take bonds from the account. Example: The bonds have a public offering price of 100 and the syndicate member's takedown price is 98.75.
2. As two words: take down is used in corporate underwritings to signify the number of shares or bonds for which a syndicate member is financially responsible. Example: Member A's take down is 150 bonds.

TAKE OUT

1. Slang: for the dollar amount an investor removes from an account if he sells one security and purchases another at a lower cost.
2. A trader's bid for the remainder of a seller's holdings that he has been selling piecemeal. Purpose: to remove overhanging supply from the marketplace.
3. Also called a "backup bid" if a Ginnie Mae dealer offers to

finance a mortgage banker's loans offered for sale at a GNMA auction. The dealer gets the right to repurchase them later at a specified price.

TAKEOVER
The acquisition of one company by another. The takeover may be accomplished with cash, with securities, or by a combination of the two.

Takeovers may be friendly or unfriendly.

As a rule, mergers cause both companies to survive. Acquisitions, or takeovers, cause the company acquired to go out of business, although its component parts become operating entities—in most cases—of the new corporation.

TAKING A VIEW
A colorful English expression for predicting the near and future prospects of interest rates, yields, and securities prices. In the United States, we would tend to use the word "forecasting."

TAKING PROFITS
See PROFIT TAKING.

TAPE DANCING
Slang used by block traders of equity securities who sometimes accommodate institutional sellers by paying ⅛ or ¼ over the last sale and then levy a larger-than-usual commission. The effect is twofold: (1) the block trader receives increased commission revenues to cushion possible trading losses, and (2) the print on the consolidated tape makes it appear that an anxious buyer is in the market to acquire stock. This can lure eager speculators.

TARGET
1. A corporation that is the object of a takeover attempt is said to be the target.
2. Slang expression for the common stock of Tenneco, a major pipeline, shipbuilder, and manufacturer. The nickname is derived from its NYSE symbol: TGT.

TARS
Acronym: Trade Acceptance and Reconciliation Service. This is an NASD-supported computer system in which uncompared trade problems in over-the-counter executions can be quickly resolved. Ultimately, TARS will provide on-line reporting of trade data for the immediate comparison of contracts.

TAT
See TEMPORARY AGENT TRANSFER PROGRAM.

TAX EQUITY AND FISCAL RESPONSIBILITY ACT
Acronym: TEFRA. A U.S. law designed to increase federal revenues through targeted levies and reform measures designed to improve taxpayer compliance. Among features having an impact on the securities industry are the requirement for a 20% withholding of interest and dividend payments under certain circumstances, sale transaction reporting of customer orders, and owner registration of debt obligations.

TAX–EXEMPT DEFERRED INTEREST SECURITIES
See TEDIS.

TAX SELLING
1. Any sale of securities made to realize a capital loss.
   See also WASH SALE and PAINTING THE TAPE (WWS).
2. A euphemism used by technical analysts to explain a market drop just before a payment date or accounting date for federal tax liabilities. Example: It is not uncommon for tax selling to occur late in a calendar year.

TAX STRADDLE
General term for a strategy whereby a client with a realized short-term capital gain could take offsetting positions in commodity futures contracts. Purpose: take a short-term loss in the same tax year as the realized short-term gain—thus, no tax on the net position—but get a long-term gain in the next tax year on the remaining position. The Economic Recovery Tax Act (1981) requires that the remaining position be considered a completed transaction (i.e., marked to the market for tax computations). As a result, tax straddles are no longer an effective strategy for negating a gain in one tax year and postponing it to the next.

TAX WAIVER
A written consent of a decedent's state of domicile stating: (1) that state inheritance taxes have been paid or (2) that it will forgo immediate payment of such taxes. As a general rule, no reregistration of securities registered in the name of a decedent can be made without such a tax waiver.

TCO
See TRANS–CANADA OPTIONS, INC.

TEDIS

Acronym: (pronounced: teddies) Tax-Exempt Deferred Interest Securities. This is a Kidder Peabody counterpart of GAINS initiated by Goldman Sachs.

See GAINS for a fuller explanation.

TEE WAY

Jargon used to identify Trans World Corporation, a major airline. The nickname is derived from the NYSE symbol: TWA.

TEFRA

See TAX EQUITY AND FISCAL RESPONSIBILITY ACT.

TEMPORARY AGENT TRANSFER PROGRAM

Acronym: TAT. A program created by the North American Securities Administrators Association (NASAA) to expedite the transfer of agent registrations between broker/dealers using the NASD's Central Registration Depository (CRD). TAT grants temporary registration to salespersons before the submission of new U-4 forms providing a termination notice, U-5 form, has been filed by the former employer and the termination was not "for cause."

TENDER

1. To submit a formal bid for a security. Example: to tender a bid in a Treasury offering of bills, notes, or bonds.
2. To submit a security in response to an offer to buy at a fixed price. Example: When ABC made an offer to buy the security at $29 per share, the client tendered his shares.

TENDER OFFER

Public announcement of intent to acquire, at a fixed price, any or all of the securities of a company. Notice of the announcement first must be filed with the SEC. The acquisition also may be by exchange rather than by a cash offer. Used often in the takeover of another corporation.

TENDER OPTION PUT SECURITY

Acronym: TOPS. A municipal security that carries a short-term put option enabling the holder the right to redeem it at par. This feature, during the life of the put, effectively turns the long-term obligation into a short-term trading instrument. The title TOPS was created by Paine Webber for certain municipal securities that it underwrites.

TENOR

A word occasionally used as a synonym for maturity when referring to the age of a debt security. Example: "That bond is not an alto, it's a tenor."

TESTATE

Legal term for someone who died and left a valid will to direct the disposition of the assets in the estate.

Antonym: intestate.

THIRD–PARTY ACCOUNT

Brokerage account carried and operated in the name of a person other than the owner. Example: Bill Jones carries and manages a brokerage account in his name that is actually the account of his brother-in-law. Such accounts are forbidden by industry regulation.

Do not confuse with power-of-attorney accounts, which are managed by a third party but which are owned and are held in the name of the person who gave such authorization.

THIRD–PARTY REPO

A dealer's collateralized financing transaction with a customer of a commercial bank, using that bank as an intermediary and guarantor of the loan. In general, the dealer pledges U.S. government securities, receives somewhat less than their current market value, and pays a negotiated rate of interest for the money borrowed, based on the amount borrowed and the time of the loan.

THREE–HANDED DEAL

Slang in municipal security underwriting: the issue will combine serial maturities with two term maturities. Four-handed and five-handed deals expand the number of term issues accordingly.

TIDAL WAVE PURCHASE

A corporate finance term that describes a cash-rich corporate raider's open market purchase of the stock in a target company. The metaphor implies that the purchase is of a controlling interest made in a short time—hence, the target is overwhelmed (better: inundated) by the raider.

TIE GAUGE THEORY

This jocular stock market indicator was developed by the well-known technical market analyst, Alan Shaw. In effect, the width of men's ties predicts the direction of the stock market: wide ties, lower stock prices; narrow ties, higher stock prices.

TIGHT MONEY

An economic situation, often orchestrated by the Federal Reserve, in which the money supply is lowered and interest rates begin to rise. Thus, credit is difficult to obtain and businesses are faced with bankruptcy and unemployment begins to rise.

The shape of the yield curve often is inverted—that is, short-term rates are higher than long-term rates. It is possible, however, for all rates to be high.

TIGR

Acronym: Treasury Investment Growth Receipt. (Pronounced as the animal: tiger.) This Merrill Lynch product comes in two forms: serial TIGRs and principal TIGRs. Both arise from "stripping" a Treasury bond of its coupons. Ownership interests are sold in individual coupons (serial) or the stripped bond (principal), and the holder receives a single distribution of cash at a specified time in the future. TIGRs are similar in concept and operation to CATS and COUGARS.

TIN

Acronym: taxpayer identification number.

TIN is a nine-digit numerical identifier assigned to all U.S. persons employed in the United States. For individuals, the numbers are arranged XXX-XX-XXXX. For corporations, trusts, and other legal entities, the numbers are arranged XX-XXXXXXX.

TIR

See TRANSFER INITIATION REQUEST.

TITLE X and TITLE XI BONDS

Title X and TITLE XI refers to sections of the Merchant Marine Act that provide for the acquisition of certain equipment that is financed and guaranteed by the full faith and credit of the United States. In the event of default, holders of the bonds purchased in compliance with Title X would receive the full amount of principal and unpaid interest. The purpose of these government-guaranteed loans is to promote international commerce for the United States.

TOEHOLD PURCHASE
Slang for the purchase of less than 5% of the outstanding stock of a company prior to the public disclosure to the SEC that the purchaser owns 5% or more of the shares.

TOM–NEXT
Jargon from the Eurodollar and foreign exchange markets for a transaction that will be settled on the next business day. The expression comes from "tomorrow next."

TOP
1. As used by technical analysts, this noun means a price level through which an issue will not trade without encountering significant selling by other owners. Example: "We anticipate a top at 32."
2. As a verb: top means that a security has reached a relatively high price and (usually) has backed off. It is anticipated that some time will elapse before that level will be reached again. Example: LMN topped at 32, backed off to 29, and is now in a period of consolidation.

TOPIC
TOPIC is a comprehensive videotex information system that is available on a subscription basis. Linkage to TOPIC is through any IBM PC terminal.

TOPIC was developed by the London Stock Exchange. In multicolor format, it provides up-to-the-minute information on U.K. equities, options, and "gilts." It also provides international information and news.

TOP MANAGEMENT
General term for the highest ranking officers in a corporation. In terms of corporate titles, the chief executive officer, the president, the chairman, and the executive vice presidents are considered top management. In practice, senior vice presidents, the treasurer, the corporate secretary, and the corporate counsel may be top management.

TOPPY
Slang for a market situation in which a security, or the market in general, has achieved its resistance level, either former or

anticipated, and is now expected to decline. Example: The market at 1452 is rather toppy.

TOPS
1. See TRIPLE OPTION PREFERRED STOCK.
2. See TENDER OPTION PUT SECURITY.

TORONTO STOCK EXCHANGE
Acronym: TSE. Common newspaper abbreviation: T or (T).

The TSE is a major exchange, subject to the regulatory jurisdiction of the Ontario Securities Commission, located in Toronto, Ontario. The TSE provides trading facilities for many lesser-known Canadian mining companies as well as for most larger and more popular companies doing business in Canada. Stocks of American companies doing business in Canada also are traded on the TSE.

TOTAL RETURN
1. Refers to the yield on a debt instrument related to the amount of money invested. In this sense, it is equivalent to yield to maturity: interest, interest on interest, and capital gain/loss at maturity.
2. Used of a client's investment objective if the client wants a combination of interest/dividend yield plus capital gains from a security investment.

TOUT
1. Slang for any highly biased recommendation to buy or sell a particular security. Example: "LMN is being touted all over the street."
2. The term also is used in a derogatory sense: of a particular registered representative who endeavors to buy or sell a particular security and thus generate commissions without regard to the financial circumstances and objectives of the customer. In this sense, tout and churn are close in meaning.

TPOD
Acronym: trade processing and operations department. (Pronounced: tee-pod.) A work area within a typical broker/dealer organization that is responsible for the processing of transactions, including all the steps between order execution and the monetary settlement of contracts.

TRADE ACCEPTANCE AND RECONCILIATION SERVICE
See TARS.

TRADES ON TOP OF
Slang used of debt instruments whose yield differential is very small or nonexistent. In effect, both instruments afford investors approximately the same basis point yield, and one investment is not preferred over the other. Example: This bond trades on top of the other, there is really no advantage of the one over the other.

TRADING DIVIDENDS
The act of buying/selling equity securities by a corporation to increase the number of annual dividends subject to the 85% exclusion of dividend income from corporate taxation.

Trading dividends is possible because the IRS requires only a 46–day holding period for a corporate holder to be eligible for the preferential exclusion privilege.

In practice, trading dividends is highly sophisticated because most corporate preferred securities tend to be priced in such a way that both seller and buyer share the advantages of the 85% dividend exclusion for corporate holders.

TRADING DOWN
The sale of portfolio securities and the purchase of securities with higher risk or lower-quality ratings. Example: the sale of investment-grade securities and the purchase of speculative securities.

Trading down generally is undertaken to increase yield or capital gains. Price volatility and increased annual income will compensate, it is thought, for the increased risk.

TRADING ON THE EQUITY
Term describing the issuance of funded debt by a corporation. Example: A corporation with equity of $5 million issues bonds with a face value of $2 million. The corporation is trading on the equity in that the interest on the bonds, as a percent, may be less than the percent return on total capital ($7 million). Thus, the corporation is leveraging its total investment.

Trading on the equity increases the risk of bankruptcy because the fixed-interest charges on debt may exceed the return on total capital.

TRADING ON THE PERIMETER
Term used when there is very active trading at a post on the floor of an exchange. Because the specialist cannot handle all of the trades, some trades are completed on the periphery of the crowd. In some cases, such trades are not known to the specialist and are not included in the volume figures for the day. Although such trades are "ex lex," they conform to the spirit of the law and generally are not a source of trading abuse.

TRADING UP
The sale of portfolio securities and the purchase of securities with higher ratings. Example: the sale of speculative securities and the purchase of investment grade securities.

Trading up generally is undertaken to better the quality of a portfolio and to reduce risk.

If done periodically to give a good impression, trading up is called "window dressing." Mutual funds often window dress shortly before they must make their semiannual reports to stockholders.

TRANCH
Term used to describe two or more debt security offerings by the same foreign issuer at the same time. Example: notes and bonds with differing interest rates and maturities. Tranches are issued to customize the issuer's capital needs and, in many cases, to conform to peculiar local requirements. Such issues are very popular in the Euromoney and capital markets.

TRANS-CANADA OPTION
Acronym: TCO. A put or call privilege traded on the Montreal or the Toronto Stock Exchanges for which the underlying stock is a corporation domiciled in Canada. The Options Clearing Corporation is the issuer of the privilege and the recordkeeper of all exchange-traded transactions.

TRANS-CANADA OPTIONS, INC.
A Canadian corporation, registered with the Securities and Exchange Commission in the United States. It is organized as an issuer of options traded on the Montreal and Toronto Stock Exchanges. In all instances, the underlying is the common stock of a Canadian corporation whose shares may be traded both in Canada and the United States.

TRANSFER INITIATION REQUEST

Acronym: TIR. This is a document issued by the National Securities Clearing Corporation (NSCC). It authorizes the transfer of a customer's assets (securities and money) from one member's account to another.

For details of the actual account transfer service, see AUTO-MATED CUSTOMER ACCOUNT TRANSFER SERVICE.

TRAPPER

An old slang and derogatory description for a registered representative. The term originated in the early 30s when securities business was slow and industry salespersons supposedly had to trap customers to survive.

TREASURY INVESTMENT GROWTH RECEIPT

See TIGR.

TREASURY RECEIPTS

Acronym: TR. These receipts, created by the First Boston Corporation, are similar to TIGRs, CATS, and COUGARs. They are stripped Treasury bonds and are, in effect, zero-coupon Treasury securities.

TRIPLE EXEMPTION

Term used to describe a municipal bond providing interest income to a holder that is exempt from federal, state, and local taxation.

As a general rule, interest income from bonds issued within the state in which the holder-taxpayer is a resident has a triple exemption.

The term *triple tax exempt,* as a feature for any holder, regardless of the state of residence, normally is reserved for municipal bonds issued by the Commonwealth of Puerto Rico or by the District of Columbia because this feature is provided in the federal tax law.

TRIPLE MARY

Colloquial name for the shares of Minnesota Mining & Manufacturing Co., a large producer of cellophane tapes, audio/video products, and industrial abrasives. The nickname is derived from the NYSE ticker tape symbol: MMM.

TRIPLE NET LEASE
Term used of a rental arrangement if the renting person pays a fixed sum to the renter and is responsible for the upkeep, utilities, and insurance on the property. In effect, the renter receives a fixed sum of income without any concern for these other expense items.

TRIPLE OPTION PREFERRED STOCK
Acronym: TOPS. A type of preferred stock that permits the holder, on a quarterly basis, to tender the stock back to the issuer and to receive, subject to the issuer's preference, either: (1) common stock valued at the preferred's par value, (2) a debt security valued at the preferred's par value, or (3) cash. The dividend rate on TOPS also is reset quarterly, based on some preset formula.

TRIPLE WITCHING HOUR
Slang for the final hour of trading immediately before the expiration for equity, index options, and index option futures contracts. The triple witching hour occurs quarterly (four times a year). There is voluminous trading as arbitrageurs and traders unwind their positions—often resulting in sharp price swings in these contracts and in the underlying common stocks.

TRUF
Acronym: transferable underwriting facility. Term is used in Eurosecurity financing if one banker is able to transfer capital raising commitments to an issuer to another bank or broker/dealer.

TSE
See TORONTO STOCK EXCHANGE.

TURKEY
Slang: a poor and unsuccessful performance. Used of the security that loses money for investors or of an offering of securities that loses money for the underwriters.

TWO–HANDED DEAL
Colloquial expression for an underwriting in which two broker/dealers are comanaging the forthcoming distribution of securities. Example: Salomon Brothers and Merrill Lynch arranged a two-handed deal for $1 billion State of California Bonds.

TWO–SIDED MARKET

This is a quotation for a security that gives both a bid and asked price.

With the exception of the market for municipal bonds, most American securities markets are two-sided and this is considered the ethical standard for dealers. The municipal market, with more than 1 million issues outstanding, does not find it practical to give both a bid and offer at all times.

Synonym: two-way market.

TWO–TIER PRICING

This term, used in conjunction with a contemplated takeover, identifies the acquisition of controlling persons' stock at higher prices than that paid to other shareholders in a tender offer.

The practice is morally, if not legally, questionable and is in litigation in several courts in the United States.

U

UKULELE

A nickname for the common shares of Union Carbide Corporation, a diversified manufacturer of chemicals. The nickname is derived from the NYSE ticker symbol: UK.

ULTRA VIRES

Latin: beyond the powers of . . .

Also: ultra vires act(ion). A corporate activity that is not illegal (contra vires) but that is beyond the specific powers granted in the corporate charter. Such actions may be rescinded to the detriment of the other party to the contract.

For this reason, corporate accounts are subject to close scrutiny. Corporate counsel, the director of compliance, or the manager of new accounts will—if there is any doubt—require a copy of the corporation's charter before certain security and commodity contracts are permitted.

UNCOLLECTED FUNDS

Financial euphemism for a customer's check that has "bounced."

UNDERCAPITALIZED

Term used of any business that has inadequate funds to conduct its day-to-day business. In and of itself, this term is neutral; it simply means a shortage of short-term funds.

Firms that are undercapitalized must increase permanent capital, either by issuing stock or through debt securities.

UNDERLYING

1. The stock subject to purchase (a call) or to sale (a put) if the holder of an option chooses to exercise the option.
2. The common stock that a corporation must deliver to a person who chooses to exercise a stock option, to subscribe to a rights offering, to exercise a warrant, or to convert a security that is convertible.

UNDERWRITE

General term for the process whereby investment bankers purchase a new issue of securities from the issuer and resell the security to the investing public. The term implies that the investment banker is at risk between the time of purchase and resale.

The term also is used more loosely of some security distributions where the investment banker acts as the agent of the issuer and has no financial risk. Example: a best-efforts underwriting.

UNIFORM COMMERCIAL CODE

Acronym: UCC. This is a nationwide set of statutes designed to standardize commercial customs, usages, and procedures of trade associations in transactions between its members.

The state of Louisiana does not conform to the UCC, and there are some local modifications.

UNIT INVESTMENT TRUST

Acronym: UIT. A UIT is a fixed, diversified portfolio of securities in which fractional participations (units) are sold to represent a pro rata interest in the underlying principal and net investment income.

Also called a "unit trust."

UITs are redeemable securities. They may increase or decrease in resale market value.

The term *bond fund* also is used of such unit investment trusts.

UNIT PRICE DEMAND ADJUSTABLE TAX–EXEMPT SECURITIES
See UPDATES.

UNIT STOCK INVESTMENT TRUST
See USIT.

UNLIMITED TAX BOND

Municipal securities term for an issue secured by the issuer's pledge of tax collections that can be levied upon constituents. In effect, the issuer may levy any rate in any amount needed to service the debt.

Antonym: limited tax bond.

As a general rule, unlimited tax bonds are issued only by states. Cities and other municipalities generally have limited taxing power.

UNSEASONED SECURITY

1. Any security that is new to the marketplace and that has not yet been subjected to the forces of supply and demand.
2. An unregistered security. Example: A Eurosecurity that is sold outside the United States. Such securities may not be resold within the United States unless they are seasoned. Seasoning is a matter of fact. As a general rule, such securities may not be sold within the United States within the first 90 days of their public offering and completed distribution.

UNSECURED DEBIT

Brokerage industry term for any customer debit that is not properly collateralized.

Unsecured debits may result from a sudden drop in market value of a customer's margin account, a maintenance call for securities or commodities that has not yet been met, uncollected funds (a bounced check), and, after settlement date, customer failures to pay or deliver. In a word, the broker/dealer is at risk because of a customer action.

UNWIND A TRADE

1. To reverse a previously established transaction: a purchase is unwound by a sale; a short sale, by a short cover.
2. To cover a transaction made in error. Example: A broker/dealer makes a sale but the client actually entered an order to buy. The broker/dealer is short the security sold—this will have to be unwound to rectify the situation. The client's buy order is unexecuted. This, too, will have to be rectified.

UP

1. Preceded by a number (e.g., 10,000 up): used to signify that there is a bid (offer) for 10,000 or more shares or units.

2. Followed by a number, such as up 2½: used to signify the dollar value of a market price increase.
3. In general, any increase in market value or yield.

UPDATES

Acronym: Unit Price Demand Adjustable Tax-Exempt Securities. UPDATES are variable-rate municipal securities with a put feature developed and sold by Merrill Lynch.

The variable rate is reset daily; interest is paid monthly. Holders have the right to redeem the security at face value; but this privilege may be exercised only once a month, or once a week, depending on the indenture of the individual securities.

UP FRONT PAYMENT

1. Any money exchanged before a deal is settled.
2. In municipal bond terminology, a synonym for the good faith deposit given by the underwriter to the issuer for a scheduled underwriting.
3. In the underwriting of Ginnie Maes, a commitment fee paid by a borrower to a mortgage banker for assurance of a future loan.

USABLE BONDS

Term used of a debenture issued as a unit with a detachable warrant. The warrant enables the holder to use the bond, at face value, to subscribe to common stock in lieu of cash at the price set forth in the initial offer.

In practice, the original bond often is issued at a discount from face. Thus, the unit represents a cheap call on the underlying.

USIT

Acronym: Unit Stock Investment Trust.

USIT is a trademark for the Americus Trust. The initial Americus Trust involved common shares of American Telephone & Telegraph before the breakup.

See PRIME and SCORE for a further explanation of the operations of the trust.

At the time of writing, Americus Trusts are proposed for the common shares of Exxon, General Motors, IBM, and other widely held common shares.

U.S. TERMS

In foreign currency transactions, the number of U.S. dollars needed to purchase one unit of a foreign currency. Example: If British pounds are offered at .6222, it means that:

$$\frac{\$1.00}{.6222} = \$1.6071$$

dollars will be required to buy one British pound. $1.6071 is a British pound stated in U.S. terms. And $.4204 could be a deutsche mark or Swiss franc in U.S. terms.

USURY

1. In general, the lending of money at interest. This meaning has become obsolete, although it is used commonly in older documents.
2. The lending of money at higher rates of interest than that allowed by prevailing state law. Conformity to state usury laws is an important consideration for broker/dealers in the conduct of client margin accounts.

UT

A frequently used abbreviation for: unit.

UTP

1. Acronym: unlisted trading privileges. Under SEC rules, an exchange may apply for permission to trade an issuer's securities on its premises even though the issuer has never requested nor filed papers for such privileges.

   Few stocks, but most bonds, are traded under UTP.
2. NYSE ticker symbol for Utah Power & Light, a prominent utility company in this western state.

V

VALUE DATE

In foreign currency transactions, value date is commonly used as a synonym for settlement date.

In practice, in spot currency transactions the value date is the second business day following the trade date.

VELOCITY OF MONEY

Economic term that identifies the turnover of money in terms of expenditures for goods and services. Example: If the money supply were $500 billion and the gross national product were $3 trillion, the velocity of money would be 6: GNP divided by money supply equals velocity of money. Needless to say, this concept is fine-tuned by using the various money components, such as M1, M2, and the like.

Also called the "velocity of circulation."

VENTURE CAPITAL

Industry term for an investment in a new, untried business venture with all of the financial risks inherent in such an enterprise.

Companies specializing in such investments are called venture capital companies and, as part of their compensation for such investments, usually demand a large portion of the equity ownership. Thus, if the risky enterprise prospers, they will be richly rewarded.

VERTICAL MERGER

A merger of businesses controlling various stages of production for a single product. Example: A merger of a paper mill with an ink producer and a newspaper publisher would be a vertical merger. The petroleum industry has many vertical mergers in that exploration, refining, and distribution often are combined.

Also called "vertical combination."

Antonym: a conglomerate—that is, a merger of businesses in disparate fields.

VSP

Abbreviation for: versus purchase. When followed by a calendar date on an order instruction to sell, or on a broker's confirmation, these initials identify the security being sold. Example: VSP 10-26-84 will identify the client's sale of securities acquired on October 26, 1984. Required in many cases because, if no designation is made by the client, the IRS requires that securities sales be considered as made on a first-in and first-out basis.

VULTURE FUNDS

A colorful name for organized pools of money assembled to purchase commercial real estate at sharply distressed prices. At the bottoms of business cycles (i.e., during recessions), such properties often are available at bargain prices and purchasers can profit tremendously as the economy recovers. Money for these purchases usually is funded by insurance companies, pension funds, and other well-capitalized institutional investors.

W

WAITER
The British equivalent of floor clerks on U.S. stock exchanges. On the London Stock Exchange, the waiters assist brokers in communicating messages, market information, and execution reports to member firms.

WARRANTS INTO NEGOTIABLE GOVERNMENT SECURITIES
See WINGS.

WARTS
Acronym: warrants to buy Treasury securities. Initiated by Goldman Sachs, these are privileges to buy a fixed amount of a specific government issue at a fixed price from GS. The life of the warrant is generally six months to a year. Large amounts can be purchased under such warrants; thus, they appeal to speculators and portfolio managers who want to hedge large debt positions.

WASH–METS
Industry slang for the bonds of the Washington Metropolitan Transit Authority.

WASH SALE
1. A sale resulting in a disallowed capital loss because the seller purchased the same, or a substantially identical, security within 30 days prior to or 30 days after the sale at a loss. Tax advice is needed.
2. Popular name of the manipulative practice of buying and selling similar amounts of a security—at the same price through the same broker/dealer without a true change of beneficial ownership—to give the impression of trading activity.

WELLS SUBMISSION
A written procedure that enables the subject of an SEC investigation to provide the commission with personal comments and opinions in an endeavor to persuade the SEC to discontinue the case under consideration.

WESTERN ACCOUNT
Term describing a corporate underwriting agreement in which syndicate members sign a contract with the issuer as a group but limit their individual liability to the specific quantity of shares or bonds that they individually underwrite.

In practice, the term often is used of corporate underwritings, although it is infrequently used of municipal underwritings that have similar responsibility features.

Also called a "divided account."

WE THE PEOPLE
This nickname, taken from the first three words of the Preamble of the Constitution of the United States, often is applied to Merrill Lynch & Company, the nation's largest brokerage firm. It also is the title of the company newspaper of Merrill Lynch.

WG
Initials used on corporate calendars, particularly if Canadian securities are being underwritten, to identify Wood Gundy, Inc., a major underwriter of securities.

WHEN ISSUED
Technically: when, if, and as issued.
1. A trade in U.S. Treasury bills after the auction is announced, but before the auction is actually held. After the auction, but before settlement, these bills trade on a when-issued basis.
2. Used to designate a trade settlement date that subsequently will be determined. Used extensively of the primary market for bonds, and occasionally for stocks. Example: The bond traded today but when-issued settlement will be in three weeks.

WHITE KNIGHT
Slang for a person or corporation who saves a corporation from an unfriendly takeover by, in turn, taking over the corporation.

WHITE SQUIRE
Merger and acquisition term used as a last resort by management to stave off an unwelcome takeover. Taking a calculated risk, management encourages significant purchases of its stock by another party whose financial interests are aligned with its own officials. These newly acquired holdings often are sufficient to discourage the unwelcome suiter.

WICKY
Slang for Warner Communications, a company engaged in the entertainment industry, derived from its NYSE stock symbol: WCI.

WIGGLEY
Slang for Washington Gas Light Company, a major utility in the Northwest United States, derived from its NYSE stock symbol: WGI.

WILDCAT WELL
A speculative drilling venture for oil or gas in unproven territory—that is, in a location in which such products have not been found previously.

The term is used extensively in conjunction with direct participation programs.

WINDOW
A time within which a person may do an action without additional cost or other adverse effects. Example: By signing a letter of intent, a mutual fund purchaser has a 13-month window within which to purchase a sufficient dollar amount of the fund to achieve the reduced sales charge for larger purchases.

WINDOW DRESSING
See TRADING UP.

WINGS
Acronym: warrants into negotiable government securities. Salomon Brothers' term for the option to buy a fixed number of Treasury notes at a fixed price for delivery at a future date. The immediate cash outlay is minimal. Used to hedge fixed-income portfolios, to establish a future price, or, in the case of foreign investors, to reduce foreign exchange risk.

WITH PREJUDICE
Used in legal settlements if the parties to the original action are prohibited from reinitiating litigation on the same matter. In effect, the case is closed.

Antonym: without prejudice. The case may be reopened in the future.

Both terms also are used in popular parlance to signify the same concepts.

WOLF PACK

Slang in corporate finance concerning some corporate mergers. It is best described as one investor purchasing a large position in a public company, then signaling others to follow suit by publicizing that company's vulnerability to potential takeover.

WORKING INTEREST

In direct participation programs, this term refers to an investor's financial interest in a partnership that is drilling and maintaining oil and gas wells. Working interest is not synonymous with equity, because working interest may include large sums of borrowed money through recourse and nonrecourse loans.

The term also is used of other tax-sheltered ventures, such as limited partnerships created for real estate, cattle and horse breeding, movie production, and certain farming ventures.

WORKING ORDER

An instruction to buy or sell a significant quantity of a stock. *Working* means that the execution is to be effected slowly and carefully on a piecemeal basis and thus not unduly change the market price level of the stock.

WORLD BANK

1. The International Bank for Reconstruction & Development, abbreviation IBRD. A multinational bank created to promote economic development in countries that are members of the organization. IBRD provides loans for construction projects and technical assistance in those member countries.
2. The debt securities issued by the World Bank, the popular name for the International Bank for Reconstruction & Development.

WRAPAROUND MORTGAGE

A mortgage loan built around two components: an assumable mortgage from the previous seller and a new loan from the carrying bank. The recipient of the wraparound mortgage has a lower average rate of interest than would be available if the entire mortgage amount were covered by one interest rate.

WRINKLE

Slang: a feature of a security that may be advantageous to the holder. Example: A company offers to exchange outstanding 11% bonds with new 10% bonds with this wrinkle: the holder may tender the bonds at par five years from the day of the exchange. Obviously, this feature would be profitable to the holder if, five years from now, interest rates were substantially in excess of 10%. He could redeem at par and reinvest at higher interest rates. Meanwhile, the company has saved 1% of its interest costs each year.

WRIT OF CERTIORARI
Legal writ issued by an appeals court to a lower court if it decides to hear an appeal. The term means that the lower court is to deliver the relevant trial or proceeding records to the appeals court. (Latin: to be informed.)

In practice, therefore, to appeal a court decision, one of the parties applies for a writ of certiorari. If the appeals court is willing to accept the appeal, it issues the writ to the original court.

WROS
Acronym: (joint tenants) with right of survivorship. A form of joint tenancy in which ownership passes to the other tenant(s) upon the death of one of the tenants. Probate thus is avoided.

Also written: W/R/O/S.

Y

YELLOW COLOR THEORY
A lighthearted market indicator. It presumes that when the popularity of the color yellow is on the rise in clothing, packaging, and home decor, the stock market is on the rise. When yellow falls out of popularity, the stock market will fall.

YEN
The primary currency in Japan. The yen is a major "hard" currency and is extensively traded in the spot, forward, futures, and options markets.

Symbol: Y.

YEN BOND
A bond, originally issued outside the United States, that is denominated in Japanese yen. Such bonds are not registered for sale in the United States, although after the bond is "seasoned" (traded for a reasonable period outside the United States) it may become eligible for trading here.

YIELD CURVE

General term for the graph depicting yields on the y-axis, and time to maturity on the x-axis, for fixed-income securities of the same class (e.g., corporates, utilities, governments, municipalities, and so on). Yield curves may be ascending (long-term bonds yield more than short-term bonds); descending (short-term bonds yield more than long-term bonds); or flat (both yield approximately the same).

A knowledge of the configuration of the yield curve and its trend is essential to intelligent fixed-income investing.

YIELD EQUIVALENCE

Term used in the completion of GNMA contracts: spot, forward, or option.

In effect, yield equivalence permits a seller to deliver various GNMA securities—each one, after all, represents a different pool—so the buyer gets the agreed-upon yield. This is accomplished by so adjusting the contract purchase price that the yield is maintained. Example: A contract to deliver a 12% GNMA at 90 may be effected by delivering a 10% GNMA at 77, if the yield will be 13.21% on either security.

See YIELD MAINTENANCE CONTRACT.

YIELD MAINTENANCE CONTRACT

Trading in GNMA securities permits the basic contract to center on yield. Thus, a contract may be settled with the specific rate designated in the contract, or with other rates, provided the yield to the buyer is that agreed upon. This will require a price adjustment if securities with differing rates are delivered against the contract.

YIELD TO MATURITY

A measurement of the compound rate of return that an investor in a bond with a maturity of more than one year will receive if: (1) he holds the security to maturity and (2) he reinvests all cash flows at the same market rate of interest.

YTM is an approximation and presumes a flat yield curve. However, it is used extensively in comparing fixed-income investments, in making fixed-income portfolio decisions, and in financial planning if an investor does not want to spend investment income but, instead, is looking for an increase in net worth.

The YTM is greater than current yield when the bond is selling at a discount, less when it is selling at a premium.

YIELD TRADING
See BASIS TRADING.

Z

ZERIAL BOND
Slang to designate a zero-coupon bond that is issued in serial form. Stripped Treasury bonds are classic examples of "zerials."

ZERO–COUPON BOND
A debt instrument that makes a single cash payment at maturity. The presumption is that such a bond will mature in more than one year and, therefore, sells at a substantial discount from maturity value. The term *discount bond* (or *bill*) is generally used of shorter-term debt securities with a single payment at maturity.

Zero-coupon bonds may be so issued by a corporation or government, or zeroes may be formed by "stripping" coupons from a bond issue and making separate sales of the coupon and principal distributions.

Tax advice is needed if such bonds are in a taxable account.

ZEROES
Popular designation for zero-coupon bonds.